Czech Conroy is Senior Research Associate at the International Institute for Environment and Development (IIED) in London.

Miles Litvinoff is a freelance editor with a special interest in environment and development.

THE GREENING OF AID

Sustainable Livelihoods in Practice

EDITED BY Czech Conroy
AND Miles Litvinoff

EARTHSCAN PUBLICATIONS LTD
in association with
THE INTERNATIONAL INSTITUTE FOR
ENVIRONMENT AND DEVELOPMENT
London

First published 1988 by
Earthscan Publications Limited
3 Endsleigh Street, London WC1H 0DD

British Library Cataloguing in Publication Data

The Greening of aid : sustainable livelihoods
  in practice.
  1. Developing countries. Industrial
  development. Environmental aspect
  I. Title   II. Conroy, Czech.   III. Litvinoff, Miles
  338.09172′

  ISBN 1-85383-016-X

Set in Baskerville
by DP Photosetting, Aylesbury, Bucks
Printed and bound in Great Britain by
Richard Clay

Earthscan Publications Ltd is an editorially independent and
wholly owned subsidiary of the International Institute for
Environment and Development (IIED)

Contents

PART 3   Appropriate Technology and Industry

CHAPTER 3   Mass Production or Production by the Masses?

PART 4   Planning Techniques for Sustainable Development

CHAPTER 4   Planning Techniques for Sustainable Development   *Colin P. Rees*

Figures, Maps and Tables

Figures

Maps

Tables

Preface

This book is based on the papers produced for the "Only One Earth Conference on Sustainable Development". The conference was organized by the International Institute for Environment and Development and took place at Regent's College, London, on 28–30 April 1987. IIED's Vice-President, Richard Sandbrook, developed the idea of the conference. The rationale for it was that if "sustainable development" was to become more than a vague, abstract buzzword it needed to be illustrated by real life projects. Only then could its implications be fully grasped, and acted upon in the development assistance process.

Special thanks are due to Ed Barbier, who helped me organize the conference and commission and edit the 40 or so papers; and to Caroline Brookes, the conference administrator, who somehow made an impossible task possible. Thanks are also due to the numerous other IIED staff and volunteers who contributed to the conference's success.

Many of those who prepared papers for the conference had to work to tight schedules, and to respond to queries and suggested changes from myself and Ed Barbier. Their patient cooperation was much appreciated. Time pressures have made it impossible to consult them all about the edited versions of their papers that appear in this book, and we apologize for any errors that may have crept in, or if any key points have been omitted from the summaries of the case studies. (The complete case studies are available individually from IIED.)

The conference would not have been possible without the generous assistance of the Overseas Development Administration, UK; the Swedish International Development Authority; the Dutch Ministry of Housing, Physical Planning and the Environment; and the European Commission. IIED is grateful to them all.

Czech Conroy
Senior Research Associate, IIED

Introduction

CZECH CONROY

There is a new jargon phrase in the development business – "sustainable development". It stems from a concern that many activities undertaken in the name of development have actually squandered the resources upon which development is based. In the industrialized countries the rapid consumption of finite materials such as fossil fuels and metals is the main concern. In the least developed countries overexploitation of natural biological resources is usually the major threat to sustainability.

Resource consumption can also have damaging environmental side-effects. In the North, chemical pollutants lead to acid deposition, ozone depletion, lead poisoning, etc. In the South the main environmental costs are usually associated with degradation of the natural resource base – deforestation, soil erosion and salinization are occurring at alarming rates. When rural livelihoods are undermined people migrate to the cities, where inadequate water and sewage services, and the degraded sites on which the poor are forced to live, pose other major environmental problems.

Definitions of sustainable development usually talk of improving people's material well-being through utilizing the earth's resources at a rate that can be sustained indefinitely, or at least over several decades, living off nature's interest rather than depleting the capital. The World Commission on Environment and Development (WCED) defined it as "development that meets the needs of the present without compromising the ability of future generations to meet their own needs" (WCED, 1987). The Commission particularly stressed the importance of meeting the essential needs of the world's poor.

General definitions are important, but they do not tell us what actions are needed to achieve sustainable development in practice. This book should help to fill that gap in the field of overseas aid. It provides specific and practical guidance to aid agencies and all those interested in ensuring that overseas aid supports countries' long-term development. It is based on papers produced for an international conference on sustainable development that the International Institute for Environment and Development (IIED) organized in April 1987 at Regent's College, London.

The people and economies of most Third World countries are heavily dependent on indigenous natural resources. Food production is a major activity for most rural people; and timber, paper, rubber and cotton textiles are but a few of the other industries based on natural resources. Thus, degradation or overexploitation of these resources directly affects economic development and human well-being.

Many of the world's most valuable fisheries have been overexploited, reducing catches to well below their previous levels. The export of timber from tropical forests can be an important source of foreign exchange, but for how long? Tropical forests are hardly ever harvested on a sustainable basis, and reforestation is uncommon.

People in the North are concerned about the huge scale of environmental destruction in the South. This has raised the question of what their governments can do to help alleviate these problems. The answer is: a lot.

They can start by putting their own economies on a sustainable development path so that their impact on the global environment (the atmosphere and the oceans), and particularly on Third World countries, is minimized. They need to reduce the vast quantities of the world's non-renewable resources that they are consuming, and to change their policies if they are having harmful effects on people in the South. They can help to change international economic relations between North and South so that they are more equitable. Finally, they can take steps to ensure that their $40 billion spent annually on overseas aid supports sustainable development and does not undermine it.

Unfortunately, there are many examples of aid projects that have disrupted the lives of local people and done serious damage to the environment; this is a second factor that has aroused public concern about aid and the environment (see, for example, Caufield, 1986; Searle, 1987). Also, a large proportion of aid projects that were intended to help conserve and enhance the productivity of natural resources have failed to do so. For instance, one report concluded that most conservation programmes in Africa ''have been unsuccessful ... structures and activities introduced are not maintained ... most programmes have been too expensive and too complex to be replicable'' (Centre for Development Co-operation Services, 1986). The record of other kinds of project, such as community tree-planting and new energy-efficient stoves, has also been disappointing.

Public discussion in the 1970s and early 1980s repeatedly emphasized these negative aspects of aid and the environment, to the point where some people must have wondered whether aid had ever benefited the environment and natural resource base. In fact, many projects *have* made a positive contribution to sustainable development, and IIED decided to gather information on some of the best and to see what lessons could be learned from them.

Thirty-four detailed case studies of aid projects and programmes illustrating sustainable development were commissioned for the IIED conference. Through these examples the conference aimed to assist aid agencies (both official and voluntary) in identifying the types of project they could fund and the key factors in their successful implementation. The case studies were grouped into six sets, corresponding to the six parts of this book. General papers were then written, reviewing each of the six sets. These six overview papers form the bulk of this book, supplemented by summaries of each of the 34 case studies. (The full case studies can be ordered individually from IIED.)

Many development projects have failed to produce their intended benefits because of the "mindset" of the people who designed and/or managed them. Development professionals tend to share certain biases that add up to what Robert Chambers has called "normal professionalism". These biases "start with things rather than people, the rich rather than the poor, men rather than women and numbers rather than qualities ... Poor rural children, women and men have been treated as residual not primary, as terminal problems not starting-points" (Chapter 1). Consequently, normal professionals have often misunderstood the "problem" and misspecified the "solution".

Many soil and water conservation projects, as their very name suggests, fall into this trap. Development professionals saw soil erosion as the problem, rather than the associated reduction in people's well-being, and designed technical solutions that people were then pressed to adhere to. The people's views were not sought, nor was much thought given as to whether these "solutions" would be compatible with their way of living. Often they were not compatible, which is why the project activities were not maintained by the intended beneficiaries.

The rural poor, in their struggle to survive, are sometimes driven to doing environmental damage. Their herds overgraze; their shortened fallows on steep slopes and fragile soils induce erosion; they are forced to cultivate and degrade marginal lands.

There is much greater awareness now that poverty and environmental degradation are often interlinked. But there has been a tendency to portray the poor as stupid and short-sighted, and in need of education on the importance of conserving natural resources. The factors that force poor people to degrade their environments are frequently overlooked. Population growth is often, and sometimes incorrectly, given as the main factor. Other factors may be more important, such as inequitable land distribution; appropriation of poor people's lands by the rich; no security of tenure; and the unavailability of credit for new and more efficient technologies.

The increased awareness of how poverty can affect the environment is welcome, but it should not distract from the harmful environmental impacts of the rich. The high resource consumption of developed countries and the wealthier groups in Third World countries place heavy pressures on natural resources (on forests, fisheries, etc.). Some people argue that this is the world's "main source of environmental destruction" (Agarwal, 1985).

Improving the livelihoods of the poor is essential if pressures on the natural environment are to be reduced. Secure resources and adequate livelihoods lead to good husbandry and sustainable management; and by combating poverty they help to slow population growth. For these reasons, most of the projects described in the following chapters are ones that have involved some of the poorest people. Although few of them are explicitly aimed at slowing population growth, many may do so indirectly.

IIED and the contributors to this book have tried to break out of the old paradigm of "normal professionalism" and to put people and their livelihoods first. We hope that this book will be a valuable contribution to the debate on how the poorest of this planet's five billion people can secure a fulfilling and sustainable living.

References

Agarwal, Anil (1985), "The State of the Environment and the Resulting State of 'the Last Person'". Fifth Annual World Conservation Lecture, World Wildlife Fund UK, Godalming.

Caufield, Catherine (1986), *In the Rainforest*. Picador, London.

Centre for Development Co-operation Services, Free University, Amsterdam (1986), *Soil and Water Conservation in Sub-Saharan Africa: Issues and Options*. International Fund for Agricultural Development, Rome.

Searle, Graham (1987), *Major World Bank Projects*. Wadebridge Ecological Centre, Camelford, Cornwall.

World Commission on Environment and Development (1987), *Our Common Future* (the Brundtland Report). Oxford University Press, Oxford and New York.

PART 1

Sustainable Rural Livelihoods (1)

CHAPTER 1

Sustainable Rural Livelihoods: a Key Strategy for People, Environment and Development

ROBERT CHAMBERS
Institute of Development Studies, University of Sussex, Brighton

Until recently the debates on environment and development have been dominated by values which reflect the "first" biases of normal professionalism. These start with things rather than people, the rich rather than the poor, men rather than women and numbers rather than qualities. They bear the imprint of interests that are urban, industrial and central in location rather than rural, agricultural and peripheral. Poor rural children, women and men have been treated as residual not primary, as terminal problems not starting-points.

The report of the Advisory Panel on Food Security, Agriculture, Forestry and Environment to the World Commission on Environment and Development (Food 1000, 1987) reverses this normal view, arguing that analysis and policy should start at the other end, with the poor, especially the rural poor, with where they are, with what they have and with their needs and interests. In developing this theme, it presents sustainable livelihood security as an integrating concept (p. 3):

> Livelihood is defined as adequate stocks and flows of food and cash to meet basic needs. Security refers to secure ownership of, or access to, resources and income-earning activities, including reserves and assets to offset risk, ease shocks and meet contingencies. Sustainable refers to the maintenance or enhancement of resource productivity on a long-term basis.

The report argues that there are both moral and practical imperatives for making sustainable livelihood security the focus for analysis and action; in the context of environmental development, these imperatives are not in conflict but mutually supporting.

That there is a moral imperative for putting poor people first few would dispute. The evidence of totally unacceptable deprivation and suffering is harder than ever for the affluent to escape. It ranges from Jan Breman's (1985) descriptions of the awfulness of life for rural migrants in Gujarat, to Dominique Lapierre's (1986) devastating book, *City of Joy*, about Calcutta, and the stark television images of the famine in Ethiopia and the Sahel.

From the point of view of environment and development, there are in addition powerful practical reasons for putting poor people first. In analysis which starts

with environment and development, population pressure on resources is a
central problem. The World Bank's (1986) estimates of the rise in population
over a mere 16 years are presented in Table 1.

Table 1 Estimated population growth in low- and middle-income countries,
1984–2000 (total population in millions)

	1984	*2000*	*Percentage increase in 16 years*
Sub-Saharan Africa	406	665	64
India	749	994	33
China	1,029	1,245	21
Other low-income	328	476	45
Other middle-income	1,040	1,427	37
Totals	3,180	5,224	37
Totals without China	2,781	3,979	43

Source: World Bank, 1986, p. 228

Without China, the populations of middle- and low-income countries are thus
estimated to increase by 43 per cent from 1984 to the end of the century, and in
Sub-Saharan Africa the figure is 64 per cent. Some four-fifths of the populations
of most of the countries concerned are rural. The pressure on urban livelihoods,
services and environments is often already intense, and much of the increase will
have to be supported in rural areas.

A common pattern in many parts of the world, rarely picked up by
conventional statistics, is a crisis of livelihoods generated by increasing rural
populations, and by social and political trends such as concentration of
ownership. Poor people respond to this through intensification of agriculture
and diversification of remunerative activities, through greater exploitation
of remaining common property resources (CPRs) and through migration.

The case studies in this part of the book and this overview chapter are mainly
concerned with resource-poor conditions. These include most of Sub-Saharan
Africa and the hinterlands and remote areas of Asia and Latin America, and
forests. Both resource-poor lands and forests are exploited by urban, commercial
and rich-country interests as well as by the poor, and often in non-sustainable
ways. It is convenient to blame the poor for deforestation, degradation of fragile
soils, overgrazing, erosion and "desertification". In fact, they are often victims in
the scramble to exploit public and common resources in which the rich and
powerful get in first.

The case for making sustainable livelihood security central for environment
and development strategies is reinforced by the need to offset such pressures on
resources both from the commercial and rich and from the poor. More and better

sustainable livelihoods in areas of high potential can reduce pressures elsewhere from outmigration by the poor. More important, and less well recognized, sustainable livelihoods in those resource-poor and forest areas are ecological and political safeguards against pillage and degradation by commercial interests and the rich. Contrary to popular professional prejudice, there is mounting evidence that when poor people have secure rights and adequate stocks of assets to deal with contingencies, they tend to take a long view, holding on tenaciously to land, protecting and saving trees and seeking to provide for their children. In this respect, their time perspective is longer than that of commercial interests concerned with early profits from capital, or of conventional development projects concerned with internal rates of return. Secure tenure and rights to resources and adequate livelihoods are prerequisites for good husbandry and sustainable management. Moreover, sustainable livelihood security is a precondition for a stable human population in the long term; for only when livelihoods are secure does it become rational for poor people to limit family size. Enabling poor people to gain secure and sustainable livelihoods in resource-poor and forest areas is, thus, the surest protection for the environment. The poor are not the problem; they are the solution.

The case studies

The five cases in this part of the book are all considered to be successful, although the case study authors are in general commendably self-critical, having mostly been personally involved. A comparative evaluation of performance, whatever criteria, would be difficult without extensive field visits. Rather than to evaluate, the purpose in this paper is to draw out lessons from the experiences gained and reported, supplemented from other sources.

The five cases are all based on initiatives in which NGOs (non-governmental organizations) played a major part. Two of them are geographically limited projects, and three are geographically extensive programmes, although they started on a smaller scale.

The two geographically limited projects are both village-sized. Sukhomajri/ Nada (Case Study 2) is an experiment in sustainable development with equity, limited to two villages in the Himalayan foothills of India; and Tin Aicha (Case Study 4) is a settlement of some 200 families of former nomads who now appear well established on the shores of Lake Faguibine in Northern Mali. Both set themselves difficult tasks; Sukhomajri/Nada began as a soil and water conservation project which expanded its objectives to encompass equitable resource management including social fencing of degraded forest land, a stake in new village resources for all villagers and sustainable livelihoods for the poorest. Tin Aicha sought to enable destitute nomads with no previous experience of cultivation to take up a settled agriculture which they despised, and create a new community from people with different origins. Both were, in the terms of their objectives, successful. Both received the intensive attention of committed senior staff with a high degree of staff continuity over the years. Both generate lessons for development and have influenced thinking and practice. Neither has been fully replicated.

The three programmes present a contrast in scale. The Lampang Applied Nutrition Program in Northern Thailand (Case Study 1), the Baudha-Bahunipati Family Welfare Project in Nepal (Case Study 3) and the Guinope Integrated Development Program in Honduras (Case Study 5) all cover wider geographical areas. Each has a larger and more dispersed staff. None has attempted as radical or difficult a transformation as Sukhomajri/Nada or Tin Aicha. Each includes elements of health and agriculture. Lampang and Guinope drew on experience gained by their organizations elsewhere and have followed tested approaches and procedures. All three have expanded their geographical areas over time and deepened the range of their activities. And all three appear replicable in certain respects.

The case studies provide the basis for four discussions. These concern, first, the bio-economic potential for sustainable livelihoods in resource-poor and forest environments; second, issues in the management of common property and private property resources; third, major practical lessons; and fourth, questions of scale and wider impact of NGO projects.

The bio-economic potential for sustainable livelihoods

One possible inference from the case studies is that the unrealized potential for sustainable livelihoods is considerable even, or especially, in environments which are resource-poor, degraded and marginal. This inference would be based particularly on Sukhomajri/Nada, Guinope and another case study (No. 9), the Yatenga Soil and Water Conservation Project in Burkina Faso. Let us consider these in turn.

Sukhomajri/Nada was under forest in the nineteenth century, but this was cut down. Under the degraded conditions before the project, each hectare of hillside was yielding 400 tons of silt per annum. Had these conditions persisted, the small dams built for conservation at the start of the project would have silted up in a few years. But with social fencing protecting the catchment there was a chance of sustaining the new system, even if some desilting was still needed. The advent of irrigation from small dams, with grass planting and protection in the catchment and other measures, led to increases in production in Sukhomajri which ranged from doubling to quadrupling earlier levels.

Similarly in Nada the poor farmers were enabled to multiply their wheat yields more than threefold. Earlier, 70 ha of hillside had been needed to feed one head of cattle, but growing bhabbar grass for ropemaking generated a potential income from only one hectare of Rs 20,000 ($1,500) per annum. The earlier regime was not sustainable and could not provide adequate livelihoods for the villagers; the new regime promises sustainable livelihoods at higher levels, and support for more than the present population.

The Guinope programme similarly, but without irrigation, enabled farmers to make a spectacular jump in production in the first year. Yields of maize which had been around 400 kg/ha often increased by three or four times through simple measures such as small drainage ditches plus either chicken manure or chemical fertilizer or both, and later with green manure. Wages, stagnating elsewhere, rose.

In Yatenga in Burkina Faso water harvesting on eroded lands led to major though less spectacular increases in yield. In four successive years (1981–4) the yields of treated plots (with contour rock bunds and other physical and management changes) compared with controls were on average 50 per cent higher.

It is important to ask whether Sukhomajri/Nada, Guinope and Yatenga are exceptional. Are these examples where the unrealized potential for sustainable livelihoods has been unusually high?

In answering this, the Sukhomajri/Nada experience must be qualified in two respects. First, institutionally, it received exceptionally intense, sensitive and sustained external support. This was probably necessary to offset and contain social and political inequalities in Nada, while Sukhomajri was unusual in being a single-caste village. It remains to be seen whether the rights and management systems established can survive without continued external support, and whether parts or all of the approach can be extended on any scale. Second, ecologically, there is the question of whether the irrigation systems are sustainable in the long term.

The Guinope and Yatenga experiences raise a different question. Both appear institutionally and ecologically sustainable. The question is whether their environments are atypical, with large gaps between potential and performance and with relatively easy ways those gaps could be closed. The Yatenga rock bunds are spreading in physically and socially similar areas, but an attempt to transplant the technology to a different environment in Mauritania ran into difficulties. With World Neighbors, the approach described by Bunch (1985) is to identify a very limited number of innovations, preferably one or two, that respond to the limiting factor in local production – in the case of Guinope, soil quality. The question is whether World Neighbors manages to choose places to work where, exceptionally, this approach can succeed, avoiding others where it would not, or whether the approach is applicable in most or all resource-poor farming conditions. Clearly, though, in some conditions quite simple low-cost changes can transform resource-poor agriculture, sharply reducing risk and lifting production on to a higher plateau.

There are grounds for a working hypothesis that in much of the arid, semi-arid and perhaps semi-humid Third World the bio-economic potential is orders of magnitude higher than is being achieved. In India as many as 100 million hectares of degraded land have been estimated to be producing less than 20 per cent of their dry-weight biological potential (Bentley, 1984, p.1). Even bad land can, through trees, provide poor people with an accumulation of wealth, giving them the basis for a better livelihood. An example is Midnapore District (population 7 million) in West Bengal. There, landless families have planted eucalyptus on degraded land allocated to them as part of a land reform. This is now producing wealth which most of them have used to buy irrigated land on which they can grow three crops a year, establishing them with the makings of sustainble livelihoods from agriculture. To the evidence of Guinope, Sukhomajri/Nada and Yatenga can be added other examples. At Kondoa, in Central Tanzania, a remarkable ecological discovery followed exclusion of livestock (Ostberg, 1986). In the Fuel and Fodder Project in Machakos District, Kenya, green oases have been produced by uprooting bush and using it to fence barren lateritic land, bulldozer-ripping that leaves hard surfaces as micro-catchments and planting trees in the rips (Bailey, Bottrall and Chambers, 1985).

Paradoxically, degradation is an opportunity for the poor, if it can be they who command and develop the degraded resources. The 35 million ha of degraded forest land in India are one such opportunity. Had the Forest Department protected it, and were it covered in a fine stand of trees, the practical potential for the poor would be less. As it is, the potential is immense for them to plant and own trees where few or none grow now, and to have them as savings banks and insurance to back their livelihood strategies, enabling them to get out of debt and to acquire other assets (Chambers and Leach, 1987). Environments with low productivity, but with high potential from water harvesting, agroforestry and green manuring, present a massive opportunity precisely because their current productivity is so low. The issue is whether governments and voluntary agencies have the imagination, will and resources to enable the poorer to realize and benefit from those potentials.

Sustainable livelihoods and common property resources

For the rural poor to realize sustainable livelihoods from the bio-economic potential of resource-poor environments requires a combination of incentives, technology and management. These questions touch on issues of policing, access, management and privatization of common property resources (forests, common pasture, rivers, bodies of water, etc.).

Basic to the discussion is an understanding of how poorer rural people contrive livelihoods. Some are locked into a single enterprise or life support, for example, full-time employees, bonded labourers, outworkers and single-species pastoralists. Most, though, rely on a diverse repertoire of resources and activities. In these, common property resources (CPRs) often play an important part, particularly in times of stress. The case studies of individuals at Tin Aicha bear this out. Water is one such resource, wood another, and grazing, browse and tree fodders yet others. But the pressures on CPRs, and their degradation, are a commonplace. Many of these pressures come from commercial interests, corrupt officials and politicians and those who are better off and more influential, especially in cutting and appropriating the wealth of trees in forests and in enclosing and privatizing common land. But poor people too are driven, often in need and sometimes desperate, to overexploit common resources. The environmental impact of Tin Aicha was bad at first as trees were cut for house frames and firewood, and brambles for fencing and cattle fodder. All too often such unmanaged exploitation of CPRs is not sustainable, and livelihoods which rely on them are therefore not sustainable either.

Approaches to the management of commons are vulnerable to simple dogma, with privatization currently in vogue. For sustainable livelihoods, and in the basis of our case studies and other evidence, four approaches stand out: government policing; equitable access; privatization; and drawing off pressure.

Government action to police and protect rarely works well on its own unless people see it as in their interests. At least three times over the previous ten years the Forest Department had planted trees at Sukhomajri and Nada, but not a single plant had survived. Innumerable attempts at government-policed grazing schemes in Sub-Saharan Africa have failed. Forest Departments have failed to protect forests adequately against either the rich or the poor.

The second approach, *equitable access*, is illustrated by Sukhomajri/Nada. Poor villagers in Nada were willing to forgo grazing by their goats in the eroded catchments when they had a stake in early benefits from protection, notably through ropemaking with bhabbar grass grown in the catchment and through their share of irrigation water from dams dependent on catchment protection. The nature and degree of equitable access in Sukhomajri/Nada hold two surprises. The first is that villagers in India could agree to allocate water rights equally to all households in the village, including the landless. This meant that landless labourers could sharecrop land of farmers who had more land than water, to the benefit of both. The second surprise was when the landless in Harijan Nada faced a fodder crisis because they were keeping their animals off the hill; those with land could feed their animals on crop residues, but the landless had nothing. The project team were ready to propose exclusive access for the landless to the new bhabbar grass which had been planted. But the landless insisted that either all families should be permitted to cut bhabbar grass from the plantation or nobody should be allowed. This is not to suggest that there should always be equal access, but rather to point to the realities of political feasibility; there are times when equality is more socially and politically sustainable than positive discrimination in favour of the poorer.

The third approach is *privatization*. Normally this takes the form of pre-emptive appropriation by the richer and more powerful. But there can be opportunities for the poorer to get in first, before the potential of the resources is realized. A sensitive, well-informed and committed programme can help the poorer here, as the Guinope case study illustrates. Since unoccupied plots around Guinope were fenced off by the landless before land values rose, it seems likely that the land use in future will be more livelihood-intensive than if the appropriation had been by wealthier farmers.

The fourth approach is *drawing off pressure* by providing alternatives. One form of this is direct substitution, growing on private land what was previously taken from common land. With the Baudha-Bahunipati project, fodder trees grown on the terrace faces of private land reduced the need for the more laborious cutting and carrying of tree fodders from further afield. Or the approach may be indirect through generating better alternative activities. The exploitation of CPRs is often hard work, involving walking far and carrying loads. Thus, poor people will only exploit them if they lack other, easier and more remunerative options, including wage labour. At Guinope, turpentine collection, which had been killing tens of thousands of pine trees, was reduced partly because the project generated a demand for labour and raised wage levels. Tree cutting for firewood was also reduced due to the increased availability of other work during the dry season.

The best mix of these four approaches varies, and combinations may often work best. Rural communities are capable of more subtle, complex and varied arrangements than outsiders usually realize. To take one example, tree tenure and land tenure can differ. In Turkana District, Kenya, at least four tree species are subject to family usufruct rights on common land. In a tribal village in South Gujarat, the village has divided up the mahua trees on the village commons to give exclusive household rights in order to avoid overexploitation. Perhaps the most important general lesson with CPRs is the need for analysis by communities, villagers and the poor themselves of their resources and their management, and assistance to support their endeavours to experiment and develop their own equitable and sustainable solutions.

Five major lessons

For the achievement of sustainable livelihoods, five major lessons can be drawn from the case studies and other evidence. These concern: (1) a learning-process approach; (2) people's priorities first; (3) secure rights and gains; (4) sustainability through self-help; (5) calibre, commitment and continuity of staff.

A learning-process approach

The first lesson is to follow the learning-process rather than the blueprint approach. This has been well described and analysed by David Korten (1980, 1984) and Dennis Rondinelli (1983). All five case studies demonstrate this approach, as also do others elsewhere in the book including the Yatenga Soil and Water Conservation Project in Burkina Faso and the Zambia Integrated Rural Development Programme (Case Study 27). All these underwent major changes of emphasis as experience was gained. To illustrate:

Sukhomajri/Nada began as a soil conservation project by outsiders. The original object was research, to find out sediment rates and the physical effects of conservation measures. The project was then transformed over time, through intensive interaction between staff and villagers, into a community process for resource management and sustainable livelihoods.

Tin Aicha evolved over time, especially with livestock ownership and management. Several systems of herd management were tried, with varying arrangements of ownership and herding responsibilities, leading eventually to marked differentiation and diversification by household in terms of livestock species (including camels, donkeys and goats) and numbers. Activities were added to the project as needs and opportunities arose.

The *Lampang* programme followed on from the USAID-funded Lampang Health Development Project which cost more than $7 million in 1974–81. That earlier project paid insufficient attention to nutrition and did not address the causes of malnutrition. Lampang started with the introduction in 1980–2 of 21 village texturizers to child nutrition centres, the experience with which convinced both Meals for the Millions (MFM) and the Thai government that only a comprehensive integrated programme would have a sustainable effect on nutritional status. The more successful MFM project followed on from this learning process.

Baudha-Bahunipati (BBP) began as a health and family-planning project, with rather little response. It became clear that people's higher priorities were agricultural livelihoods. BBP then changed both its emphasis and its main supporting institution to give attention to cultivation and livestock, with special attention to agroforestry and tree fodders. Working with farmers, lessons learned included the need to transplant fodder trees in June so that they would grow out of reach of animals by the time fields were fallow.

The *Yatenga Soil and Water Conservation Project* began as an agroforestry project. Trees were planted on eroded and infertile common land using square bunds made of earth. This was unsuccessful; farmers were not much interested in growing trees in common land in square bunds or in bunds made of earth. The project evolved, learning with and from farmers, to emphasize the growth of crops on less infertile private land using contour bunds of stone.

The *Zambia IRDP* began with a major survey and consultants' report and a blueprint-style approach to development, but evolved into a project for strengthening local government.

The *Haiti Agroforestry Outreach Project* (Case Study 10) grew out of a social anthropological analysis of soil erosion and reforestation projects over the previous 25 years, which were generally unsuccesful. Learning from that experience, a highly successful programme was devised.

In these examples, the ability to recognize, embrace and learn from error and failure, and even to change objectives, was the key to success. Conversely, many of the persistent failures in development owe their lack of success to adherence to blueprints and a dogged commitment to non-learning.

People's priorities first

The second lesson is to put people's priorities first. It seems strange, as late as 1988, to have to make this point. All the case studies were successful because sooner or later they managed to identify and meet people's perceived needs. The account of Lampang speaks for the others in stressing the importance of involving villagers in defining the goals and process of the programme. All too often, the learning process is a process of learning for outsiders in which they only gradually come to understand what people's priorities are. In the experience of the case studies, these were linked with livelihoods: fodder for animals and agriculture rather than family planning in BBP; incomes from ropemaking with bhabbar grass and from irrigation in Nada; fodder for animals in BBP; goats, donkeys and camels as well as or instead of cattle in Tin Aicha, where it was also recognized that transhumance from a fixed base was a long-term goal for most; food and incomes from soybeans, ducks, beekeeping and so on in Lampang; savings bank reserves in the form of privately owned trees in Haiti; sharply increased yields and incomes in Guinope.

The sensitivity to people's needs extends to the manner and timing of how they are consulted. While this is not stressed in the case studies, the personal style, patience and demeanour of outsiders are crucial; too often outsiders prevent themselves from learning from the poor because they adopt the role of teacher or disciplinarian. The timing of consultation also matters. Three of the projects are known to have held meetings in the evenings or at night because that was more convenient for villagers, although probably less convenient for staff.

Soil conservation efforts are a striking example of the costs of not consulting farmers and not putting their priorities first. Decades of soil conservation programmes, whether in Haiti, India or the Sahel, foundered because they were not what farmers wanted. In their review of soil conservation in Sub-Saharan Africa, the first of eleven lessons drawn by Reij, Cullis and Akililu (1987, p. 5) is that "Not outsiders but farmers should determine which conservation techniques will be promoted". For many years official programmes in West Africa tried to construct earth bunds with singularly little success. But "It is not surprising that farmers... show a preference for stone bunds. Stone bunds are less fragile than soil bunds, they are easy to design and they can absorb run-off from outside. Stone terraces and stone bunds are the most common indigenous conservation techniques in West Africa" (ibid., p. 5).

In contrast to past resistance to earth bunds, the contour rock bunds of the Yatenga project are even being adopted by some farmers spontaneously and without any external assistance.

Guinope was not included in the learning-process section because it appears to have gone straight to a successful solution which met farmers' priorities. Perhaps it is significant that Guinope drew on other earlier learning gained elsewhere. Putting people's priorities first shortens the learning process. The experience brought to Guinope, and the insights of social scientists into farmers' priorities in Haiti, not only avoided costly errors; they went straight to the point in starting self-sustaining processes.

People's own priorities, especially those of the poor, will often include substantial early gains. Nevertheless, the dramatic increases in yields and incomes in Sukhomajri/Nada and in Guinope are exceptional, and should not discourage others who can only hope to achieve less. The poor, contrary to much popular belief, are able and willing to make longer-term investments for lesser rewards. Outsiders should not assume that they know what poor people want, but should undertake a persistent, patient exercise of asking them, and then going on asking them, again and again.

Secure rights and gains

The third lesson concerns secure rights and gains for the poor. Sustainable resource use requires that the users take a long-term view. Once their very basic subsistence is assured, poor people's ability to take a long-term view depends on how secure they judge their future rights and gains to be. This aspect of their rationality has been persistently overlooked, perpetuating the myth that the poor are somehow negligently incapable of taking a long view or making long-term investments. Without secure rights to resources, it makes no sense for them to do so.

Rights to trees make the point. In contrast with Tin Aicha's community trees, the shade trees planted within compounds were well tended. Almost universally, trees on private land are better cared for than community trees. Evidence from Kenya and Haiti confirms that when peasant farmers are secure in their ownership of land and their rights to do what they like with trees, they are likely to plant them in considerable numbers. Conversely, in parts of the Sahel and of India, where government regulations restrict rights to cut, peasant farmers are reluctant to plant. The Haiti Agroforestry Outreach Project makes the point clearly. When farmers were told, "You will be the owners of any trees planted", and "As far as we're concerned, you can cut the trees when you want", and when they believed this, they planted many times the numbers of trees anticipated.

Secure rights can be communal, and, as Sukhomajri/Nada suggests, new equitable allocations of rights to CPRs may be sustainable. In general, though, individual rights to property tend to be more secure. While this is not an overwhelming argument for privatization, which is anyway not always feasible, it suggests that sustainable livelihoods will often best be achieved through secure and exclusive family or household rights to resources which ensure that those who stint, invest and manage, and their children, will be those who gain.

Sustainability through self-help

The fourth lesson is to achieve sustainability by starting with self-help. All the major case studies stress self-help, and contributions from people. In Sukhomajri half the cost of land levelling was born by farmers. Each family contributed an equal share of labour for laying water distribution pipes. The villagers agreed to desilt dams, and so on. In Tin Aicha villagers made the bricks for the school, dispensary and co-operative store. With BBP, there were labour and cash contributions to building irrigation and water supply systems. Von Mehren and Seo's account of Lampang stresses at the outset that the individual projects encompass a wide range of self-help activities whose objective is sustainable development. Guinope, however, is where the emphasis on self-help is strongest. In recounting that 31 km of contour rock walls had been built by farmers in the process of protecting some 449 ha of hillside land from erosion, the study observes that none of this work was paid for or done by the programme; it was all done by the farmers, who were convinced it was in their own interest.

The link between self-help and sustainability is strong. Subsidies, for example through food-for-work, may sometimes be necessary or desirable, but they often diminish the relevance or sustainability of a programme; relevance is less because people who are being paid in food or cash are prepared to undertake work in which they have neither interest nor faith, and because of the expectation of further support for further work. By inducing people to do what they are not really interested in, subsidies also inhibit outsiders' learning; they are misled into thinking people want what they do not. In contrast, the first key factor emphasized in the Guinope study, as also in *Two Ears of Corn* (Bunch, 1985) is that "All forms of paternalism should be avoided … work should be accomplished for the sole reason that villagers have seen success achieved and have become enthusiastic enough to work toward achieving it for themselves."

This advice cannot be applied universally, especially with deeply impoverished populations. The Central American countries in which the World Neighbors approach has been developed are not among the poorest. None the less, one universal lesson can be drawn from this: within humane and practical limits, to restrain subsidies and to encourage self-help, in order to improve the relevance, maintenance and spread of a programme.

Self-help and sustainability go further than this, however, in the enhancement of people's capacity to innovate and adapt, and so to help themselves in the future. The experimental capacities and practices of small farmers are now well known (see, for example, Richards, 1985). In Harijan Nada families experimented with different crops. In Tin Aicha the American Friends Service Committee (AFSC) looked particularly to nomads who were experimenting with a mix between agriculture and herding. With BBP, farmers were found to be evolving their own planting practices for ipil-ipil, which led to modification of project recommendations. Again, Guinope goes furthest; one of the project's objectives is to enhance farmers' own experimental capacities, so that "farmers can continue to develop their own agriculture long after the program has closed its doors". After the programme, what would be sustained is a loose-knit federation of village-level agricultural clubs in order to coordinate experiments each year and then share experimental results.

Staff calibre, commitment and continuity

The fifth lesson is the importance of calibre, commitment and continuity of staff. Calibre refers to sensitivity, insight and competence. Commitment refers to determination, self-sacrifice and dedication to working with and for the poor. Continuity refers to working consistently over at least several years. The argument is liable to be circular; if a project is good, the staff involved must be of high calibre and commitment. But the element of continuity is more verifiable. P.R. Mishra, Madhu Sarin and others who worked with Sukhomajri Nada were involved for a matter of years, the first two for an exceptionally long time. As the case study reports "the complete devotion and involvement of a band of dedicated workers made the success of Sukhomajri and Nada possible". Tin Aicha had an AFSC staff member in post from 1975 who gave "unforeseen continuity" compared with the turnover in government staff. For Lampang, the vital link was provided by a Thai nutritionist who had attended MFM's training course in Santa Monica, California, in 1979. Until he left BBP in 1979 John Carr "was the project ... not only administrator, manager or supervisor, but also doctor, nurse, motivator, clerk, driver, peon, porter, sweeper and labourer" (Ghimire, 1980, p. 8); in addition, one of the field co-ordinators was with the project since its inception. In Yatenga the continuity and work of Peter Wright and Mathieu Oedraougo, and the support they received from Oxfam, were critical. And it is difficult to imagine that the *tour de force* of Guinope would have been possible without exceptional leadership, including that of farmers from other projects as extension agents.

Calibre, commitment and continuity of staff reinforce the ability to implement the other lessons – the learning process approach, putting people's priorities first and especially those of the poorer, securing rights and gains, and enabling self-help for sustainability. It is usually impossible for government field staff to have the combination of assured continuity and freedom of action needed, and ✳ difficult for them to have a close relationship with the local people. NGO staff may also be better able to understand and represent the point of view of rural people (for example, the desire of Tin Aicha's former nomads to be transhumant) or to adapt local custom, as with Lampang's extension of traditional feeding of Buddhist monks to feeding of children. The "new professionals" who are capable of such sensitivity and reversals of normal values are often most at home in NGOs and are increasing in number. Without such people, these case study successes could scarcely have occurred.

Sustainable spread

Some of the case studies present details of unit costs. These, however, take a narrow view of effects. On the negative side, much development has losers as well as gainers, and the losers usually receive less attention. On the positive side, good effects, as the cases demonstrate, are usually wider than unit costings indicate. A criterion here is whether there is a sustainable spread of good effects. These can take at least three forms: institutional spread; spontaneous or induced diffusion; and impact on analysis and policy.

Institutional spread

Institutional spread of a successful or promising approach developed by an NGO can occur in three ways: expansion of the NGO and its activities; adoption by other NGOs; or adoption by and incorporation in government organizations. All three are represented in the cases. Neither of the two projects – Sukhomajri/Nada and Tin Aicha – has been replicated, but elements in their approaches are adoptable: Sukhomajri/Nada has encouraged other NGOs, for example the Aga Khan Rural Support Programme in Bharuch District in Gujarat, to adopt the principle of water rights to all villagers including the landless.

In contrast to the two projects, the three programmes – Lampang, BBP and Guinope – expanded or extended their influence in more institutional ways.

Sukhomajri/Nada had prolonged and difficult negotiations with the Forest Department, and Tin Aicha had a "bumpy ride" with local government authorities. In contrast, both Lampang and Guinope made close relations with government departments part of their strategy. Lampang seems to have been outstanding in the care taken to work with the Thai Ministry of Public Health. An evaluation of Lampang noted a willingness to subordinate private-voluntary-agency identity to Thai government interests and desires of beneficiaries; it also noted that

> MFM efforts gave ownership of the project to national and provincial departments of health, the governor of Lampang and village leaders, stimulating improved response among field staff and villagers. . . . This building of responsibility has produced measurable increases in the quantity and quality of activities. It also improves likelihood of institution-alization and sustainability.
>
> (Pines and Becht, 1985, pp. 24, 30)

Partly in consequence, another factor being low unit costs, the programme was widely replicated without any financial support from MFM. Similarly, Guinope worked with the Honduran Ministry of Natural Resources from the start, was chosen as a national model for agricultural extension work and had eight other programmes in Honduras modelled on it. Whatever dilution or distortion there may have been with these expansions, both Lampang and Guinope thus achieved institutional spread and sustainability, promising much wider impacts.

Factors contributing to such spread and sustainability can include those enumerated above as the five lessons. Others, more specific to these two examples, appear to be: using tried methods based on experience gained in other countries; working with government from the start; adoption of a low profile (Lampang); low recurrent costs. Also, neither Thailand nor Honduras is among the poorest countries; neither is likely to be suffering stringent constraints on recurrent expenditure. To the contrary, Thailand's economic growth must have made it easier for the government to accept any additional costs. Institutional spread through adoption by government will be harder in countries hit by debt and economic decline.

Spontaneous or induced diffusion

The spontaneous or induced diffusion of technologies outside a project or programme area is a non-institutional form of impact. Visits by farmers, officials and NGO staff to project and programme areas play a part in this. Extension and training are also undertaken. The smokeless *chulas* (stoves) developed in Sukhomajri/Nada were diffused elsewhere by Harijan women from Nada as extension agents. The spread of Guinope's technologies, of Lampang's soybeans and ducks, of BBP's ipil-ipil and of Yatenga's water harvesting technology all occurred spontaneously, with no project costs, as well as through extension efforts.

Planning and working for spontaneous diffusion are especially important in resource-poor areas of the lowest-income countries where institutional spread is difficult to sustain and subsidies and recurrent expenditures constrained. Good innovations which spread on their own bring benefits without costs. Few NGOs or governments pay adequate attention to this.

Impact on analysis and policy

Much of the impact of the case study projects and programmes had been, and will be, on analysis and policy. Sukhomajri/Nada, though not replicated, has had a big impact on official thinking in India, not least through an analysis of lessons conducted for the Planning Commission (Chowdhry *et al.*, 1984); and Guinope and the World Neighbors approach to agricultural innovation and improvement, as also the Yatenga experience, present a challenge to normal agricultural research and extension. Guinope and Yatenga open up the question whether farmers have a comparative advantage over normal scientists in resource-poor conditions, being able as they are to experiment flexibly with many variables simultaneously, using common sense, experience and intuition, unconstrained by statistical scientific methods. If farmers do indeed have such advantages, and if big advances in resource-poor agriculture require more complex simultaneous innovations, the analytical and policy implications are immense.

Conclusion

To imply, as the title of this chapter does, that sustainable rural livelihoods are a key strategy for people, environment and development complements the normal view of resource-poor peripheries as seen from resource-rich cores. This normal view sees pollutions and exploitations spreading out from urban, industrial and rich-country cores to harm rural, agricultural and poor peripheries. To restrain and reduce the spread of such bad effects is essential, but the dominant view from the resource-rich cores is unbalanced. The other view, from the periphery to the core, is neglected. Yet it is vital, both to represent the needs and priorities of the majority of the world's poor and to see what best to do and how best to do it. A strategy for the resource-poor peripheries must aim to reduce the pressures and miseries of outmigration, to diminish debt and to enable people to build up self-reliance, self-respect and independent power.

Resource-poor conditions require their own approaches. Insensitive analysis and action based on the values and techniques of the resource-rich world do not fit well and often harm. Resource-poor and ecologically vulnerable people, and the environments in which they live, need new forms of development that enable them to gain a secure and decent living for themselves and their children, where they are and with the resources they can command. It is by starting with the priorities of the poorer, and enabling them to gain the livelihoods they want and need, that both they and sustainable development can best be served.

References

Askew, Ian, and John Carr (1986), *An Analysis of Community Participation in the Bouddha-Bahunepati Family Welfare Project, Nepal: A Report to the Bureau of the Indian Ocean Region.* International Planned Parenthood Federation, London.

Bailey, Charles, Anthony Bottrall and Robert Chambers (1985), "Notes and reflections on three agroforestry projects in (Lake) Baringo District, Kenya", typescript. Institute of Development Studies, University of Sussex, Brighton.

Bentley, William R. (1984), "The uncultivated half of India: problems and possible solutions". Ford Foundation Delhi Discussion Paper Series 12. Ford Foundation, 55 Lodi Estate, New Delhi 110003.

Breman, Jan (1985), *Of Peasants, Migrants and Paupers: Rural Labour Circulation and Capitalist Production in West India.* Oxford University Press.

Bunch, Roland (1985), *Two Ears of Corn: A Guide to People-Centered Agricultural Improvement*, 2nd edn. World Neighbors, 5116 North Portland, Oklahoma City, Oklahoma 73112.

Chambers, Robert, and Melissa Leach (1987), "Trees to meet contingencies: savings and security for the rural poor". IDS Discussion Paper 228. Institute of Development Studies, University of Sussex, Brighton.

Chowdhry, Kamla, *et al.* (1984), *Hill Resource Development and Community Management: Lessons Learnt on Micro-Watershed Management from Cases of Sukhomajri and Dasholi Gram Swarajya Mandal.* Society for Promotion of Wastelands Development, Sucheta Bhawan Annexe, 11–A Vishnu Digamber Marg, New Delhi 110002.

Food 2000 (1987), *Food 2000: Global Policies for Sustainable Agriculture. A Report of the Advisory Panel on Food Security, Agriculture, Forestry and Environment to the World Commission on Environment and Development.* Zed Books, London and New Jersey.

Ghimire, J. (1980), "A study of Badha Bahunepati family welfare project of Family Planning Association of Nepal", mimeo. Cited in Askew and Carr, 1986.

Korten, David C. (1980), "Community organization and rural development: a learning process approach". *Public Administration Review*, 40, September/October, pp. 480–510.

Korten, David C. (1984), "Rural development planning: the learning process approach". In Korten and Klauss, op, cit., pp. 176–88.

Korten, David C., and Rudi Klauss (eds) (1984), *People-Centered Development: Contributions toward Theory and Planning Frameworks.* Kumarian Press, West Hartford, Conn.

Lapierre, Dominique (1986), *City of Joy.* Arrow Books, London.

Ostberg, Wilhelm (1986), "The Kondoa transformation: coming to grips with soil erosion in Central Tanzania", *Research Report No. 76.* Scandinavian Institute of African Studies, Uppsala.

Pines, James M., and James N. Becht (1985), *Evaluation Report: Meals for Millions, Thailand.* Management Services for Health, Suite 700, 1655 North Fort Myer Drive, Arlington, Va 22209.

Reij, Chris, Adrian Cullis and Yacob Akililu (1987), "Soil and water conservation in Sub-Saharan Africa: the need for a bottom-up approach". Paper for the Oxfam Workshop on Arid Lands Management, Cotonou, 23–27 March.

Richards, Paul (1985), *Indigenous Agricultural Revolution: Ecology and Food Production in West Africa*. Hutchinson, London.

Rondinelli, Dennis A. (1983), *Development Projects as Policy Experiments: An Adaptive Approach to Development Administration*. Methuen, London and New York.

World Bank (1986), *World Development Report 1986*. Oxford University Press for the World Bank.

Wright, Peter (1985), *Soil and Water Conservation by Farmers*. Oxfam, Ouagadougou.

CASE STUDY 1 *Lampang Applied Nutrition Program, Thailand*

PHILIP VON MEHREN

Programme Associate, Asia, Meals for Millions/Freedom from Hunger Foundation

and JOHN SEO

Regional Director, Asia, Meals for Millions

Since 1982 Meals for Millions/Freedom from Hunger Foundation (MFM) has been co-implementing, with the Thai Ministry of Public Health, an Applied Nutrition Program (ANP) in Lampang Province, Northern Thailand. The ANP's broad goal is the improvement of the nutritional status of the 86,000 people in Ngao and Sobprap districts, especially children 0–4 and pregnant and lactating women.

The ANP was planned to foster sustainable development, and with both government and village-level organizational structures seen as crucial to this strategy, and to demonstrate to government fieldworkers the effectiveness of intersectoral co-ordination and a bottom-up approach. Within villages the programme sought to promote management and technical skills. Fieldworkers, volunteers and the villagers themselves seem prepared to manage the development process in the wake of MFM's phase-out in 1988. Local control over day-to-day programme management, the ANP's methodology and the relatively small amount of foreign financial assistance have contributed to the programme's long-term effectiveness.

The manner in which the ANP was implemented in Lampang is a clear indication of MFM's commitment to local participation and control. Two factors coalesced to prompt the project's inception. The first was consensus among decision-makers in the Thai Ministry of Public Health, following a large-scale project funded by USAID, that Lampang Province needed a nutritionally focused, intersectoral, grass-roots development strategy. The USAID project had created an excellent health infrastructure in the province, but by neglecting nutrition, food security and income generation it failed to maximize impact. The second factor was a shift in the programmatic orientation of MFM, away from simply nutrition training, to an Applied Nutrition Program.

Context and approach

Lampang Province is situated on the south-central edge of the hills dominating most of Northern Thailand and has roughly 650,000 inhabitants of whom 86,000 live in Ngao and Sobprap. Sobprap has gentler hills and wider river valleys than

Ngao, making more land available for cultivation of the main crop, rice. In Ngao, with its teak forests, steeper hills and narrower valleys, the Yaw and Cairn hill tribes practise slash-and-burn agriculture, primarily cultivating corn. Thai villagers dominate the valley floors in Ngao, growing rice as a staple.

Among the hill tribes, ANP and government field staff have attempted to promote intensive agriculture; soybeans were promoted as a highly nutritious crop that improves soil quality, encourages long-term cultivation *in situ* and thus discourages slash-and-burn. Efforts were made to show the hill tribes the health and nutritional benefits associated with permanent settlement.

The ANP evolved through six stages: (1) initial feasibility study; (2) collection of baseline data and defining objectives; (3) creating detailed plans for specific projects; (4) initiating programme activities; (5) evaluation and adjustment; (6) replication in other communities. The ANP methodology has stressed throughout the importance of involving government ministries and villagers in an interactive process.

The programme comprises a variety of projects and training activities aimed at improving the people's health and nutrition, including the creation of family latrines and food cabinets, and the promotion of soybean cultivation and duck raising. Data on child growth are collected by health workers to identify families with malnourished children.

Project activities

In most of the 82 villages, monthly sanitation campaigns are now part of the regular cycle of rural life. Sanitation has improved considerably. A traditional Thai practice of feeding the Buddhist monks was the catalyst. After gaining the monks' support, ANP staff pointed out to villagers that their dirty kitchens and villages were contaminating the food given to the monks. As a result, the villagers organized to clean up their environment. Simple bamboo trash cans, mounted on poles, have displaced the open dumping of garbage. Homes are cleaner, with less cow dung where small children play. Kitchens are also cleaner now that villagers understand the causal link between poor sanitation and morbidity.

The promotion of soybean cultivation and attempts to increase duck raising and the types of vegetables available progressed slowly until a concerted effort was made to teach village women new recipes and cooking techniques. Women are now preparing soy milk, tofu, duck-egg soup and other nutritious recipes using the new food sources.

The interrelationship between improving nutrition and protecting the environment for human use has led to a programme that is environmentally sustainable. The ANP has emphasized the management of contaminants in the area's agro-ecosystems through several main foci: (1) using organic or biodynamic means to increase soil fertility; (2) supporting sanitation projects and environmentally sound means of waste disposal; (3) introducing simple techniques for storing and preserving foods and water. Soybeans were introduced because they both yield needed dietary protein (especially for weaning foods) and replenish nitrogen in intensively cultivated soils, decreasing the need for chemical fertilizers. Villagers received training in the use of natural waste products, including the nutrient-rich run-off from the fishponds; and mulching of vegetable and animal wastes, which further increase soil fertility while improving environmental sanitation.

The villagers are now independently removing garbage, including cow dung (which contributes to high levels of diarrhoea), from areas near the household and using it, if appropriate, for mulch pits. Inside the households, kitchens are now kept clean by using simple drains and thoroughly cleaning cooking utensils.

The villagers have also learned non-contaminating techniques of pest control for food storage and preservation. A simple wooden cabinet is used for food storage with each leg set in a split coconut shell filled with water and a thin film of vegetable oil. Ants and other ground insects drown trying to reach the food, and the film of oil prevents mosquitoes from breeding in the water. The improvement of water storage was also achieved with simple techniques; the Thai government provided a mould of a slow sand filtration tank that many villagers quickly learned to reproduce and use.

The ANP revolving fund furthers the programme's self-help philosophy. Villagers are loaned in-kind grants of ducks, soybeans, etc., and are expected to repay the programme after the loan matures. During 1986 the ANP began training the villagers in loan fund management. The programme will have much greater sustainability when the revolving capital becomes owned by a local, village-based organization.

Prior to 1985 not enough targeting of "at risk" families occurred. But project staff have since learned to help each other identify "at risk" families and to design interventions for them.

Training

Village women and schoolchildren have been given classes on basic food groups, balanced diet, weaning foods, nutritional problems and nutritious foods that can be grown in backyards. Training has also been given to Health Post Volunteers (HPVs) and Health Communicators (HCs) in the creation of community and individual growth charts for the identification of malnourished children.

Costs and benefits

The overall programme costs were modest. A total of $598,598 was spent from July 1982 to August 1986. Annual per capita costs range from $1.64 to $1.99 per beneficiary. The Thai government supported the programme with an estimated $175,000 from 1982 to 1986, and a number of non-govenmental organizations donated a variety of inputs.

The ANP has had a considerable impact on its beneficiaries: 80.4 per cent of the families now have latrines, 69.0 per cent have food cabinets, 49.2 per cent have some system for collecting and storing clean water, 48.0 per cent have vegetable gardens, 16.1 per cent are growing soybeans, 9.7 per cent are raising ducks, 2.9 per cent have a fishpond and 1.0 per cent are raising bees. The benefits are most dramatically expressed in nutritional terms; in a little over four years the ANP has contributed to the overall reduction in child malnutrition in rural Lampang.

The training component of the ANP has had an impact in four major areas: (1) government workers are now sensitive to nutrition concerns and the importance of intersectoral collaboration; (2) an overwhelming majority of the 82 villages have improved their sanitation; (3) HPVs and HCs now run an efficient child growth-monitoring system; (4) village women are more conscious of how to prepare a balanced diet for infants and the rest of the family.

Institutionalization and sustainability

Several institutional structures are steadily assuming some of the functions of the ANP, thereby demonstrating their ability to promote sustainable development: (1) Thai government ministries have begun to adopt the applied nutrition approach; (2) village women's groups are beginning to organize nutrition activities independently; (3) HPVs and HCs are replacing paid staff in monitoring child growth and advising families on child nutrition; (4) the revolving fund has good prospects of becoming community-managed. Also, hundreds of farmers are now choosing independently to grow soybeans, raise ducks, etc.

When the ANP began in 1982 the government's rural development efforts were characterized by a top–down approach. The ANP has successfully demonstrated a more participatory development strategy. The ANP is being replicated, without any financial support from MFM, in all 12 districts in Lampang Province, and the government's field staff have received instructions to foster participation.

Within villages, the ANP has promoted the emergence of three organizations important for sustainability: the women's clubs, the growth-monitoring and health-promotion system run by HPVs and HCs, and the revolving funds. The main activities of the women's clubs include cooking classes, the monastic feeding programme and kitchen sanitation. Many of the HPVs and HCs have begun taking leading roles in nutrition projects in their communities; as a vital link between government fieldworkers and the people, they should play a pivotal role in sustaining the ANP after MFM's phase-out.

CASE STUDY 2 *Social Security through Social Fencing, Sukhomajri and Nada, North India*

P. R. MISHRA and MADHU SARIN
Development Consultants

The Shiwaliks are foothills of the Himalayas in North India. By the end of the nineteenth century most of their vegetative cover was gone. New settlers clearing land for agriculture, unrestricted tree felling and the cattle grazing of nomadic herdsmen were the main causes of this devastation. Vegetative destruction led to the formation of gullies and to once perennial streams being converted into hundreds of *choes*, ever widening river-beds which remain dry most of the year but flood suddenly during the monsoons.

The Shiwaliks are fairly densely populated. The rain-fed cultivation of maize followed by wheat is unable to ensure even subsistence, and most villagers rear livestock for sale, mainly to the plains. Most of the cattle are let loose for grazing in the hills. Overgrazing has led to severe erosion, low grass production and poor quality of cattle. The end result of the vicious cycle is that 50 per cent of the average annual rainfall of 1,200 mm ends as run-off from bare hill slopes, carrying an estimated 100 to 150 tonnes per ha of sediment to the plains.

Sukhomajri: origin of the project

In 1958 a dam was built across the Sukhna Choe to create an artificial lake as a recreational facility in the new city of Chandigarh. By the early 1970s Sukhna Lake was silting at the rate of 3 per cent annually. By 1974 about 60 per cent of the lake's storage capacity was filled with sediment. Chandigarh administration sought help from the Indian government's Central Soil and Water Conservation Research and Training Institute (CSWCRTI).

To find the basic cause of such a high sediment rate, the CSWCRTI team, then headed by the first author, decided to survey the entire catchment of the lake on foot. Senior officials of Haryana state's Forest Department also participated in this exercise. Degradation of the hills near Sukhomajri, where one of the two tributaries feeding Sukhna Lake originates, was the most acute in the whole catchment of the lake. Barely 5 per cent of the slopes had any vegetative cover. Out of 85 ha of hilly area, planting could be considered on only 7 ha. The hills were totally cut up into pieces with tall, bare, vertical walls.

Sukhomajri is inhabited by Gujjars, professional graziers. They kept large herds of cattle, including small cows and goats, which were let loose for grazing in the hills. Most families also owned small landholdings on which they practised rain-fed agriculture. Due to land hunger caused by economic insecurity, many villagers had started clearing hill slopes to bring them under the plough. This yielded little and reduced the land's water-retention capacity; the fertile topsoil was getting washed away.

Construction of check-dams and planting of trees had been undertaken near the village many times, but without the support of the people, and nothing had survived. The villagers wondered suspiciously if the government project was a guise to deprive them of their land or evict them from the village. The challenge was to ensure the people a reasonable standard of living from their limited land so that they could be persuaded to stop overexploiting the hills.

First attempts and new problems

Two small earthen dams were built, one in the catchment releasing water towards Sukhomajri. The catchment of this dam was intensively treated with contour trenches, grade stabilizers, check-dams and planting, to find out the degree to which the sedimentation rate could be brought down by intensive treatment of slopes, gullies and streams. The second small dam was built on Sukhna Lake's side. No treatment was given to this dam's catchment, the objective being to get an idea of the existing sediment flow.

The earthen dam built on the Sukhomajri side, whose catchment had been treated, collected some water during the 1977 monsoons. It was decided to use this water for providing supplemental irrigation to the adjoining fields for the winter wheat crop. The owners of these fields were also provided improved seeds and adequate fertilizer. Yields increased sustainability. The enthusiasm of the villagers was tremendous.

A village leader showed the team another location where a larger amount of water could be stored by building a bigger dam. Outside the catchment of Sukhna Lake, the location and topography were ideally suited for providing gravity-fed irrigation to a larger area of the village's cultivable land. The suggestion was taken up. It was realized that the siltation problem of Sukhna Lake could be tackled by working in a different watershed, provided it made it in the villagers' interest to stop grazing their animals in either watershed. Mutual benefit of the watershed and its command area could be ensured by tying up the interest of the people in the command area with protecting the watershed, since the latter could yield life-saving water for the crops.

Thus a second dam was built in Sukhomajri in early 1978. Because this dam was to collect water for irrigation, mostly grasses were planted in the catchment to permit greater run-off. An underground pipeline was provided to take water to a command area of about 40 acres. The undulating fields were levelled to maximize the benefits of irrigation, with the landowners contributing half the cost.

The first supplemental irrigation from dam no. 2 was provided to the winter wheat crop of 1978–9. Improved seeds and fertilizers were also provided to the farmers at cost price. Crop yields increased dramatically and have increased further since then as the farmers have learned better management of irrigated agriculture.

Some villagers continued to graze their cattle in the hills. One day, when a villager was asked to stop bringing his cattle to the hills, he threatened to burn the CSWCRTI field tent in the village, objecting to outsiders seeking to deprive villagers of their traditional rights without providing any benefits in return. Inadvertently, the project had increased inequality among the villagers, providing irrigation for only some of the village land. In 1981, therefore, the water pipeline was extended to the unirrigated area.

The only way of getting every family's co-operation in stopping grazing in the hills was through ensuring an equitable distribution of water, irrespective of landownership or size of landholding. This proposal was presented to the villagers in 1980. The villagers had reached the same conclusion on their own.

It was also decided to constitute a water users' society. A representative from each family could become a member of the society and gain a right to an equal share of water. Any member whose cattle was found in the hills would lose his or her right to water. The society was given responsibility for maintaining the dams and their catchments, distributing water and maintaining records.

Even those owning very small amounts of land were to get the same amount of water, and it was suggested that they could either sell their surplus water at a higher price to those short of water or sharecrop using their water on part of the land of those short of water.

The birth of "social fencing"

Most families in Sukhomajri gradually sold off their goats, the animals that do maximum damage to the hills, replacing them with high-milk-yielding buffaloes bought without any outside subsidy. The villagers decided to stall-feed them instead of letting them loose for grazing. The concept of "social fencing", whereby villagers decide to protect the hills from grazing through self-restraint, was born.

Stoppage of grazing initiated regeneration of the hills. Newly planted saplings took root, and the output of natural grass started showing a dramatic increase. Greater availability of fodder, from both the hills and the villagers' fields, resulted in a substantial increase in milk production.

Seeing the output of grass in the hills rise, the Haryana Forest Department (FD) felt that the villagers deserved the benefit rather than an outsider. In 1985 FD agreed to give joint management of grass-cutting rights to the Sukhomajri and Dhamala (an adjoining village) societies rather than, as previously, to a private contractor.

In 1986 the FD also decided to subcontract the right of cutting the commercial bhabbar grass from its nearby compartment to the Sukhomajri/Dhamala societies. When they have learned how to manage such a large-scale operation, they hope to buy some ropemaking machines to convert the grass into rope within the village before selling it. Sukhomajri and Dhamala should be able to make a substantial income from bhabbar, and many underemployed villagers will get employment.

The learning process has led to a decided change in the attitudes of the Haryana FD, which has appointed an assistant conservator of forests to help set up similar societies in other villages. It was planned to set up 40 societies by the end of 1987. In some of the villages the FD has also built dams, after obtaining agreement from local villagers to protect the catchment. These new societies are being given the right to cut grass and bhabbar on the Sukhomajri pattern. The FD does not need to play a policing role any longer, and its expenditure on fencing is reduced drastically; and with villagers protecting the hills, productivity is increasing.

In 1985 the name of the Sukhomajri Soil and Water Conservation Society was changed to Hill Resource Management Society. All the new societies formed since then have this name. The Sukhomajri experience indicated enormous possibilities of growth through better management of hill resources. Water and grasses were only two of these. Fish could be grown in the water of the dam to generate further social revenue. If this was ploughed back into the hills to grow carefully selected species of trees and grasses, and the villagers processed their output into higher-value products such as oils, rope and paper, the village economy could become almost self-sufficient.

Exploring replication in Nada

By 1979 a self-sustaining development model, capable of radically transforming the economies of poverty-stricken hilly villages in many parts of the country, was taking shape. To explore the viability of the model in a different setting, the project was extended to Nada village.

Unlike Sukhomajri, Nada is quite spread out, with four separate hamlets. Upper, Middle and Lower Nada are inhabited by a caste called Lavana. Nada Choe, which is a dry river-bed most of the year, cuts the village into two parts. A fourth hamlet, on the other side of the *choe*, is inhabited by low-caste Harijans.

Practically all the Lavanas own some land. Besides agriculture and livestock farming, the Lavanas earn their living from other activities such as transporting stone on their camels from the Ghaggar river-bed to nearby stone-crushers.

Whereas the Lavanas had 235 acres, the Harijan hamlet had only 6 acres of unirrigated land, of which the crafty Lavana village *sarpanch* (headman) had bought off about 1.5 acres. Five Harijan families were completely landless and the other 12 subsisted on 4.5 acres of land supplemented with income from daily wages.

The hills behind the Harijan hamlet presented a scene of severe denudation. The yield of natural grass here was very low. The situation was truly daunting; the concept of social fencing would be severely tested.

In 1980 three dams were built around Nada. Two of the sites were to the south of the village and suitable for gravity-fed irrigation of the Lavanas's agricultural land. The catchments of these had reasonable vegetative cover. The third was near the Harijan hamlet and could irrigate their land. This watershed was severely denuded.

The irrigation system of the Harijans was kept separate from that of the Lavanas. It was feared that if the Harijans were made members of the same society, they would be cheated of their rights. From the beginning the villagers were offered the package deal of getting water only in return for protecting the watersheds of the dams. Some of the bigger landowners resisted the idea of each family being entitled to an equal share of water, but village meetings effectively resolved such conflicts, with the help of neutral project personnel and the Sukhomajri example.

The yield of the first irrigated wheat crop harvested in 1982 was three times that from rain-fed agriculture. Two threshers were brought from outside to thresh this yield. In 1983 the village had six threshers operating for the same crop. Two local farmers subsequently bought their own tractors and threshers.

Progress in Harijan Nada

Establishing rapport with the Harijans was begun through the women, who were keen for income-earning opportunities within the hamlet, being prevented from going out to work by social taboos. The first author thought of persuading the women, particularly the landless, to take up rope production, using the local bhabbar grass, *Eulaliopsis binata*. Processed into rope, and selling in the market at Rs2 to Rs3 per kg, its value would increase four to five times. One hectare of denuded hilly land brought under bhabbar could then generate an income of Rs20,000. The landless families, once persuaded to take up this work, could then be persuaded to protect a plantation of their raw material in adjoining hills.

On 1 July 1980 two foot-pedal-operated machines, some bhabbar from the research farm and an instructor arrived to teach six women how to use the machines.

Getting rope production established was not easy. Problems included breakdown of the machinery, marketing difficulties and seasonal fluctuation in demand. Through persistence and building up a collective spirit and basic technical competence, the battle was ultimately won. In November 1981 three new machines were bought at the request of younger women who now saw the other women earning and achieving greater economic independence and improved social status.

Bhabbar was a material the villagers were already familiar with and knew how to process before conversion into rope. They enjoy the right to cut the grass from hills under the Forest Department, and produce rope by hand for their own consumption. The biggest advantage was that the rope has a large local market. Villagers use it for making the widely used *charpais* (a kind of hammock) and for tying thatch roofs and bundles of harvested crops.

By the end of 1980, with 6 out of 17 families engaged in rope production, thought was given to revitalizing the denuded hill behind the Harijan hamlet. For the other families, fuel and fodder trees could be planted as an incentive to protect the land from grazing. The land belonged to the Forest Department, which feared that as soon as the villagers were given special rights to the produce of forest land they would bring the land under the plough. Fortunately, by designating the plantation a research project, the Harijans could be provided special rights on an experimental basis. They would get priority rights to the produce, with a share going to the FD. The villagers' major contribution was to be protection; they had to stop grazing their own animals there and also help keep out the animals of other villagers. Until the plantation started yielding fodder they could take their cattle for grazing in other parts of the hills. The Harijans accepted the deal.

But the stoppage of grazing produced strains among the villagers. Now someone had to take the animals much further away and ensure that they did not wander into the plantation area. The FD guard started impounding animals caught in newly planted areas. With the beginning of the hot dry season in 1982, while the landowning families got wheat straw as fodder, the landless ones started complaining about fodder scarcity. The landless men, who worked on daily wages, had no time to take their animals for supervised grazing. The project team proposed that in the near future only the landless families should be allowed to cut bhabbar and other natural grass growing in the plantation area. The team was totally taken aback by the villagers' response. While the landowners were willing to let the landless have this special right, the landless rejected it, saying they did not want any exclusive rights, which would make them the objects of envy and resentment. The project team had to bow to their wisdom.

In November 1982 the first harvest of bhabbar for ropemaking took place. This was the hamlet society's first clear-cut responsibility, which it managed efficiently. Between 1982 and 1986 the quantity of bhabbar harvested quadrupled.

As in higher-caste Nada, the Harijans were told that water from the dam would be distributed to each independent family unit on an equitable basis. But the situation in the hamlet was considerably different from both Sukhomajri and higher-caste Nada. The Harijans had a lot of water and very limited land. Almost a third of the families were totally landless. Even the landowning families were very poor, with tiny holdings on which they could barely use their own share of water. Who would be interested in the landless's share of water?

It was suggested that the landless could raise fish in the dam, retaining their water share there. Or maybe they could sharecrop on the *sarpanch*'s land or sell him their water at a higher rate. But raising fish required learning a new skill, and no one felt strong enough to deal with the domineering *sarpanch*.

Project staff made further suggestions to the Harijans about how to maximize the output from their limited land now that they had plenty of water. The Harijans also started experimenting themselves. One family put aside a small area for planting vegetables. Seeing the problems of marketing a perishable vegetable such as tomatoes, they instead tried *arbi* (a root crop like sweet potatoes). This took only five months to mature, and they were able to sell the yield for Rs500.

The catchment of the Harijans' dam was in the most denuded condition. Its siltation rate continued to be high, and by 1984 the water outlet from the dam was completely choked with silt. Time for sowing wheat was approaching fast, there was no rain to provide the necessary soil moisture, the dam was full of water, yet the Harijans could not use the water. Desperate, they tried to borrow or hire a pump to pump the water out to their fields, but this proved impossible. They decided to buy a pump using the society's social fund and an informal loan. This way, the Harijan Nada Society acquired its first major asset, a 10 hp motor, which can even run a thresher. Now the society is planning to buy its own thresher.

Benefits and wider impact

Sukhomajri's daily milk sale has increased almost ninefold, with at least 300 kg of milk retained for daily consumption within the village. The average annual crop yields in both Sukhomajri and Nada have increased four to five times. Whereas Sukhomajri had earlier to import grain, now it has a surplus to sell. Through the practice of social fencing the average sediment flow into Sukhna Lake has fallen dramatically. The recreational facility of the lake has been saved for the residents of Chandigarh.

Social and economic security of people in both villages has increased, and they have acquired a sense of dignity through helping change a destructive development cycle into a productive one. The villagers have started taking control of their own development. There has been a qualitative improvement in women's daily lives, since cattle fodder is more freely available. The generation of an annual social fund in both villages has created a possibility for the villagers to continue the development process.

The concept of social fencing is now being extended to other villages of Haryana and Punjab and to some villages in Gujarat, Bihar and Rajasthan. The complete devotion and involvement of a band of dedicated workers made the success of Sukhomajri and Nada possible, and support by several senior government officials was also crucial. The model continues to face resistance from the established "development" infrastructure, however; that remains the main obstacle to its wider implementation.

CASE STUDY 3 *Baudha-Bahunipati Family Welfare Project, Nepal*

TOM ARENS and GOPAL NAKARMI
World Neighbors, South Asia Regional Office

The Baudha-Bahunipati Project (BBP) is a project of the Family Planning Association of Nepal, covering 48 *panchayats* (a *panchayat* is a political/administrative division with a population of 2,000 to 9,000). World Neighbors provides support in 19 of these *panchayats*, covering a population of about 80,000. The project began in 1973 in the small village of Bahunipati, on the bank of the Indrawati river. The Majhi (fisherman) village above Bahunipati's bazaar has been a focus area for income-generating demonstration and activities.

The project started with assistance from the International Planned Parenthood Federation, of which the Family Planning Association of Nepal is a federated member. In 1975 World Neighbors was requested to provide supplementary assistance for agricultural development and expansion of the health work. It was felt that an integrated approach in this rural, remote area would increase family planning adoption.

The increasing reputation of the region is placing growing demands on the available natural resources (for food, fodder and firewood). This is leading to outmigration, threatening living standards and degrading the environment. To counter these trends the programme has set itself the following goals: (1) to reduce the birth rate and improve the health of children and mothers; (2) to increase agricultural productivity and family income, particularly of small farmers; (3) to improve basic curative and preventive health services until the area is adequately served by alternative services. The programme places a strong emphasis on community participation in programme design, implementation and management and on the integration of its activities with other agencies and the Nepalese government.

The project expanded out from Bahunipati to surrounding *panchayats* over the years. Programme planning originates with the local community and *panchayat* worker, and development activities depend on local interest and relevance and on available local/external resources. The project has achieved one of the largest contraceptive use figures in Nepal, an average of 28 per cent of the fertile couples (twice the national average); and the average birth rate is well below the national average.

Income-generating activities

Acceptance of family planning in the Majhi village started simultaneously with income-generation activities in 1977, although the clinic was offering services as early as 1973. Luxmi Majhi, the first female acceptor of family planning (temporary and permanent methods), now has the largest number of ipil-ipil trees, has increased her income with livestock and is the village health worker for the Majhi village.

In Bahunipati fodder and livestock development was given priority, and the Majhi community identified as the focal point. Aside from limited fishing, Majhis have few income-generating options. Those who are small farmers have only rain-fed lands with generally poor soils; and at the time of starting the programme livestock was limited to pigs and a few goats. A goat, buffalo and swine upgrading programme has been carried out in the community, along with fodder tree and grass extension; veterinary services are now available.

Livestock numbers increased 40 per cent between 1983 and 1986. Yearly sales of livestock have also increased steadily, showing that the village not only maintains but also sells more livestock. Animal mortality is roughly 25 per cent of the figure in 1983. Animal improvement (percentage of upgraded animals) has increased tenfold.

The irrigation canal, constructed by 34 Majhi farmers to provide light irrigation for a summer crop on about a third of the villagers' dry land, has demonstrated to farmers what community participation can achieve. With a project investment of $275, and an active "user" group, the community has increased its food production an estimated 25 per cent among the poorest farmers. Self-sufficiency in food production has more than doubled since 1983.

The drinking water system for one section of the Majhi village followed the irrigation canal and provided convenient year-round protected water to 34 houses (different from the irrigation families). Out-of-season vegetable gardens have increased from zero to almost every household. With the exception of pipes, cement and fittings, all costs were borne by the community, including a monthly house tax for water system maintenance.

Health care (Luxmi Majhi's teaching, clinic services for referral and selected immunization services) has contributed to lower child mortality and the community's overall better health. The other factors noted above have also contributed, including increasing family-planning acceptance. Male and female Mahji children increasingly attend the local school.

Agroforestry

When the project first started to assess potential income-generating development inputs in Bahunipati, particularly in the poorer-income Majhi village, there was a need for fodder in the community. The forest across the river was disappearing. Land quality was deteriorating. Animal mortality was largely related to poor forage and malnutrition. Manure was insufficient for crop production, especially improved varieties, and livestock numbers were limited because of fodder unavailability. What was needed was a magic species which grew on terrace faces (a quarter of the country's cultivated land is unused terrace face), could be cut to prevent shading, was deep-rooted to prevent competition with crops for moisture and nutrients and was multi-purpose, providing fodder, green manure and fuelwood.

In 1977 a few ipil-ipil (*Leucaena leucocephala*) seeds of Peruvian and giant varieties were obtained and sown in plastic bags. Initially project staff had little idea if the tree would survive or produce enough forage to attract farmers, and which varieties would be best suited to different altitudes.

The trees did survive and averaged 8 to 10 feet growth the first year. A small nursery was started in 1978 to produce seedlings for distribution to farmers in the Bahunipati area. Numerous varieties have been tried over the years; K8 and *Leucaena diversifolia* have proved to be the best, the latter at higher altitudes than Bahunipati.

An extension programme was then planned to demonstrate that ipil could be grown by farmers in large numbers on terraces along with crops, and without competing for moisture or sun, unlike most local fodder trees. It also aimed to show that ipil could be cropped heavily – particularly in the dry season when forage is in short supply – to permit the farmer to increase livestock quality and quantity. By developing the planting of large numbers of trees on private land it was hoped that there would be a growing acceptance of stall feeding and decreasing pressure on forest lands for fodder.

In June 1978 there still remained many unanswered questions about ipil under Nepal conditions, such as altitude limitations, diseases (if any) and effect on nearby crops; so the extension programme was started slowly. Ipil was treated like a crop; planting and management practices were meshed with the farmers' cropping and labour practices. Farmers were ready to modify traditional fodder-collecting practices if they could be convinced of the new practices' value and it did not mean replacing food crops with fodder trees.

Five farmers were selected to plant large numbers of trees. All had to agree to plant a minimum of 400 trees each, a figure set as the minimum number of trees required for providing 50 per cent of the forage for one large animal in the dry season. Ipil trees were provided free of cost by the nursery.

Out of the five farmers, three were successful, with an average survival of 80 per cent, and follow-up intensified the second year to improve their results. The trees did not compete with their crops, and they grew out of the reach of livestock in six months, before the time of year when they were allowed to graze the fields. This impressed the farmers and encouraged others to plant more trees in 1980.

Extension work has focused on a few farmers, who were followed up at least once a month to ensure they were successful and all the steps were being followed. These successful farmers now perform the basic extension role of teaching other farmers. Starting in 1980, farmers in the same community, and those from other *panchayats* and districts, were given a tour of farmer demonstrators and involved in field-level discussions.

As the programme progressed, it was seen that farmers in Bahunipati were evolving their own planting practices, and initially with a small number of trials it was possible for the project staff to modify recommendations before expanding the programme over a wider area. For example, it was recommended earlier that trees be cut 2 ft from the ground when grazing was controlled. But some farmers complained of neighbours' animals grazing trees during the crop fallow months and started lopping at 5–6 ft to allow the tree to branch out above the reach of cows or goats. This is now the recommended practice, and the multiplication is more successful because the package of practices represents the farmer's personal farm experience.

Ipil was chosen because it is non-competitive with crops, in terms of shade and fertilizer, and because it can grow beyond the reach of animals within six months of planting. Few, if any, local species have these characteristics. The greatest attraction of ipil, however, is its coppicing characteristic, so it can be cut low, and its ability to provide fodder year round (compared to once a year for most local fodder trees). Now that ipil has been planted so extensively, and most Bahunipati farmers meet a good proportion of their own fodder requirements, grazing practices are changing. Stall feeding is easier than grazing. People see results (milk, meat) of better-quality fodder versus former grazing on stubble and common land. Animal upgrading has introduced higher-quality animals that are too valuable to risk grazing by a small boy.

The demonstration approach has proved a successful extension strategy. As of 1986 out of 102 families in Bahunipati's Majhi village 88 per cent had planted ipil fodder trees, 10 per cent had planted more than 400 trees per large animal and 22 per cent had more than 400 trees. At least 30 per cent of farmers are now self-sufficient in fodder and fuelwood. Several have trebled their livestock numbers. There has been reduced pressure on fodder and fuelwood in the nearby forest. Terraces have been stabilized by extensive planting of ipil and grass, and soil erosion reduced.

The future

We feel that the fodder trees programme, without a continuing staff presence or project nursery, can be sustained in Bahunipati. The nurseryman is the only full-time village staff person, and he could produce horticulture and other varieties of trees to become self-supporting. Another local Majhi was trained in livestock and veterinary care and could become self-supporting from the sale of services and veterinary drugs.

However, the project feels it should maintain a continuing presence over the next two years: (1) to diversify ipil with other, preferably local, fodder trees to offset any effect of pests or diseases on ipil and reduced fodder in the community; (2) to use the community demonstration and impact in Bahunipati, and its successful farmers, to replicate this success to other communities, particularly among low-income groups.

Changing grazing patterns offer the opportunity in the next few years to identify, test and demonstrate varieties of local fodder trees which will supplement ipil on the terrace face. People prefer to plant varieties not as susceptible as ipil to grazing, and the project will assist local farmers to identify species, and provide seedlings, which meet needs for supplementary terrace planting and common land use.

A training methodology has evolved for extending the ipil programme. Called "home nursery", it has been used extensively for several years in *panchayats* around Bahunipati. "Home nurseries" teach nursery skills to many people, enabling them to be local resources in the future for seed, inoculant and training if they become successful demonstrators. These local nurseries produce seedlings near the planting area, a further incentive to plant trees.

The number of fodder tree seedlings planted annually on private land as a result of the project rose from 1,000 in 1978 to 150,000 in 1987, most produced by the farmers themselves. Replication to other *panchayats* has taken place in the past three years, and 23 *panchayats* had ipil training and demonstrations in 1986. Also in 1986, six *panchayats* had goat-upgrading activities, eight had drinking-water supply systems, two had irrigation canals, two had pig upgrading and nine had improved citrus trials. Following successful demonstration and extension, outside staff time is redirected elsewhere; local people must sustain the level of adoption in the community with minimum staff input.

CASE STUDY 4 *Tin Aicha, Mali*

STEPHEN MORRISSEY
Consultant to the American Friends Service Committee

As rain returned after the Sahelian drought of 1968–74, close to 2,500 destitute herders remained in the government relief camp at Goundam, Northern Mali. Goundam's *commandant* (district chief administrative officer) had seen them succeed in growing potatoes in the dry channel bottoms around the camp. He believed that, desperate to regain their independence, they would try farming. The *commandant* granted 100 volunteer families 100 hectares along the northern shore of Lake Faguibine, at a place called Tin Aicha (see Map 1). The regional government agreed to give them seed and other help, and to take them to their new farms.

Representatives of the American Friends Service Committee (AFSC) visited

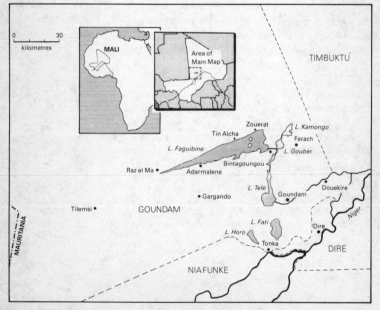

Map 1: Tin Aicha, Mali

Mali in 1973-4, meeting the *commandant* of Goundam and finding his ideas and initiative impressive. The Tin Aicha project grew from discussions between him, AFSC staff, the national livestock service and Malian government ministries. It proposed to integrate agriculture with animal husbandry, and to offer modern education and health-care facilities to its participants. The government invited AFSC to provide funds and technical advice, but Tin Aicha was to be managed and decided by Malians.

AFSC agreed to provide a community development worker, livestock for herd reconstitution, seed grain, medicines, agricultural and educational materials, a vehicle and salary supplements for the project's civil-service personnel. The Malian government gave Tin Aicha its director, its agricultural and veterinary extension agents, two teachers and a school, a nurse and a dispensary, a social worker and housing for this staff.

The primary objective was the economic rehabilitation of Goundam's drought victims. The government tended also to see project success as the sedentarization of nomads; but AFSC felt that improved health and education and new skills would stay with the nomads whether or not they remained settled.

In late 1974 102 nomad families moved by truck to Tin Aicha. They pulled nets for the lake's Bozo fishermen in return for fish, a new food, and they began to work their slope of lakefront.

Faguibine is the largest of the Niger lakes. They flood with the rising of the river and then shrink through the long dry season, and the families' fields could measure several hectares or disappear entirely beneath the water. The farmers are often sharecroppers, and the lake's arable land can be redistributed annually. The first Tin Aicha families held about a kilometre of shoreline.

In early 1975 an AFSC staff member arrived in Tin Aicha, finding the beginning of a village. Straw houses had begun to replace tents, and Tin Aicha had brought in one harvest.

Life at Tin Aicha remained precarious, but at the end of the year a second 100 families joined the first. They settled half a kilometre from their neighbours (in what was then called the "second village") and farmed a second stretch of lakefront.

The people were helped by Tin Aicha's project staff. But the staff felt themselves overburdened; turnover in the project's early years was rapid. The AFSC staff member therefore gave unforeseen continuity; she trained a local social worker and three young women villagers as health/nutrition aides. The agricultural extension agent schooled five young men in new techniques of cultivation, and they worked with the rest of the villagers.

Project activities: agriculture, livestock and reforestation

Farming was alien to Tin Aicha's participants, whose cultures viewed it as demeaning. It was also very hard physical labour for people weakened by malnutrition, and the immediate post-drought years brought plagues of rats, birds and insects. Tin Aicha could never rely wholly upon agriculture; its harvest, even in good years, could feed the villagers only for about six months. In the project's first years, yields were low. As the villagers became farmers, however, and the drying lake uncovered more fertile land, yields rose. In 1976–7 they were almost twice what they had been.

At the 1975 harvest Tin Aicha's inexperienced farmers sold much of their crop to itinerant merchants, from whom they were forced to rebuy it at doubled prices in early 1976. They therefore agreed to sell to the community co-operative at nationally fixed prices, and they then could repurchase it at cost. The Tin Aicha grain bank was always undercapitalized, and the villages never had enough land to produce surpluses.

The extension agent organized a demonstration farm, where new techniques and new crops were tested. As the new farmers of Tin Aicha learned, they began to put together some of the rules of an agricultural community. They fined villagers whose animals ran loose in the fields and expelled villagers who abandoned their fields for more than three months.

Herding of livestock met economic and nutritional needs, and it kept alive the traditional culture of Tin Aicha's nomads. Animals were distributed to project families early in 1976. The villagers had agreed to return to the project in four years the number of animals they had received. The repaid animals could then be given anew to future villagers.

Despite its advantages, the livestock work created problems and ill will. Tin Aichans wanted goats before any other animal, but the Malian government would not allow them. The project's managers also chose the sheep and cows which were purchased, and they were not as careful as the nomads themselves might have been. Although the animals were owned by individual families, they grazed together in a communal herd, because the project's decision-makers did not want Tin Aichans leaving their fields to travel with their livestock. Several systems of herd management were tried, none being completely satisfactory.

In 1978 Tin Aichans requested an early and modified repayment of their livestock loans. The villagers remained dissatisfied with the care their animals received and, as they became more independent themselves, wanted to be able to make their own economic decisions. They suggested that, given the significant losses the communal herd had sustained, each family repay only one cow and one sheep. And they suggested payment in cash rather than kind, for early reimbursement and young animals meant few available offspring. They then proposed creating with the money collected a village herd. With its profits they would meet urgent needs (e.g. well repair, school supplies and medicines) when outside funding ended.

With government agreement these plans took shape in early 1979, when Tin Aicha's Fédération de Groupements Ruraux (FGR) bought a modest herd of cows and goats and hired a herder. The villagers found it difficult to accept the herd as a common asset. As it continued, however, it became more convincing. In the early 1980s the villagers discussed plans to take loans from the herd to rebuild their family holdings. They began to consider sales strategies, pooling their resources for better bargaining, and the possibility of travelling together to distant markets.

As an agricultural population in a semi-desert environment, Tin Aichans continued to find herd management difficult. They needed to keep their animals nearby through as much of the year as possible in order to realize the greatest profit from them, yet keeping them close to the lake during the dry season damaged newly sown fields. The most successful herders have been those who, because of family composition and herd size, can allow some family members to move from pasture to pasture with their animals, returning to the villages only for short periods. This sort of transhumance from a fixed base was a long-term goal for most.

As Tin Aicha was settled, villagers felled trees for house frames and firewood. They cut brambles for fencing and cattle fodder. Even without goats, they were creating a disastrous situation; they viewed vegetation as an expendable resource. By the end of 1979 the state of the environment began to alarm both villagers and the local forestry service. The agricultural extension agent established a tree nursery with the help of ten young workers paid from project funds. But the FGR, by vote of the population, was unwilling to pick up the workers' salaries as AFSC withdrew. The reforestation project will therefore deteriorate. But trees planted around the new school buildings are cared for by the students, and within family enclosures shade trees are well tended.

Project activities: health, nutrition and education

In mid-1975 Tin Aicha's first villagers moved from the lakeshore to a cleaner and drier spot half a kilometre from the lake. There the project's first real well (15 metres deep) was dug. The creation of a second village brought a second well, and these began to make Tin Aicha a centre for all of north Faguibine's nomads.

The government nurse at Tin Aicha became a magnet, like the village wells, serving people in the 50 km radius where he was the only health worker. The AFSC staff member organized a nutrition programme, using vegetables from the demonstration garden and other foods new to the villagers. She also developed health and child-care materials which the social worker and her assistants used.

Malian nomads are by reputation resistant to modern education, but Tin Aichans accepted the value of a government school from the beginning. The school was unusual; it was in the village itself, and its teachers were Tamashek. No longer did parents have to send children to boarding-schools in the towns or fear that the children would be alienated from their own culture. The school began with one class; from 73 students in 1975, it grew to 189 in 1979. Teachers were generally available, although in some years classes had to double up. Supplies and books, usually sent by the regional government, were rarer.

The school lunch programme, which exists in all Malian schools, was supported at Tin Aicha by the project, the World Food Programme and the villagers themselves through the demonstration farm. It improved health and encouraged attendance, but it is costly to sustain without outside funding.

Farming, herding and handicraft work were added to the traditional French educational system. Tin Aichans also wanted part of their own tradition in their school, and a Koranic scholar teaches both children and adults.

Tin Aicha is the only school in the district of Goundam (and one of a very few in the country) a majority of whose students are nomads. The rate of passage from class to class is high, and absenteeism is low. Nomads from all over Goundam find it the most promising investment the project made.

Village infrastructure

The Tin Aicha co-operative began as a seller of staple goods (tea, sugar, cooking and lamp oil, soap and cloth) at reasonable prices to the villagers. Its capital came from AFS, and it was managed by the social worker. In 1978 it became an FGR under the national co-operative service, and its operating capital was transferred to an elected council which hired a full-time manager from the village. It began to sell a wide range of goods and make a small profit.

The FGR manages the monthly grain allotments to the village's civil servants. It loans seed money to Tin Aicha's farmers, who repay in grain at the harvest; it manages the demonstration farm, which has become a communal field; it oversees Tin Aicha's livestock co-operative and village herd.

The construction of permanent buildings to house the school, the dispensary and the co-operative store dominated the final phase of the project (1977–80). Professional builders came from Goundam. They were assisted by between 25 and 50 local workers chosen by the village council.

The co-operative store housed a sales room, offices and storage areas. The FGR began to buy in bulk and to buy goods it had never been able to stock under the old straw-mat buildings, such as grain and seed crops. The dispensary offered treatment areas, offices and a pharmacy for the nurse. The school compound had two classroom buildings, an office, a store and toilets.

Several workers emerged as qualified professional builders. Some local women developed pot- and brick-making skills. Local transporters (who carried adobe from the lakeshore to the building sites by donkey) established ongoing businesses moving grain and commodities. The buildings gave Tin Aicha a sense of stability and permanence.

Tin Aicha has been administered from its founding by village chiefs and councillors elected by the residents annually. It was not at first a recognized village. Its people remained administratively attached to their former homes, through which they paid taxes and received services. Few Tin Aichans wanted to cut themselves off from their origins, and all battled with a traditional prejudice against villages. They accepted, however, that their life at Tin Aicha could continue only if it became an official village, which it did in 1981. The village administration demands the interaction of a number of popularly elected bodies: the governing groups of the youth movement, the women's movement, the co-operative store, the market and the school.

In 1976 Tin Aichans suggested establishing, outside the project, a weekly market. A chain of markets around the lake allows commerce among several populations. In April 1978 several important merchants set up simple shelters near the lake, and Tin Aicha's Monday market entered the Faguibine commercial calendar.

The market's most important functions are economic: new opportunities, increased incomes and better living standards. For the people of Tin Aicha, however, it has brought greater interaction and understanding among neighbouring villages and camps.

Assessment of the project and its influence

Tin Aicha offered its participants both a framework within which to make new economic choices and the resources to carry them out. The project enabled drought refugees to regain their dignity without compromising their cultural values, and it gave them new skills. Better medical, educational and agricultural services have grown from the contributions of Tin Aichans and project staff. Village initiative has spurred cohesiveness, stability and a sense of community. Tin Aicha's administrative services, school and dispensary have made the village a local centre, and the project has had an impact far beyond the village itself.

Although the villagers were very little involved in the early design of the project, local involvement gradually increased. People began to choose for themselves and, managing their own resources, they began to profit. Tin Aicha's land has never been as fertile or as plentiful as a full agricultural economy would demand, but it remains the villagers' most valuable asset. They now point with pride to their crops and their ability to adapt. Whether the project has succeeded in sedentarizing nomads, however, is open to debate.

Although replication of the project proved unfeasible, AFSC continued to work in Northern Mali, trying to help pastoralists improve their economic lives, increase food self-reliance and develop water resources. The project has had a major influence on some aspects of the AFSC programme. When Tin Aicha parents asked the Malian government to create a middle school in the village and asked AFSC to support its construction, AFSC financed a new classroom building, dormitory and staff housing; these were built in 1982–3 by local workmen who had learned their trade as part of the project. The school serves all of northern and western Goundam district. Building on work at Tin Aicha, AFSC has continued to support Tamashek literacy programmes in Timbuktu region.

CASE STUDY 5 *Guinope Integrated Development Program, Honduras*

ROLAND BUNCH
Central America Regional Office, World Neighbors

History and chronology

In January 1981 the Guinope Integrated Development Program was initiated as a tripartite effort between World Neighbors, the Honduran Ministry of Natural Resources and the Association for the Co-ordination of Development Resources (ACORDE), a Honduran private voluntary agency. It was based on a similar World Neighbors programme in Guatemala. The root problem in the Guinope area was severe soil deterioration caused by erosion and the continual monocropping of corn. Much of the area's topsoil was gone, so average yields were extremely low (around 400 kg/ha). Many farmers were walking for hours, or taking buses to other parts of the country, to find arable land; others had left permanently; malnutrition was increasingly noticeable.

The first year, yields often increased by three to four times previous levels. Word of this success spread rapidly. During the next five years, some 50 new villages requested the programme's training, and the programme has done at least a year's training in a total of 41 villages across a wide area.

The extension methodology has been as follows. A very limited number of innovations (preferably one or two) that respond to the limiting factor in local agricultural production (in this case, soil quality) are introduced through field demonstrations and the use of farmer-run, small-scale experiments on the people's own land. These technologies must be inexpensive and easy to understand, produce significant increases in yields and be directed at the traditional crop(s) of the villagers (i.e. they must be truly "appropriate" technologies). They include soil conservation practices and the use of chicken manure and/or chemical fertilizer.

These technologies are taught largely in the fields through hands-on activities of the farmers, the emphasis being practical rather than theoretical. All classes are taught by village farmers who have previously had success with the same technology.

As agricultural success increased basic grain supplies beyond what was needed locally, incomes rose, and people wanted to grow cash crops, as well as to prepare more varied and healthy meals for their families. A series of classes in nutrition and hygiene was begun, as well as training in growing vegetables, both for local consumption and as cash crops.

Costs and benefits

The programme is not involved in any kind of paternalism, either donations, subsidies or doing things for people. All agricultural production costs are carried by the farmer. Except for a small revolving fund used to buy and sell necessary equipment, the programme makes no expenditures for labour, equipment or raw materials. In that the technologies are kept simple and locally replicable, there are no important requirements; nor is there any need for replacement parts or maintenance that are not locally and cheaply available.

The programme has spent $254,000 on agricultural extension work, approximately trebling the per-hectare basic grain production of some 1,200 families, thereby at least assuring them ample basic grain supplies for the ensuing year. On average, this programme has trebled basic grain production of small farmers at a cost of less than $212 per family.

After the first year or two of producing large surpluses of basic grains, farmers realize that corn and beans are not particularly profitable cash crops. They then normally reduce the land planted in corn and beans to an area sufficient to assure them a year's supply and either let the extra land lie fallow or plant it in a cash crop (coffee, oranges and, increasingly, vegetables).

The programme has achieved a good deal more than merely trebling grain production. The techniques used have also probably assured that productivity's permanence; and this has further been assured by the farmers' having learned how to experiment and adapt to changing circumstances.

Another major benefit has been the training of some 60 local villagers as agricultural extensionists. Even after the programme leaves, these new leaders' agricultural knowledge, commitment to improved techniques, outside contacts, teaching and organizational abilities and willingness to teach others will remain in the communities.

Also included in the cost of $212 per family is the training in vegetable production given to some 400 of the area's farmers, many of whom are now helping to provide three full truckloads a week all year round to the programme's vegetable store.

A further $34,500 has also been spent on the Boutique Agropecuaria (Agricultural Boutique), the programme's vegetable and fruit store in Tegucigalpa, the nation's capital. The benefits accruing from this include the marketing of some $6,000 of vegetables each month (a figure increasing almost monthly), the making of contacts with other vegetable retailers, the full-time, well-paid employment of six people from the Guinope area and the gaining of experience by Guinope area farmers in vegetable marketing and quality control. If the Boutique continues to be profitable, it will gradually repay this entire sum to the programme.

The $44,000 spent on health work has enabled at least 100 families spread across five villages to improve their everyday diets and the hygiene of their home environments.

The programme's design is aimed at reaching and benefiting the very poorest. Even the landless and nearly landless (not common in this area) have benefited through an increase in wages arising from the increased demand for labour that the programme has brought about. This increase in local wages, plus the opening up of new land previously thought useless, has attracted a lot of new residents to the area. A large number of previously abandoned homes in and around Guinope are now occupied, and dozens of new houses are being built. The new population includes at least 30 Guinope families who have returned to the area from Tegucigalpa's slums.

Early on in the programme, extensionists talked individually with the very poorest, the landless farmers, telling them that land values were going to go up, and that if they wanted their children to have a decent life they should fence off a piece of unoccupied land (thereby establishing their right to it by Honduran law). A good many of these people did, and in the mountains above Guinope dozens of two- to five-hectare plots have been fenced off in the last two years.

Environmental benefits

The programme has improved the environment in a number of ways.

(1) Land fertility has been increased, and probably ensured on a long-term basis, by the near elimination of agricultural burning; by the introduction and widespread use of chicken manure; by the use of locally produced cow manure and compost; by the introduction of a number of tropical green manure crops; and by a more informed use of chemical fertilizers. Over 198 km of contour or drainage ditches, 80 km of contour grass barriers and 31 km of contour rock walls have been built by local farmers in the process of protecting some 449 ha of hillside land from water erosion. None of this work was paid for or done by the programme; all was done by the farmers, convinced it was in their own interest.

(2) Air and water quality have been improved. Tons of chicken manure used to be dumped into the rivers around Tegucigalpa, but the demand for this product has now virtually eliminated the practice. The near elimination of agricultural burning has greatly reduced the quantity of smoke in the air from February to May.

(3) In various ways the programme has had a significant impact on the quantity of forest around Guinope. By controlling erosion on people's land, the need for migratory agriculture has been eliminated (ending migratory agriculture could save millions of hectares of forest around the world, and is much more easily accomplished than has been previously thought). Increased productivity has meant that most farmers are now actively farming less land than they did before, so that land above what a farmer can use intensively either has been left idle to grow back gradually into pine forest, or is being used in a more extensive (less labour-intensive) manner. Thus hundreds of hectares previously used for agriculture are now covered by trees.

Every year, agricultural fires "got away" from Guinope area farmers, burning gradually through hundreds and hundreds of hectares of forest, killing the vast majority of small trees. Now that agricultural fires are rare (and villagers actively fight the spread of those that are set, because of their new respect for the value of forests), the forests are once again beginning to regenerate naturally.

Turpentine collection, formerly a major source of employment around Guinope, was killing tens of thousands of pine trees. Now turpentine collection has been greatly reduced, partly because the programme's influence in increasing demand for labour and wage levels has made it a relatively less remunerative activity. Similarly, the increased availability of well-remunerated work during the dry season has greatly reduced the need for small farmers and the landless to cut firewood as a source of income.

Sustainability and replication

By using small-scale experimentation, keeping simple accounts of their experiments and then sharing their results with each other, large numbers of small farmers can continue to develop their own agriculture long after the programme has closed its doors. What will be sustained is a loose-knit federation of village-level agricultural clubs that will co-ordinate experiments and share results. The vegetable producers' association will continue to run the vegetable store in the event that alternative marketing channels do not grow around Guinope's now proven record of high-quality vegetable production.

Most of the technologies used in Guinope's agricultural development either were replicated from previous World Neighbors agricultural programmes in Guatemala or were standard practices of non-mechanized agriculture. But one major technology, that of small-farmer-adapted green manure crops, was largely developed by the Guinope programme and its sister programme in El Rosario.

The technology is now being applied by at least a dozen development agencies throughout Honduras, and major government programmes now use contour ditches, grass barriers, rock walls, green manure crops and villager extensionists. The government has also sent many of its agronomists to the Guinope programme for training, and has initiated four new programmes that are attempting to apply the overall Guinope approach.

The programme design used in Guinope is virtually the same as that described in a World Neighbors book (Roland Bunch, *Two Ears of Corn: A Guide to People-Centered Agricultural Improvement*, Oklahoma City, 1985). Other programmes have adopted this approach after experience with it first-hand in Guatemala or Honduras, as in the case of programmes in El Salvador, Honduras, Nicaragua, Peru and Togo. Others have established programmes that follow this methodology through contact with the book alone, as in Bolivia, Kenya, Indonesia and the Philippines.

Key factors in programme success

The key factors in the programme's success, which can be applied to programmes in most of the Third World, are as follows.

(1) All forms of paternalism should be avoided, including giving things away, subsidizing farmer activities or inputs or doing anything for the people. All work should be accomplished for the sole reason that villagers have seen success achieved and have become enthusiastic enough to work towards achieving it for themselves.

(2) Such programmes should start slowly and start small, so that local people can participate in planning and execution from the start.

(3) The programme must use a limited technology, so that: villagers can learn and begin to teach it as soon as possible; a maximum number of villagers will be reached; great socioeconomic differences are not created among the population; and efforts can be concentrated on a few ideas to assure success.

(4) The technology should be locally appropriate. The first technologies taught should almost always deal with traditional food crops and solve the limiting factors in their production. Technologies should be simple to learn, inexpensive, usually labour-intensive and oriented towards a good market. They should use locally available resources and provide rapid, recognizable successes, also being consistent with the ecological well-being of the area's food-producing systems.

(5) The technology should be taught through a system of small-scale experimentation. The teachers should whenever possible be villager farmers who have already experienced success in their own fields. Training should be done in one- to two-day sessions in the farmers' villages, with most of the class time consisting of practical work in the fields.

(6) A multiplier effect must be an important component of any agricultural extension programme, whereby successful, well-motivated villager farmers become the trainers and eventually take over the programme.

(7) Programmes usually do best by gradually becoming integrated, responding, one at a time, to other felt needs of the various members of the farm family, including health, infrastructure, family planning, participation in the political system and environmental improvement.

PART 2

Sustainable Rural Livelihoods (2)

CHAPTER 2

Sustainable Rural Livelihoods: Enhanced Resource Productivity

JOHN MICHAEL KRAMER
Director of Agriculture and Natural Resources, CARE, USA

Sustainability: what is it? How is it achieved? Whose sustainability is it? Someone looking for sustainability will find in nearly every situation these questions have a unique answer. This is inevitable because ecological and social systems are dynamic. People working in international development must recognize this. Some suggestions on how they might achieve more sustainable systems is the first objective of this chapter. A second objective is to describe the characteristics of a sustainable land-use management system. A third is to indicate what development agencies can do to fund more successful projects of this kind.

The foundation for the analysis is the six case studies of natural resource management projects presented in this part of the book. Where appropriate other project experiences are brought in. Together they offer a cross-section of how governmental and non-governmental institutions work with local people to achieve lasting improvements in their farming system. The fundamental problem all the projects address is similar: farm families at risk due to the rapid degradation of their farm's soil and microclimate. The projects all aim to reverse the ecological decline and improve the well-being of the people depending on the affected land.

This chapter deals with a comprehensible and manageable level of sustainability: the farm. Until the farming systems of the world reach a sustainable footing, true development will not be possible. This applies equally to the "developed" as to the "developing" countries.

The case studies

Indonesia: irrigation and water-catchment protection (Case Study 6)

The Dumoga valley experienced rapid population expansion in the 1970s, resulting in forest clearance for farming. This threatened both wildlife and the watershed on which new irrigation systems depended. The systems would not be able to provide a steady, adequate supply of water if deforestation was not halted.

In 1980, with urging from the World Wildlife Fund, the World Bank attached a watershed protection component to a loan to expand the irrigation command area. This led to the creation of the Dumoga-Bone National Park.

Establishing the National Park brought disruption and suffering to a few hundred people, but protection of the watershed has benefited thousands of downstream irrigation system users and a unique biological reserve has been saved for the benefit of all. Whether or not this project will be sustainable remains to be seen.

Kenya: soil conservation (Case Study 7)

The governments of Sweden (SIDA) and Kenya have since 1974 collaborated in a soil conservation programe. The programme has a relatively small budget matched to the counterpart agency's absorptive capacity and does not have a fixed completion date. It has trained over 120,000 farmers in soil conservation. Altogether one million farmers have been reached.

The programme has shown that large-scale application of simple techniques is possible. Donor agencies can best support such efforts by working within existing governmental structures and with a long-term commitment to fund the programme.

Niger: dry-season gardening (Case Study 8)

In 1976 Lutheran World Relief (LWR), in response to the Sahelian drought, began a project to help villagers and farmers achieve sustainable food and water availability. LWR helped communities dig large-diameter concrete-lined wells to supply water for vegetable and fruit-tree cultivation as well as livestock and domestic use. The method requires a small investment and provides a reliable and safe way to reach the water table.

LWR also helped farmers with techniques such as live fences, agricultural inputs, irrigation training, marketing services and fruit trees.

In the Niger mini-droughts of 1984–5 people gardening around the concrete walls were able to remain in their villages, and LWR's dry-season gardening projects were made the national programme of the year.

Burkina Faso: soil and water conservation (Case Study 9)

In 1979 Oxfam began an agroforestry project in Burkina Faso. This region had been misused for years, resulting in heavily crusted and nearly impermeable soil. Crop yields had fallen disastrously. Farmers were at the mercy of the next drought. The project initially encouraged farmers to plant trees in micro-catchments, a simple technique designed to increase water available to the seedling and improve tree survival and growth rates. The farmers soon discovered that water harvesting had a remarkable effect on crop yields, and this shifted the project's emphasis away from agroforestry.

The farmers abandoned the labour-intensive micro-catchments in favour of traditional rock bunds, low rows of rocks placed along the contours. They are permeable and act to slow run-off, allowing more rainfall to percolate into the soil. The rate of rock bund construction has doubled each year since 1983. Yields have increased. The total cost of Oxfam's investment is very low, and Oxfam's participatory approach made it possible for the farmers to influence the project's technical package so that it met their needs. This has resulted in the identification and widespread voluntary adoption of a more sustainable farming system.

Haiti: agroforestry outreach (Case Study 10)

In 1981 USAID provided funds to three international NGOs – Pan-American Development Foundation (PADF), Operation Double Harvest (ODH) and CARE – to support the extension of agroforestry to combat land degradation. Previous failed soil conservation projects were studied by an anthropologist who developed a new strategy to protect the soil and increase farmers' incomes. The strategy was simple: provide millions of inexpensive tree seedlings and ensure that the farmers owned the trees and benefited financially from selling the trees' products.

The farmers' response has surpassed expectations. During the first five years 27 million seedlings were planted by 110,000 farmers. Tree cropping is becoming an established practice, and ecological degradation is being reduced.

Niger: Guesselbodi bushland management experiment (Case Study 11)

In 1980 USAID and the Nigerien Forest and Wildlife Service began an effort to manage a 5,000 ha forest reserve 25 km east of Niamey, the capital. The reserve was under pressure from overgrazing, neighbouring farmers seeking new, more fertile fields and from woodcutters. The project's goal is to halt the degradation and find a sustainable and balanced use of the Guesselbodi forest reserve. Its strategy is to create a natural resource management system run by the local community to cost-effectively and sustainably exploit the forest reserve.

The project is an experiment to find an alternative to previous Sahelian reforestation projects that cleared hundreds of hectares of thorn scrub and planted them with fast-growing exotic trees. Unfortunately, the exotics were often not so fast-growing and did not benefit the local people.

The project began with a physical inventory and socioeconomic analysis of the forest reserve. About the same time field staff began to discuss with local people problems, needs and thoughts about the reserve's use. This resulted in a management plan and a series of land-use management techniques that the users undertook in return for direct payment or accrued future benefits. Treatments included: soil and water management, range management, controlled firewood harvesting, agroforestry and plantations.

The project has pioneered a new approach to natural forest management that should provide important lessons for future projects.

Designing for sustainability

The case studies provide some insight into the questions. They also offer suggestions as to characteristics of a sustainable system. There are multiple levels of sustainability, and the sustainability of the entire system is limited by the least sustainable level. Consider, for example, three levels of concern to most development projects: farm, locale and region.

The farm is the focus of most development projects. Here our ultimate goal is expressed, e.g. to increase income or health status of farmer and family. The farmer depends directly on the second level, locale, for resources and services. Locale refers to the surrounding natural environment. It includes the farmer's community, her neighbours and the systems that support them. The locale may exert a drain or a boost to the sustainability of the farm as well as the region, the third level. Region refers to a group of communities that act in a co-ordinated fashion to allocate goods, services and the means of production. It is appropriate to speak of region rather than nation, as this allows a functional rather than a political definition.

The three levels are interdependent. However, the foundation of sustainability for the system is the farm. A farm family that does not contribute a surplus of commodities and/or services to its locale is not supporting the sustainability of the system upon which it depends. The farm that does not contribute to the locale is not sustainable. It exists only by drawing on the resources of the locale or the region.

The question then is, what makes it possible for a farm to make a net contribution to its locale? We come back to soil and climate, nutrients and water. We must think in terms of closed-loop cycles, the natural means of recycling elements that biological processes depend on. Without closed loops there can be no sustainability. Farming systems can be sustained by external inputs of fertilizer, pesticides and irrigation, but for how long and at what cost? These costs are often too much to bear. A farming system dependent on external inputs can be sustained only as long as these inputs are subsidized. A closed-loop cycle can offer an affordable and indefinitely sustainable alternative.

A closed-loop cycle means that the elements and compounds that plants depend on are continuously recycled. As plants are primary producers, a closed-loop cycle for plant production will foster a sustainable system for animals, including humans. While closed-loop plant nutrient cycles occur essentially on the farm, water cycles involve the farm, the locale and the region. The case studies provide good examples of land-use management techniques that foster closed-loop nutrient and water cycles.

All the case studies deal with conservation and management of soil and water and, through this, the plant component of the farming system. The principle behind the practices is to hold soil in place mechanically and biologically. This will improve the nutrient and water recycling and sustainability. The replacement of nutrients is also practised in several of the projects. Farming systems incur some losses of nutrients, and these must be replaced to maintain productivity. In Haiti, CARE and PADF are planting trees that fix atmospheric nitrogen in the soil and, through leaf drop, increase organic matter. In Niger, LWR is helping farmers replace soil nutrients by introducing practices such as composting. The fields protected by contour bunds in Burkina Faso are manured to replace lost nutrients. In Guesselbodi the regenerative power of natural forest is used to replenish nutrients removed for crop, wood and fodder protection.

The farmer can do much to control the microclimate on her farm. The input and retention of water are important practices. Oxfam and the farmers of Yatenga have provided an example of how far simple water management can go to improve sustainability. LWR has helped hundreds of farmers increase their supply of water by digging low-cost wells; and live fences and mulching help improve microclimate and conserve water. The Dumoga-Bone National Park has assured farmers downstream of a sustainable supply of water.

The surrounding locale and the people residing there are the practical vehicles for development assistance to reach the farmer. Extension of techniques for managing land must first deal with the community leadership and receive its permission to operate. Thus the structure of communities and the social rules that bind them together influence the potential for a successful project. The key factor for the sustainability of a community is its ability to make its own decisions and manage its own resources.

The number of projects continued by counterparts in the absence of donor funds is abysmally small. When community management of the people's activities is nurtured, activities at that locale at least have a chance of being sustained. The Yatenga and Haiti projects allow the farmers decision authority over the key element of the practices; this has led to their widespread adoption. Dry-season gardens in Niger succeed because the communities can provide for the maintenance the wells require. In Yatenga the community chose the water-harvesting technique it wanted to use, and people working together have obtained a rapid increase in contour bund construction. Community-managed nurseries in Haiti are replacing centralized nurseries in preparation for the withdrawal of external support.

At the regional level another element of sustainability enters: replicability. If a practice that increases sustainability is proven effective, should it not be replicated? Many NGO projects have been criticized for lacking the element of replicability. It is the major challenge facing development. Arguably the land management techniques and even community management approaches needed to achieve sustainability are known. However, widespread adoption does not seem to be making as much progress. Why?

The answer lies in the failure of development agencies to treat communities and farmers as fully capable of achieving their own sustainable management of resources. Policies, institutions and infrastructure all too often work at cross-purposes to sustainable local resource management. Examples abound:

- Policies that favour urban populations by keeping farm produce prices low. Low prices prevent farmers making long-term investments.
- Forestry agencies have traditionally viewed farmers as threats, despite evidence that community management of forests can be cheaper and more effective in protecting resources.
- International aid agencies have funded the construction of large irrigation

systems without taking into account who will ensure the equitable and effective operation of the system.
- Voluntary agencies have installed thousands of pumps on wells without regard to how they will be maintained.

There is growing awareness of the mistakes of the past and a growing resolution to redress these. Enough examples have been found of successful resource management techniques. The challenge is to apply these on a broad scale.

Design of sustainable resource management systems

The case studies suggest that we can successfully design and undertake systems to support rather than undermine the environment we depend on. It requires knowledge of the ecological relationships, sensitivity to local conditions, patience and faith, but it can be done.

A sustainable land-use system must have the following characteristics:

- *Flexibility*. It must be able to adapt to changing social, economic or natural conditions. Project design should establish a process that will allow the implementors (with emphasis on the local variety) to select the appropriate path as the project progresses.
- *Incremental*. Usually only two or three new activities can be adopted at a time.
- *Diversified*. A sustainable resource system must include a range of elements to spread risk and see it through seasonal and yearly changes.
- *Responsive*. Adaptive processes must be fairly rapid. Projects that respond slowly can lose the support of the people. Worse, they can cause harm.
- *Locally based*. Land-use practices must be locally derived to obtain an appropriate mix. A local base is required for the supply of goods and services needed to maintain the system at reasonable cost.
- *Concerned with limiting factors*. Managers must be prepared to deal with a series of limiting factors. The proper sequencing of interventions to overcome limiting factors is important.
- *Economically cost-effective*. Often a natural resource management system may appear to be sustainable but turns out to have hidden subsidies. An example is the well-meaning agency project that supports tree planting with nursery operations subsidized through free material inputs from the agency. Until the nursery can be put on a self-sustaining basis, or an alternative to seedlings can be found, the project has not achieved sustainability.
- *Socially sensitive*. The needs, capabilities and desires of the community must be considered for a project to be accepted by the people and taken as their own. Unless corruption is a serious problem, traditional decision-making processes should be used.

A project that incorporates these elements is more likely to achieve an increase in sustainability than one which assumes it can impose a packaged set of interventions. However, at the project level our best efforts will from time to time be undone by a mistaken policy or misguided project. Yet people and environments are, within limits, resilient. With perseverance we can expect to achieve more sustainability in resource management systems.

International agency support for sustainability

This chapter's third objective is to discuss actions international agencies can take to foster sustainability of people and their ecosystems. Projects undertaken by official assistance agencies and non-governmental organizations have been described. What are the strengths and weaknesses of these two sets of agencies? What synergisms can be found between them to use available resources more effectively? Can a significantly increased level of international donor support, as is being proposed for forestry, be absorbed satisfactorily? What concrete steps can international agencies take to address issues of sustainability?

Non-governmental organizations (NGOs)

Development NGOs have been increasingly concerned with environmental issues even as environmental NGOs have been taking an increasing concern for people. The time is appropriate to strengthen further the ties between them. Agency strategies should be re-examined, and appropriate elements of each should be woven into the other's programme. NGOs must take steps to increase their professionalism in sustainable development. Recommendations on how this may happen follow:

Adopt requirements for and guidelines to environmental analyses for NGOs' development projects. Development NGOs have for the most part avoided the requirements for environmental impact analyses (EIA). The rationale is that NGOs do small projects with little potential to do harm and they are, by and large, environmentally sensitive anyway. This argument, however, loses validity as NGOs take on larger projects. This is not to say that NGOs should adopt full EIA requirements, rather they should take a simple analytical look at the potential negative environmental impacts of their projects. They should examine the major ecological systems: soil, vegetation, water and animals. If serious potential for a negative impact exists and for another reason the project still should be done, then a more complex environmental analysis should be undertaken. The analyses could be limited to specific types of projects, e.g. road construction, potable water development (especially in arid lands) and irrigation projects, and should be scaled to the size and cost of the project.

Place staff with strong natural resources and environmental technical qualifications in positions of programming responsibility. Although increasing numbers of NGO field staff have been technically qualified, this trend has not reached into the programme staff of NGOs' regional and headquarters offices. Apparently NGOs fear they will be left with narrowly focused specialists who have little regard for sociological considerations. However, today natural resources managers are often doing pioneering work in people-centred development. Careful selection of personnel should prevent NGOs hiring inappropriate natural resources specialists. This will give credibility with environmentally interested donors and field agencies.

Prepare long-term natural resources development strategies for geographic regions of NGO interest. CARE has prepared two such strategies, one for Northern Kordofan Department of the Sudan and one for Honduras. Developed jointly with counterpart agencies, the plans serve as a basis for developing programming activities. They help address donor-agency, NGO and local government questions about strategy and future activities. These agencies are then more willing to commit the long-term funding needed.

Undertake pilot projects in sustainable resource management, especially sustainable agriculture. NGOs have the flexibility to try high-risk, experimental activities at small scales. They should develop projects that test and compare in the field various resource management interventions and strategies. The advantage of field-based action research arises because farmers have a vast, untapped storehouse of adaptive knowledge of their environment and its management. In the beginning donor agencies will have to lower their expectations for quantitative output, but this should be acceptable if the NGOs become more rigorous in analysing and disseminating lessons learned. Research institutions can have a role to play in supporting these action research projects. A useful collaboration that downplays the traditional NGO suspicion toward academics would be for the researchers to train NGOs in action research and support them with graduate student interns, educational opportunities for staff of NGOs and their counterparts and short-term technical assistance.

Engage in dialogue with host-country governments. International development NGOs have shied away from engaging in detailed policy dialogue with host governments. This undercuts their model-making role, as NGO programmes are overlooked when governments set plans and priorities. Yet NGOs have field experience often poorly represented in policy setting, and less political baggage than many agencies. They should begin to talk to their partners about the policies that affect their programmes and the people they are concerned with. This might induce acceptance of NGO programming values in local government programmes and foster adoption of more people-centred programmes.

Official assistance agencies (OAAs)

Multilateral and bilateral agencies should further their efforts to complement and support NGOs. The NGO weaknesses presented above can be corrected, but it will require action and funding. Will OAAs continue to act in the old ways that have had questionable effects on sustainability? Or will they improve the effectiveness of their efforts in achieving sustainable resource management? Here are a few recommendations:

Increase support for local and international NGOs. Official assistance agencies have in the past preferred to work through government agencies. In the future governments are not likely significantly to increase support for the poorest and most marginal land users. On the other hand, NGOs have demonstrated their willingness and ability to accept increased funding from OAAs with the added benefit of being able to reach the poorest people. OAAs should provide an incentive and challenge for NGOs to increase their professionalism by offering them the prospect of increased funding. Local governments are likely to object to significant changes in funding patterns. NGOs can relieve some of this concern by working through government counterpart agencies.

Grant funding for NGOs often requires significant co-funding from the NGO. However, unless OAAs are willing to adjust or waive co-funding requirements it will be impossible for NGOs to accept greatly increased funds from them. This problem can be reduced in various ways. One government can accept another government's contibution as co-funding. They can make allowances for non-auditable contributions to the project, e.g. community labour, host-country counterpart staff or volunteer service. But if OAAs wish to increase funding through NGOs they will have to reduce or, in certain cases, eliminate their co-funding requirements.

It will remain difficult for OAAs to deal directly with local NGOs. They are too numerous, require amounts of funding beneath the threshold of OAA ability to consider and are weak in areas such as accounting, proposal writing, and formal evaluation. The best means for OAAs to work with local NGOs may be through international NGOs. PADF–Haiti is one model that OAAs should consider. It offers the advantage that both groups receive funding, which should minimize competition. However, OAAs should demand that international NGOs should, when used as intermediaries, strengthen local NGOs' management structure to increase their sustainability. IIED has taken on this role, particularly with Latin American environmental organizations. Its experience should be made widely available to other international NGOs.

Seek to increase community management of development assistance through land reform. When communities manage their own resources and the people directly receive the benefits, the likelihood of achieving sustainability is increased. It will be difficult for OAAs to ensure directly that this will happen. Working through NGOs is one means, but other examples can be found. OAAs can do a great deal to support community management of resources by supporting land reform.

Redirect International Agricultural Research Centres to sustainable resource management programmes. OAAs can bring pressure on International Agricultural Research Centres (IARCs) to hasten the shift begun towards research on crops for marginal land, soil conservation and sustainable ecological systems. IARCs can also be funded to support NGOs' action research activities through training and guidelines. They can also improve their information dissemination in practitioner-oriented manuals. CARE has prepared one such manual, entitled an *Agroforestry Extension Training Sourcebook*.

Increase support for small-scale bilateral aid projects. There are considerable constraints to increasing support for small OAA projects. To reduce administrative costs, multilateral banks and the larger bilateral aid agencies tend to programme ever-increasing amounts of funds per project officer. Staff are rewarded for amount of funds programmed rather than the impact of those funds. This reduces capacity for flexibility and quality control. However, it is not impossible for a bilateral agency to act small. In the case of Guesselbodi Forestry and Land-Use Project, USAID operated in much the same way that an NGO project might have. It had a relatively small budget and just one long-term expatriate adviser who fought for and won a remarkable degree of flexibility. It had recurring assistance from social scientists, and achieved a high degree of success. OAAs should institute systems for funding small, experimental projects by reducing requirements for preparation, funding approval and administration.

The urgent need for action to counter widespread degradation of the Earth's natural resources and the poverty that both creates and feeds on an unhealthy environment has been recognized. The means to decrease the vulnerability of the world's poor to their marginal environments are known. Failures in the past have often been due to the failure to rely on the internal resources of the people and their environment. Development agencies must become more people-centred and environmentally sensitive to help correct the downward spiral of environmental decay. It can be done. Who will take up the challenge?

CASE STUDY 6 *World Bank Irrigation and Water-Catchment Protection Project, Dumoga, Indonesia*

JAN WIND
National Park Planner, World Wildlife Fund/International Union for Conservation of Nature and Natural Resources

and EFFENDY A. SUMARDJA
Directorate of National Parks and Forest Recreation, Indonesia

The Dumoga valley is an area of approximately 30,000 ha of fertile land at 200-250 m above sea level, located in the middle of the north arm of Sulawesi (Celebes) Island, Indonesia (see Map 2). A number of projects were implemented in the 1970s that radically changed life in Dumoga. A highway was built in the centre of the valley, making it suddenly accessible from the east. The Kosinggolan weir (dam) was finished at the end of 1976, and a transmigration project brought 960 families from Java and Bali. A temporary bridge was built to cross the Dumoga river, improving access for the further exploitation of timber and other forest produce. The expectation of the forthcoming Toraut irrigation scheme attracted many spontaneous migrants into the valley. These high-investment projects induced several other developments such as building and rice and timber mills, establishment of ships and transport facilities. Good job opportunities in the government projects and cheap land attracted new inhabitants. In five years the population almost doubled to more than 32,000.

Political decisions were made that provided a basis for the protection of tropical rain forest, catchment areas and the sustaining of water resources in Dumoga. They initiated one of the most effective forest protection programmes in Indonesia. But the explosive growth could not be contained yet. The forces leading to a rapidly growing occupation and forest clearing were too strong and complex. Forces behind the high speed of valley occupation were related to spontaneous migrants, original inhabitants, absentee landlords, claimants, heritage, land speculation and local traditions. Other reasons include high soil fertility, high agricultural profits and high population pressure in neighbouring regions.

In 1977 a team from the World Wildlife Fund and PPA (the Indonesian Nature Conservation Department) made an identification survey for new reserves. The tropical rain forest of Dumoga was classified as very rich in species and a proposal was forwarded to the government to establish a nature reserve there. The area would comprise the catchment areas of the Dumoga headwaters

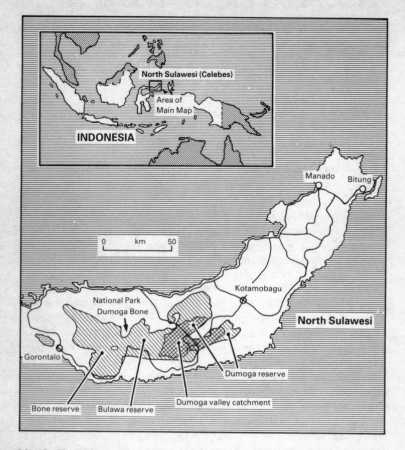

Map 2: The Dumoga valley, Sulawesi (Celebes), Indonesia

vital for the future water supply and irrigation schemes of the valley.

Ratification of the proposal for the Dumoga Reserve by ministerial decree took place two years later. The consensus grew that development options for forest logging, forest protection, transmigration and irrigation had to be reviewed and related. In 1978 WWF/PPA proposed to establish another two reserves, Bone and Bulawa. The proposal for the Bone Reserve was also ratified in December 1979.

It was expected that forest clearing in uphill areas of Dumoga would ultimately cause failure and economic loss of the Kosinggolan irrigation scheme. Water volumes at the weir dropped sharply and reached much lower levels than anticipated. Flood risk also became an issue. A flood destroyed a transmigration village 1.5 km upstream of the weir, killing three people, in 1977. Floods at the Bone river caused substantial economic loss.

Reviews of forest concessions in order to establish the Bulawa Reserve and to protect the headwaters of Bone and Dumoga were requested by WWF/PPA in 1978-9. A World Bank appraisal team for the Toraut irrigation scheme expressed its concern about the need for water-catchment protection. The local government agreed to cancel forest concessions in the Dumoga headwaters and to halt forest cutting on valley slopes. On this basis the World Bank would give its green light to a loan agreement.

Brainstorming by consultants and government officials led to the idea of creating a forest protection project. WWF forwarded a proposal to the World Bank to include a water-catchment protection component under the development credit agreement for irrigation. The proposal included project inputs such as the establishment of guard posts, purchase of equipment and expertise to prepare a management plan. This came into effect in 1980.

Forest concessions were revised by the central government, and the Bulawa Reserve was created, forming a bridge between the other two reserves. The three reserves formed a continuous area of approximately 300,000 ha; they were proposed to become a National Park.

These decisions showed a radical change in development plans. The most important aspect is the underlying new policy to sustain the rain forest, its genetic resources and the natural water resources. Many parties had been instrumental to the new set-up, in particular the project-oriented local government. Expatriate irrigation and wildlife conservation consultants provided vital ideas and data on land-use development options and environmental impact. The bargaining power of the World Bank had been used to make disbursement of the loan dependent upon forest protection in order to guarantee sufficient water flows to the irrigation areas.

The World Bank-funded fieldwork on irrigation and water catchment started in 1980. Consultants were contracted for the irrigation planning, and a WWF consultant was appointed for the water-catchment protection project. The total loan initially allocated was US$45 million, $44.3 m for irrigation development and $0.7 m for catchment protection. (The latest revision shows a final allocation of $19.19 m divided into $18.49 m for irrigation and $0.7 m for water catchment.)

The Kosinggolan scheme was completed in 1984 and Toraut in 1986-7. The water-catchment project completed most of its initial tasks in 1983. The scope of work was, however, extended in 1982 from the initial 100,000 ha of Dumoga catchment to the new Dumoga-Bone National Park of 300,000 ha. This project was completed in 1986-7.

The major task was to combine efforts at field level to halt forest cutting in catchment areas. The local government had started boundary marking as soon as the Dumoga Reserve was declared. Some 100 km of forest boundaries were initially marked. Part of the boundary was put far uphill and in steep terrain, excluding areas already cleared and cultivated, in order to avoid disputes with settlers who claimed the land. Large forest blocks on hills, which should have been included in the reserve for reasons of water-catchment protection, were left out. Elsewhere the forest boundaries were marked at lower elevations and included almost all of the catchment.

The reserve boundaries, consisting of small concrete markers at 300 m intervals and a path 60 cm wide, did not stop settlers from encroachment. The number of farmers who invaded the reserve and made huts on reserve land increased. The total number of people who claimed land inside the Dumoga Reserve at one stage or another is estimated at more than 750 family heads, up to 8 per cent of the valley population.

The original plan for Kosinggolan was to irrigate a net area of some 5,000 ha, based on expected water supplies averaging 8 m³/sec. However, the water discharge at the weir dropped to less than 2 m³/sec in 1982 and 1983, and only some 2,200 ha could be irrigated. The decreasing water supplies at Kosinggolan coincided with the increasing deforestation and numbers of settlers in the reserve. This led the people of Dumoga to link the lack of constant water supply to the inroads made by illicit farmers into the forested catchment.

In the early 1980s the World Wildlife Fund prepared the park management plan for the Indonesian government, and this formed the basis for the development of the proposed National Park. The government officially declared the Dumoga-Bone area a National Park in October 1982. After much preparation the local government evicted more than 400 families from the park area in April 1983.

Factors that made forest protection effective

The following steps contributed to a more effective forest protection programme.

World Bank evaluation missions were held at half-yearly intervals. Meetings with the provincial and district government were used to discuss constraints hampering project execution and to indicate ways to integrate planning between departments. The possible failure of the irrigation projects because of deforestation was always mentioned as well as the promise given by the government to halt forest cutting in the catchment areas.

The Indonesian Nature Conservation Department implemented intensive monitoring of the water-catchment and National Park project. Representatives organized visits to the park and meetings with the local government several times a year.

The provincial government established a task force to end illegal forest encroachment, including military, police, justice and government representatives.

The district government replaced virtually all duty stations of the *camats* (sub-district heads). These changes were instrumental in breaking historical ties to land clearance permits and land acquisition. The first priority of the new *camat* of Dumoga was the protection of the National Park. He strengthened the government's action to solve conflicts related to land tenure.

Close co-operation was established between the local government offices, its agencies and the park authorities. The district forestry cancelled all local forest concessions at park borders as soon as park boundary locations were marked.

Local government extension programmes were implemented through formal and informal local leaders, teaching people about forest protection and its link with irrigation.

WWF and PPA contacted the government to discuss options, progress and constraints concerning the development of the park. Meetings were initiated to prepare resettlement plans, to recommend improvement of land registration, to halt encroachment and local logging and to request law enforcement.

A number of court cases led to the imprisonment of group leaders of land speculators and invaders in the park. Park guards were often asked to act as witnesses; many had received police training funded by the World Bank project.

New and long-established environmental, conservation and forestry laws and regulations were made available to the local department of justice.

Boundary rehabilitation programmes included regular repair of boundary markers and boundary paths. Fast-growing trees were planted by the park staff along the boundary lines where boundaries had been faded away by cultivation. People could not excuse their encroachment on the grounds that they did not know where the boundary was.

Evicted farmers accepted their fate as an act of justice because everyone had undergone the same treatment. The action did not have any serious repercussions on the park or its staff, nor did it bring evicted farmers severe difficulties as far as is known. Early warnings to settlers had made them refrain from large investments within the park.

Final results

All major development objectives and expectations were accomplished. The Kosinggolan and Toraut irrigation schemes boosted rice production and helped convert the province from a rice-importing to a rice-exporting region. The forest protection programme has provided the guarantee for a constant water flow which in turn is a basic source for rice production and the welfare of the valley people. The initial scheduled irrigable area of 11,600 ha in total will nearly be accomplished.

The transmigration schemes in the Dumoga valley are regarded as among the most successful in Indonesia. There has been an integration of people from many different tribes. An additional result, initially not anticipated, was the development of the National Park and its stimulation of regional recreation, international forest research and tourism.

The major products directly related to the World Bank loan were:

(1) *The water-catchment protection project.* The creation of the National Park meant that the project exceeded its initial goal to develop the 100,000 ha Dumoga Reserve. Park headquarters were built, including an office and staff quarters. Guard-posts were established along the boundary. Park personnel increased from 3 in 1980 to 104 in 1986. Personnel were recruited and paid by the project till March 1984, after which they came on the government payroll.

Park development for education, recreation and tourism exceeded planning goals. Visitor centres, a guest-house and camping grounds, nature trails and shelters were established. Exhibitions were held and education materials prepared. A combined training centre and research complex is being built.

Development for research has been much faster than initially scheduled. Some 135 foreign scientists from 15 countries and some 70 Indonesian students and scientists did research in the park from 1979 to 1986.

The operating cost of the whole park is US$120,000 per annum and will increase to some $150,000 in 1990. The park is rated a high-priority conservation area by the Indonesian government. This may guarantee sufficient funds, despite periods of economic recession.

(2) *The Dumoga irrigation projects, Kosinggolan and Toraut*. The loan provided so far to the Dumoga irrigation project amounts to US$16.2 m (December 1986) against an allocation of $19.19 m. Two or three rice crops per year can be grown in most of the irrigated areas. The average rice production increased from less than 2 tons per ha in 1980 to 4.55 tons per ha in 1986. Farmers' annual incomes in irrigation areas have doubled or trebled since 1980.

Lessons and conclusions

The timing of conservation measures was about 3–5 years too late for the protection of the southern part of the valley and the Kosinggolan catchment and just about in time for the northern part and the Toraut catchment. The establishment of the reserve and the marking of boundaries and recruitment of forest guards were unusually fast.

The pressure upon forest could have been less if more attention had been paid to the culture of the local population and its adaptability to change. The original inhabitants, traditionally used to dry-land agriculture and clearance of forest for new land, could not adapt in time to a more profitable and intensive form of agriculture with wet-land rice cultivation. Some of them were bought off their land, needed for the transmigration projects. Others sold their land to speculators, absentee landlords, transmigrants and migrants. The "project transmigrants" were settled on some 5,000 ha under the irrigation schemes. The local inhabitants, together with dry-land farmers of the region who came as spontaneous migrants, were the main groups who invaded the protected land.

Local people should preferably have been included in the project areas to increase their profit from the new facilities of access and irrigation. Extension campaigns and self-help programmes would have prevented them from false expectations and speeded up their adaptation to intensive forms of agriculture.

The main victims of law enforcement and forest protection measures were local inhabitants, migrants, absentee landlords and land speculators. The social costs were high, in particular to those losing all their land, who had to return to their home village.

The economic costs are hard to assess. The government cost includes resettlement costs ($0.24 m), extension campaigns, law-enforcement action, court cases and imprisonment of land speculators. Most of the illegal farmers had the profit of 1–3 years' crops, which balanced the price of the land. The loss of water, irrigable area and produce of rice caused by deforestation cannot be assessed. An early plan for conservation could have saved part or all of the cost mentioned above. On the other hand, both irrigation schemes might have become an economic failure if no forest protection programme had been implemented or if implementation had been less speedy.

The ecological gains were many. The high goals set for irrigation made it possible to claim large forest areas to be protected as catchment. Lowland areas, otherwise hard to include in reserves, were set aside as integral parts of the National Park. The combination of irrigation development and water-catchment protection underlined the ecological link of forest–water–rice production and facilitated planning on an ecological basis.

The applicability of a combined irrigation and development and catchment protection project elsewhere is high. Also the relation between projects for hydropower plants and forest protection, drinking water and forest protection seem obvious. New approaches with farmer groups living at park borders and the establishment of buffer zones/ boundary plant zones are a promising way to advocate conservation, grow firewood, mark boundaries and enlist co-operation with villagers. Such approaches, however, will work only if there is a project with a budget and the support of the local government. The main restriction to application of catchment protection projects is the lack of regional land-use plans and the lack of government control on private agricultural land.

CASE STUDY 7 *Soil Conservation Programme, Kenya*

DR NORMAN HUDSON
Silsoe Associates, Bedford, England

This is a long-term programme which will continue as long as the assistance is welcomed by the Kenyan government. The policy is to work entirely through the existing government structure and within existing government policies, although the programme may seek to give a lead where it feels that changes would be beneficial.

The main components are institution building and strengthening through a staff training programme. There is also an operational programme of field soil conservation, with a major component of technical training for farmers. The assistance is all grant, not loan. The budget is not large (currently about US$2.75 m per year). The limitation is not how much is available but how much can be usefully absorbed.

The government of Kenya (GOK) has defined soil degradation as a major national problem. In 1973 the Swedish International Development Authority (SIDA) agreed to second an adviser to the Ministry of Agriculture to advise on setting up a soil conservation programme. In 1974 Professor C. G. Wenner arrived to fill this post. Dr Wenner has made a powerful and consistent contribution to the project. The programme started modestly in 1974 with pilot areas in four districts, and 16 government technical assistants (TAs) were trained. By 1986-7, 39 out of Kenya's 41 districts were covered.

Technical assistance

The provision of technical assistance has been low in cost but vital to the programme's success. The expatriate Swedish technical staff have always been based in Nairobi, although they spend most of their time in the districts. They have not had counterparts in the usual sense of a one-to-one working relation, but have filled specific posts within the ministry. This means that there is a lack of continuity and a major hiccup when these specialists are replaced at the end of their tour of duty. Also, if the technical assistance component were discontinued there would be major problems in replacing the role of the expatriate specialist. The lack of counterparts is probably not GOK policy but rather because suitable staff are not available.

There are three expatriate staff, usually covering training, nurseries, and monitoring and evaluation. There is also a co-ordinator of SIDA agricultural projects in the Swedish Embassy, who helps in the management and disbursement of the part of the budget (30 per cent) not handled through GOK.

Training

The training component is also small in terms of budget but an essential feature of the programme strategy. The approach is to educate and train at all levels: within government service, technical training appropriate to the level of all employees, suitable training for chiefs and sub-chiefs and for teachers at all levels in the educational system, and practical instruction for farmers. This component must be rated as successful, but because of the size of the problem it will have to continue for many years, particularly the training for farmers. Training is closely linked to the training programme for the Regional Soil Conservation Unit based at the Swedish Embassy in Nairobi which covers East Africa.

Extension

The SIDA programme makes direct intervention only through expatriate specialists at headquarters level and supports improved training of conservation staff down to division level. At lower levels the soil conservation operations depend on the location extension officer at technical assistant (TA) grade and the JTAs at sub-location level. Smooth co-operation with the extension services is therefore basic to the programme. The programme has aimed to provide technical training in soil conservation to all the extension staff.

A T&V (training and visit) system was introduced in 1983, because it is not physically possible for the JTA to maintain regular individual contact with all the farmers in his sub-location. The last stage of the dissemination of extension messages must therefore be through groups of farmers. A JTA will typically have up to eight groups of about ten farmers, one of whom is the contact farmer. The extension worker meets each contact farmer, and as many as possible of the farmers in that group, at the same time and place during each two-week period. The period also includes one training day for the TAs and JTAs at District HQ, where the district officer teaches them the topical extension message for the next period. District officers go for regular training to Provincial HQ, and provincial officers to National HQ, so there is constant upgrading of the extension service, and its message varies with the seasons. The TA has a manageable number of contacts, meets them regularly on the same day every alternate week and has a simple message to put over. The difficulty is that the TAs' time is completely taken up by this programme, so there is no time for them to do their soil conservation work of talking to individual farmers or pegging out terraces and grass strips, or supervising work involving a number of farms. The second problem is that extension through T&V can deal only with a small number of simple practices which can easily and quickly be put across to the contact farmer and his group. This difficulty of combining soil conservation into the T&V system of extension is found in many countries. Since there is no real alternative to T&V in countries with a huge population of farmers it becomes a question of trying to work in as much soil conservation as possible. In Kenya the SIDA programme is assisting this integration in several ways. The 1986 budget includes a large increase in the provision for transport of all kinds, to increase the effectiveness of the service, and increased training of staff to improve the general understanding of soil conservation work.

Tree nurseries

The achievement has been disappointing here, with a large variation in the achievement of different nurseries. The main problem would appear to be lack of proper management and of labour.

On-farm operations

This component is for the direct payment for works which benefit a number of farmers. The programme will provide all the technical advice on conservation works free of charge. Cut-off drains usually cross several properties, and the full cost of labour to dig them is paid by the programme, after all the beneficiaries have signed an agreement to maintain the works and to build terraces on the land protected by the cut-off. There seem to be few problems with maintenance. For the construction of the cut-offs hand tools are provided by the programme, on either temporary or permanent loan. Payment may be by piecework or by daily wages, either direct to individuals or to a group which has agreed to undertake the work between them. For work on individual farms, the TAs provide only advice, and the construction is done either by the farmers or more commonly by a group which works together in turn on the fields of each group member.

Costs and benefits

The budget for the SIDA input to the programme is modest: US$2.75 m for 1986–7. The total cost of the project to date, i.e. SIDA's costs plus the regular expenditure by GOK, is approximately $15.25m, and the number of farms treated is 540,000, giving an overall cost of $28 per farm.

The most important achievement is the change in the approach to the conservation of natural resources at all levels from the President to the peasant farmer. It is impossible to calculate how much of this is the result of the SIDA intervention and how much is due to the national philosophy of *harambee* (let us all work together), or indeed to the President himself, who spends several days each year leading a work-force of many thousands to carry out conservation work.

Number of farms terraced. Between 1974 and 1983, 290,000 farms were terraced, out of the 750,000 farms estimated to need terracing. By 1985 the number terraced had increased to 490,000 and the number needing it to 1,100,000. The programme was gaining ground in spite of the rapid increase in the number of farmers. This is an extraordinary achievement compared with what is being achieved elsewhere in Africa.

Farmer training. The number of farmers receiving some instruction in conservation methods has increased rapidly. In 1981–2 it was 7,510; in 1982–3, 8,500; in 1983–4, 15,736; in 1984–5, 49,510. This is another outstanding achievement. In 1986–9 greater emphasis will be placed on better training for government staff. The programme will continue until a total of 1.5 million farmers have had some introduction to the principles of soil conservation.

Benefits. National GNP and agricultural production have increased considerably, but the effects of the SIDA programme cannot be separated from other factors. There are also unquantifiable national benefits: the rate of degradation has been slowed, and government employees and farmers are better informed.

For the individual the most practical result of conservation farming is increases in yield. Studies that have been made of the economic benefits of soil conservation show that there is definitely an increase in the yield of most crops after terracing, although none provides accurate and reliable data for economic analysis. Other benefits to the farmer may be as important as yield increases. Conservation farming can lead to greater reliability of yields, a better yield per unit of labour input, better cash flow and better nutrition of farm families.

Durability and expansion

The widespread acceptance of the programme by the farming community is a powerful indicator that it will continue to be successful. This shows in several ways. First, the growth of farmers' associations and self-help groups as a means of getting done those things too ambitious for the individual to tackle (related to this is the growing use of these groups for transmitting the extension message through T&V); second, the strong response to the offer of training courses for farmers, and farmers' days and visits; third, the absence of problems with maintenance, which usually plague soil conservation projects. Another noticeable factor is the strong role played by the women.

The programme is open-ended and will continue until GOK no longer wishes it to continue. GOK is already declining to accept some of the offered assistance, particularly any more expatriate specialists and the use of outside consultants. While this may sometimes cause frustration and slow down the rate of progress, it must be remembered that the objective of institution building leads logically to a situation of no technical assistance. At the end of the SIDA programme GOK will probably be faced with substantial additional recurrent costs. The 1985 review led to material changes in the 1986–9 programme, namely:

(1) To restructure the tree nursery programme, with a smaller number of sites given stronger support.
(2) To strengthen the extension programme, making available more transport, strengthening the training programme and introducing more soil conservation into the extension system.
(3) There are also two new components, formalizing a trend apparent for some years. One is to push harder for greater emphasis on biological

soil conservation through farming systems, in addition to the existing programme of mechanical works. This will include more attention to livestock management and agroforestry.

(4) The other will be a pilot semi-arid project.

(5) Another development, also formalizing an existing trend, is to introduce more variation across the country.

SIDA is considering increasing its activity where it has a long-term commitment to assisting soil conservation programmes, particularly in Zambia, Tanzania and Ethiopia. The "Kenya model of soil conservation" is also becoming known over a wide area in Africa. When considering the possibility of applying the Kenya model in other countries and by other aid agencies, we should keep in mind that although other projects may be able to profit from the lessons learned there is no magic package which can be picked up by another agency and dropped down in another country. Some factors, such as long-term financial commitment, will not be acceptable to all agencies, and the principle of bottom-up and self-help movements may not be acceptable in centrally planned countries.

Factors affecting the success of the programme

This is a long-term programme, and this results in several benefits. There is no anxiety on either side about the continuation of the programme and no need to do things in a scramble before a deadline. The mobilization period setting up the programme is small in comparison with the programme's duration. The long-term commitment by SIDA allows long-term planning and training of specialists to meet future requirements and the training of Kenyan officers is made more effective.

The SIDA funding is a grant not a loan. Kenya already has a severe balance of payments problem, and it is undesirable to add to its burden of debt repayment.

SIDA retains control of about 30 per cent of the expenditure. This enables it to insist on administrative problems being corrected by holding up funds until action is taken. It also enables the programme to cut through red tape that is unnecessarily delaying the programme.

The programme has consistently maintained a good relationship with the government, and there is no element of paternalism.

CASE STUDY 8 *Dry-Season Gardening Projects, Niger*

ROBERT COTTINGHAM
Africa Program Director, Lutheran World Relief

The Lutheran World Relief (LWR) programme in Niger started in 1974, arising from the urgent need to replace seed grain stocks consumed during the Sahelian drought. A project was designed to truck seeds from Nigeria to the southern parts of Niger and Chad. However, the government of Niger had received 20,000 tons of seed grains from international donors but was unable to distribute the seed swiftly to rural areas. The LWR project was revised to focus on responding to that need. A team which included several people fluent in Hausa distributed 1,600 tons of seed in a few months.

The team's travel throughout Niger exposed them to the long-term efforts which would be needed to avert a similar disaster later. LWR gave the team a new assignment: to design a long-term programme that would be responsive to local needs. The design process involved extensive survey and dialogue with villagers, village councils, national and regional government officials and extensionists. LWR approved the first project in autumn 1976 and a second six months later.

Thanks to a group of unusually dedicated field staff, the programme expanded steadily along the local priorities of increasing water and food production on a sustainable basis. Getting rural people to talk about how their lives have improved or deteriorated is a start for development practitioners in their efforts to approach agricultural change and environmental regeneration. Such discussions lay the basis for prioritizing what rural people themselves think is important.

Project background

By 1974 it became obvious that a return to normal rainfall in the future was not going to occur. In Niger local food production was at least 30 per cent less than it had been the previous decade. The government pledged up to 50 per cent of its resources for the rural sector. NGOs were encouraged to create or fund projects and programmes that would help the country towards self-sufficiency in food.

LWR policy guided its staff to seek out the poorest of the poor and work with them to clarify their needs and establish their priorities. Anyone who has been involved in rural development in Africa knows this is no small feat. The poor in most settings have little or no voice or power, and in the rural areas they are excluded from decision-making village councils. The largest number of rural poor are women and children.

The second mandate was to work with this poor class in helping them produce more food for personal consumption in a manner that would help regenerate the environment. In 1974 this was seen as growing trees for firewood and constructing traditional shelters, and occasionally wind and sand-dune control. Food, water and trees are not components but rather the three basic, inseparable elements that must be present in all programmes if they are both to meet acute food needs and to help the environment move back to pre-drought conditions.

Early project sites were in places devoid of markets, on marginal land and with nomads and semi-nomads who were left destitute in many areas as drought took their animals. These people looked for new ways to survive until their herds could be reconstituted. Satellite images showed that "albedo" ("haloes") appeared around villages, reflecting vegetation loss, erosion and the break-up of soils. The most pronounced erosion has occurred on land exposed to running water in places where rainfall was and is too low to keep plants alive but still great enough to run over the soil.

Gardening around these low-lying areas intensified. Only moist sand enriched by erosion of topsoil from higher elevations remained in which to grow tomatoes, okra and manioc. During the long dry season these staples kept the village people alive. Many men migrated south in search of employment. Those left began to hand-dig shallow wells down the centre of the dry ponds, and these crude, wood-reinforced traditional wells recharged almost up to 12 inches of water overnight. Polluted as it was, it was better than using energy provided by one meal a day to walk 5–6 km for a pail of water.

Dry-season gardening

The villagers' immediate need was for vegetable seeds. While tomato and okra seeds could be dried and collected, and manioc cuttings could be replanted, other vegetables which would broaden the diet and nutritional base were generally not available. Composting was almost unheard of and difficult in dry areas, and with the loss of livestock and their manure these people were left to grow a few food items in low-quality soil. These factors generated the first few modest project attempts. The larger amounts of food grown using chemical fertilizer gave encouragement to the men and women involved, but success was short-lived.

The following elements brought new challenges: insects on the plants; nematodes in the soil; strong, constant, dry winds sucking the life out of green leafy vegetables. All took their toll. Poorly consructed wells were a constant source of danger from cave-ins. To meet these challenges, insecticides in small amounts were imported to control the nematodes. Villagers were encouraged to hand-exterminate external pests, while the Nigerien agriculture services demonstrated the safe use of insecticides and distributed them. It was rediscovered that nitrogen-fixing legumes (chickpeas) not only provided nutritional vegetables for additional food but were easy to dry, store and replant. If intercropped with other vegetables they provide nitrogen to the needy soil and cut down on nematode infestation.

Strong, hot wind caused erosion and sand dunes and sapped the life out of vegetables struggling to survive the intense heat. In response, a number of indigenous trees and bushes were planted on pond perimeters and around garden plots. These local varieties of hedges became a simple, effective way to keep out livestock and counter the relentless winds. The effect was to reduce water consumption, to add the new colour of green on vegetables and to strengthen wilting varieties of legumes; the shade given to the earth in the gardens greatly lowered ground temperatures.

Traditional well problems took longest to solve. The design team determined that the placement of a substantial number of wells providing water for human and animal consumption, as well as for irrigation, would be appropriate and that shallow wells would not pose a threat to the ecosystem. Work was begun on designing a simple technology to meet the requirements of local replicability and durability.

The result was the development of steel-reinforced concrete rings 1 m high and 140 cm across which would sink into the ground as soil was excavated from within them. These wells resembled steel-reinforced concrete culverts used to divert water under roads. The method provides a reliable way to reach ground water tables safely and easily. Test results gave a 50-year average lifespan to each well at a maximum depth of 19 m. In 1986 the total cost of a 6 m × 140 cm well (including well-diggers' salaries) was US$400 – far less than the cost of wells made by the government service.

In the first eight dry-season garden project sites, 237 shallow wells were constructed. By the end of 1987 more than 3,200 had been completed in communities where LWR supported work and eight other NGOs have constructed a large number. The methodology employed in initiating the well construction was to train teams of Nigeriens, who in turn trained villagers in construction. The principal labour was done by villagers. Steel moulds, concrete and reinforcing rings were provided by LWR, initially as a grant and later on a partial loan basis.

This technology solved well cave-in and dirty water problems and had the advantages of low cost, simplicity and ease of maintenance. The basic design of the wells has been modified over time, and with few exceptions they are still producing water. The simple irrigation techniques used in LWR-sponsored gardens should be tested in other areas of West Africa. The use of small, earthern irrigation canals saves time and labour in daily watering. Many garden projects fail to use this practice and as a result are so labour-intensive that gardeners lose interest. Without small irrigation systems gardeners are reticent to expand their gardens, live fences, fruit trees and wood lots. Fruit trees and other species producing edible leaves have been associated with garden vegetable production. Often the fruit and leaves from the trees surpass the nutritional and economic value of the vegetable.

The dry-season garden projects have also had inputs from health, literacy, community development and agriculture extension components. Literacy focuses on gardening information, weights and measures and numeracy. Animation agents inform people about the programme and help them participate. Health inputs provide medical supplies to local health workers and information on nutritious use of newly introduced vegetables, especially as weaning foods for small children, which has had a great impact on infant mortality rates.

Benefits

The most easily measured economic impact is the increased availability of garden vegetables. People have increased food for themselves, which was LWR's primary goal, but most gardeners have surplus vegetables to sell.

During the earlier years, farmers had access to highly subsidized seed, fertilizer and insecticides. As the various projects matured, gardeners began to pay larger percentages of the costs. Labour provided largely by family members is estimated to involve 20 person-months per hectare per season. Many families who were previously landless now own land. People have mastered skills and learned new methods of producing and diversifying their production for good nutrition, as well as providing greater income security. Where farmers have concentrated on selling part of their produce they have been able to generate considerable cash.

Less easily measurable economic benefits are increased production of animal feed from the use of windbreaks and live fencing; literacy and numeracy helping people market their produce more skilfully; and health and/or strength from a more available and diversified food supply. Animal watering wells prevent potential animal weight loss. Village wells make better-quality water available at more convenient, time-saving points. Wells which replace traditional wells also save construction time, upkeep and scarce wood.

Gardeners say that their garden plots provide an economic alternative to the search for jobs in slum-choked cities. Nomads who lost their herds during the drought have settled into gardening. LWR's involvement in vegetable gardening has legitimized activities that some individuals and families had undertaken on their own and has helped farm families establish themselves on sites originally open to common uses.

Environmental effects are positive. Live fencing utilizing indigenous species is possible and within the capabilities of local people. Its use has reduced pressure for the use of live and dead thorn-tree branches.

Some of these garden projects are in villages where government reforestation projects were attempted without much success. People were not able to grasp the need to protect the environment. On the other hand, when it came to planting windbreaks, live fences and fruit trees, they perceived the immediate need to stop the wind and keep animals out of their gardens, and the short-term future possibility of having fresh fruit for consumption and sale. These garden sites are the only green areas for miles in the Sahel.

These efforts at environmental protection may point the way to an educational process that will allow gardeners to think on a more national scale. This will be especially true among the women, who must walk kilometre after kilometre for firewood. They have fully appreciated the ability to trim live fences and use the branches for cooking fuel and the leaves for animal-fattening.

Reasons for success

Twelve years' experience in Niger has shown that these dry-season gardens are self-sustaining. People are aware that rain-fed agriculture may never be as it was in past years because of the decline in rainfall. They are beginning to comprehend that a new way of life must come about. Gardens can help local people become more "drought-proof".

In the Niger mini-droughts of 1984–5 people who were gardening around concrete wells were able to remain in their villages. As a result LWR dry-season garden/well projects were made the national programme of the year. Every prefecture in Niger put together resources in promoting gardens and wells. Drought has not been the sole stimulus for entry into gardening. The rapid environmental degradation of agricultural lands and low market prices for food crops have made farming an increasingly marginal occupation. Dry-season gardening promises supplemental food and cash incomes.

LWR believes that the full participation of villagers in every step of the process – from design to evaluation – may be one of the most important factors contributing to programme effectiveness. In the LWR programme in Niger this has not been possible. Allowing the project design team up to 18 months to develop relationships and trust, and to establish rapport with people at village and government levels, has perhaps contributed to positive working relationships. The time invested to examine the technology which would be utilized and to make it replicable and foolproof was wise.

The future

Dry-season garden projects and wells have been replicated in more than 20 areas of Niger with the same success as in the original 8. In 1986 Burkina Faso, Mali, Senegal and Western Sudan were surveyed for areas with water tables that would allow replication of most of the components of these dry-season gardens.

CASE STUDY 9 *Soil and Water Conservation in Yatenga, Burkina Faso*

CHRIS REIJ

Working Group for Resource Development in Africa, Free University, Amsterdam

The Yatenga region is one of the most densely populated of Burkina Faso. In 1975–6 the area cultivated per inhabitant averaged 0.5 ha only. In many villages most of the territory is under cultivation, which means that there is no possibility of expanding the agricultural area; fallow is virtually absent. Population and livestock pressures have led to extensive degradation of soils and vegetation, exacerbated by drought. The rural population of the Yatenga region seems to have only one choice: improve the land or migrate.

The Projet Agro-Forestier (PAF) started as a forestry project in 1979. Micro-catchments were introduced to increase water availability to trees, but survival rates were low due to intense grazing pressure. Villagers showed more interest in conserving soil and water than in planting trees. The focus of the project shifted towards testing simple soil and water conservation (SWC) techniques on farmers' fields. A key development was the introduction of a water tube level to determine contour lines for rock bund construction, a technology cheap and simple enough for the farmers to use themselves. Without this technology it is difficult to determine the contour because the land is quite flat, and an improperly laid contour line will channel water to its lowest point, possibly causing a gulley to form. Attention was paid to the use of organic manure and soil tillage. PAF aimed at the harvesting of run-off water, whereas all previous SWC projects had made an effort to deviate "excess" run-off water in order to reduce damage to conservation works. This was a key factor in its much greater effectiveness.

The first phase of PAF (1979–82) was characterized by a search for simple SWC techniques applicable by farmers with a minimum of external support. Farmers showed a clear preference for rock bunds, so at the beginning of the second phase (1983–6) emphasis was laid on designing and testing methods for farmer training. About 1,750 farmers in 339 villages have been trained in the use of the water tube level and rock bund construction. The number of hectares treated with rock bunds by the farmers is estimated to be about 2,400.

Farmer training and extension

The first step in farmer training is to organize a meeting with all the inhabitants of one or more villages to discuss the degradation of the vegetation, run-off and erosion. Representatives of the villages then pay a visit to fields which have been treated. Here they can discuss with other farmers their experiences and results obtained. Next comes the organization of a training course at village level. Participants usually come from various villages where they have been selected by the villagers for training. Upon return, the trainees are expected to engage, and assist other farmers, in rock bund construction.

Farmer training also comprises: (1) use of a scale model to demonstrate the importance of respecting contour lines; (2) training in the use of the water tube level; (3) practical training in rock bund construction; (4) group discussion about how to organize bund construction, treatment of individual or communal fields, etc. Government extension agents play an important role in monitoring at village level. Government staff are involved in PAF's activities from the field level (extension agents) up to the level of the director.

Aspects of rock bund construction

Farmers prefer rock bunds for several reasons. Unlike earth bunds they are not quickly damaged by run-off, which reduces maintenance; they are permeable barriers, so not only the crops planted in front of the rock bunds benefit from run-off but also those planted behind them; and they increase yields considerably. The water retained by the bunds gradually permeates the soil, much of which is covered by a hard crust that would otherwise have prevented infiltration of water.

Rock bund construction permits an expansion of the cultivated area through the reclamation of abandoned land. The number of hectares treated has approximately doubled every year since 1983, reaching 1,300 hectares in 1986. The question is whether this trend can be maintained.

There are three possible organizational approaches: individual treatment of private fields; collective treatment of private fields; collective treatment of communal fields. The large majority of the communal fields treated collectively by the villagers showed poor crop stands compared to the private fields. Farmers first of all devote their labour and organic manure to their own fields to assure food availability at family level and only then do they tend communal fields. The communal fields are also usually of poor quality.

PAF encourages collective treatment of individual fields. Traditionally those who work collectively on the fields of individuals are remunerated in the form of food and drink. PAF put a small stock of maize flour at the disposal of the more organized groups as a revolving stock. Members of the group can get a loan in the form of maize flour to prepare food for those who help them with bund construction. PAF is different from most SWC projects in Burkina Faso in that it does not give food aid or cash to farmers who undertake SWC. The prospects of short-term yield increases are sufficient motive for farmers to engage in rock bund construction. PAF does provide limited material support for farmers in the form of water tube level, shovels, pickaxes, wheelbarrows and some donkey carts. Committees have been formed to manage the equipment.

Women play a major role in rock bund construction, because many men migrate in the dry season. Women have an important indirect benefit from it since yield increases on family fields improve availability of cereals at family level, which means that women have to contribute less from their own private fields to the family food supply. In general, women's private fields are of poor quality. In some cases women have treated their private fields, with a considerable improvement in quality.

Complementary measures

A survey conducted in 1984 of 313 fields treated by farmers using the water tube level revealed that 58 per cent of the fields received no other soil treatment, 9 per cent were ploughed with animal traction and 33 per cent were treated with *zai* (water pockets/pit farming). *Zai* further reduce surface run-off and permit efficient conservation of water. The second major constraint to be alleviated is poor soil fertility. Farmers over the last decade have increased efforts to fertilize their fields, and both rock bunds and *zai* conserve manure, most of which used to be washed away by the first big rains. The same survey indicated that 60 per cent of the treated fields were manured, and those farmers who dug *zai* always associated manure with the pockets.

Cost and benefits

Project costs were 13.6 Central African francs in 1983 and 10.4 million in 1985. The average (project) cost per hectare in 1983 was about 90.700 CFA, but only 17.300 CFA in 1985. This does not, however, include the costs incurred by the farmers in terms of labour and inputs. Labour for construction of rock bunds is the most important cost component for farmers.

Rock bunds have increased crop yields considerably. They also seem to provide high-yield security by reducing the impact of low-rainfall years on yields.

Why is PAF successful?

(1) PAF is farmer-oriented in its approach; the techniques promoted are essentially improved traditional techniques. (2) Rock bunds permit the reclamation of long-abandoned, degraded fields and lead to impressive yield increases in a short time. (3) Adequate attention has been paid to designing a training and extension programme. (4) PAF benefited from the presence of two highly dedicated and capable staff members.

Wider impact

In the project's third phase (1987–9) the number of staff will be increased to five. This will permit an expansion of the training programme and an extension of the project to other regions. Other organizations now promote the same techniques, and many farmers are adopting them spontaneously. So even if PAF were stopped, rock bund construction by farmers would continue.

PAF's extension and training model, as well as its emphasis on simple improvements in indigenous techniques, can probably be replicated elsewhere in sub-Saharan Africa, even where population density, soils, topography and rainfall characteristics differ from those in the Yatenga. PAF's technical package, however, is much more difficult to replicate. Chances are best in regions where population density is high, rocks are abundant and the slopes not too steep.

CASE STUDY 10 *Agroforestry Outreach Project, Haiti*

FREDERICK J. CONWAY
Development Consultant / Social Science Adviser

The Haiti Agroforestry Outreach Project (AOP), designed and primarily funded by USAID, provides tree seedlings to peasants to plant on their farms. Between 1982 and 1986 approximately 110,000 farmers planted more than 25 million seedlings through the project. These figures far exceed the original goals of the project. The project has made substantial progress in helping farmers establish the practice of cropping trees, with the expectation of increasing their incomes, contributing to the productivity of their land and relieving pressure on the natural stands of trees currently cut for fuel and housing.

The AOP is implemented entirely through non-governmental organizations. The first phase (1981–6) consisted of grants to the Pan-American Development Foundation (PADF), CARE and Operation Double Harvest. The largest of the grants was to PADF, which in turn makes sub-grants to other NGOs interested in farm forestry. The AOP has introduced practices for the sustainable production and protection of natural resources in Haiti on an unprecedented scale.

Project design

The AOP grew out of a concern for the increasing environmental degradation of Haiti, with rapid deforestation, extensive soil erosion and declining agricultural production. The magnitude of these problems was exacerbated by the indifference of the Duvalier government. Most of Haiti's rural families own and farm some land. Their extreme poverty prevents them from taking much action, but they have a personal stake in increasing the productivity of their land and preserving their soil.

The design of the project emerged from an anthropological analysis of soil erosion and reforestation projects in Haiti over the previous 25 years. Few of these projects could claim more than very limited success. USAID staff sensed that another approach to the country's severe problems was needed. A USAID social science adviser, Polly Harrison, promoted the use of social scientists with experience in rural Haiti. In 1979 USAID contracted anthropologist Gerald

Murray to review 19 erosion control projects to identify what had led them to success or failure.

Murray found that increased income was the prime motivation for participation by small farmers. In most cases this motivation was not related to the institution of sustained erosion control practices but to wages paid in cash or food for work in the project. He concluded that agroforestry on small farms, with the cropping of trees, was the practice related to soil conservation most likely to be adopted on a sustained basis. Cash cropping is universal in Haiti, and the harvesting and sale of wood are an important element in the rural economy. Murray proposed the joining of the two behaviours; instead of cutting natural stands of trees, a way could be found to enable the small farmers to produce the food they sold. Tree cropping could become a new central element in the rural economy. Instead of focusing on the physical aspects of erosion control and viewing the peasant as an obstacle, Murray focused on the economic system and viewed the peasant as a positive element, the only possible agent of environmental restoration in Haiti.

Three social scientists, including the author, were hired to study wood production, marketing and use. Their work helped USAID evaluate the feasibility of cash cropping trees and predict the effect of the project on potential beneficiaries. This extensive use of social science research was rare in the design of USAID rural development projects.

One important, and at the time controversial, decision made by USAID was to implement its major reforestation project in Haiti through NGOs. In the project design, PADF was intended primarily as an intermediary by which resources could be channelled to NGOs working in rural areas, without burdening either them or the donor with direct administrative contact. This structure is one of the most replicable elements in the project.

Project activities

The CARE and PADF agroforestry projects differ in central organizational structure, but their activities in the field are similar.

Farm forestry extension

Extension agents. After consultation with local people, extension agents are hired. The extension agents are usually literate peasants residing in the locality where they work. They know most of the project participants personally and are familiar with the planting sites. After training, the extension agents explain the project to local farmers and register those who want to receive seedlings. Potential participants are told of options for integrating trees into their farms, e.g. intercropping, border plantings, hedgerows and woodlots. The extension agents visit the sites where the seedlings will be planted to collect information, provide advice and see that the ground has been prepared. They organize delivery and distribution of seedlings or arrange for participants to receive their seedlings at a nearby nursery.

The planting is organized by the participants. The extension agents follow up with visits to advise the planter and monitor the growth and survival of the seedlings. Subsequent training is provided in management and harvesting techniques.

Extension messages. Extension messages emphasize the potential of farm forestry for increasing peasants' incomes. Participants are asked to plant a minimum quantity of seedlings (about 150) to ensure they will have a visible economic impact. The project emphasizes the rights of planters to all benefits from their trees, as well as complete control of how they are located, managed and harvested. To ensure that participants feel secure in the rights to their trees, CARE and PADF ask them to plant seedlings on land they own.

The project delivers seedlings on the day and at the place arranged. This factor cannot be overestimated in a country where many false promises are heard.

Nursery production

Most of the seedlings are produced in regional nurseries supported by PADF and CARE. The nurseries produce small, easily transportable seedlings, in sharp contrast with previous nursery technologies. A person can carry 500 of these small seedlings, and the ground can be prepared for them without much labour. By late 1986 the 39 nurseries were producing about three million seedlings a year, usually for two planting seasons. About 40 species were produced.

PADF sub-grants to other NGOs

CARE implements its extension activities directly and works intensively in its region. PADF makes sub-grants to other NGOs, taking an active role in defining project activities. PADF's regional teams have worked with more than 170 NGOs in many areas of the country. Each of these NGOs had already been working in Haitian rural communities, but they differ in resources and experience. PADF has also helped NGOs establish more than 30 regional nurseries.

Changes in project activities

Expansion of project goals. The response of farmers and NGOs to the resources provided by PADF and CARE exceeded expectations. PADF's four-year goal of three million seedlings was nearly quadrupled to 11.8 million seedlings and was met.

PADF regional nurseries. In the original project design, seedlings were to be produced in a central nursery and delivered by truck to planting communities. The production in this nursery increased tenfold, but distribution problems became serious. For this reason, PADF initiated the nursery development sub-projects described above.

Discontinuation of incentive payments. At first an "incentive payment" was made to planters on the basis of the number of seedlings that had survived 6 and 12 months after planting. The response of farmers to the project was so overwhelming that PADF and CARE decided to discontinue the payments.

Diversification of species. In the first year, nursery production concentrated on five exotic fast-growing hardwood species. The number of species offered to peasant planters has since increased. Planters have indicated their preferences for a species mix that includes familiar indigenous hardwoods as well as exotics. This has entailed a reorientation from fuelwood production to multiple uses of project trees; it also reflects planters' willingness to make longer-term investments in tree cropping. The NGOs have refined their ability to respond to requests for particular mixes of species for given sites.

Emphasis on agroforestry. The emphasis in the first two years of the project was on the quantity of seedlings distributed to farmers. Gradually the emphasis has shifted towards the quality of agroforestry associations supported by the project. This is reflected in the refinement of training and extension messages and increased interest in tree/crop associations and soil protection by planters.

Research and monitoring. Probably the greatest problem in the original project design was insufficient attention to monitoring and applied research. In 1985 research was commissioned to rectify this situation.

Costs

The total cost of the extended AOP (1981–6) was estimated to be US$ 16.2 m, of which USAID contributed $11.5 m. The PADF project has received additional support from other donors. An economic analysis showed that the project should have a good rate of return.

Limitations of the project

The project is not the "solution" to the environmental problems of Haiti. It can succeed only on land which is privately owned or at least securely held by an individual family. Much of the most degraded land in Haiti is owned by the government or held in common by a local population.

Participation in the project

Motivation for participation. Participation in the project generally appears to be an economically viable decision for most planters. AOP participants generally plant and maintain trees because they perceive them to have economic benefits. Many planters plan to use their trees as a form of savings, harvesting them when the need for cash arises. The logic of the harvest will be based on needs for cash or wood rather than a complete rotation of the tree crop. Many planters value their trees for their potential multiple uses rather than for a single product which can be sold.

The potential of trees for reducing uncertainty has become as important an attraction to many planters as their ability to generate income. Mature trees are generally neither as dependent on the seasonal cycle nor as vulnerable to climate as annual crops. Many planters are interested in cultivating trees to use themselves. They substantially reduce the costs of building a new home, a highly valued accomplishment. Trees are valued too for their potential role in soil conservation and moisture retention. Where lack of labour is a constraint on agricultural production, tree cropping can be an attractive alternative to food crops.

Local decision-making. Community-based groups are new and still rare in Haiti. Recognizing this, the AOP has worked primarily with individual farmers and has guaranteed them complete freedom in making decisions about the resources the project makes available to them. Participation is voluntary. Where community-based groups exist, PADF and its sub-grantee NGOs work with them. The preferences of participants for the species they receive have been reflected in nursery production. Both extension agents and intermediary NGOs are channels for feedback from planters, and PADF and CARE staff meet frequently with planters to discuss their experiences.

Sustainability of the project

Economic sustainability. Some steps have been taken towards reducing subsidies to AOP planters. Elimination of the incentive payments was an important advance. The ability of most peasants to pay for any farm inputs, however, is limited. Since wood harvesting has only recently begun, it is still too early for planters to pay even a nominal price for seedlings. Nevertheless PADF and CARE are likely to begin introducing cash payments for seedlings on a pilot scale before the end of the second phase of the project.

If all subsidies were removed, the number of peasants able to practise tree cropping would be sharply reduced. If only wealthier peasants have access to seedlings, disparities in rural income will increase. Disparities in the value of land and access to land improvement will also increase, leaving poorer peasants yet more marginal. From the point of view of environmental restoration, as well as equity, it is desirable to include as many landholders as possible.

Environmental sustainability. The integration of trees as perennial crops on farms can be expected to have a number of beneficial effects on the environment. Among these are reduction of soil loss on slopes, retention of rainwater in the soil, creation of micro-environments with reduced evapotranspiration, increase of organic matter and (with some species) fixation of nitrogen in the soil. Wood from project farms will replace wood cut from natural stands, many of them in fragile zones.

Organizational sustainability. For the foreseeable future, farm forestry in Haiti will be a subsidized activity. A significant step has been for sub-grantees to receive grants directly from donors. The most important of these is a Canadian International Development Agency grant to CODEPLA, the development arm of the Council of Evangelical Churches of Haiti, which has projects in several rural communities.

Conclusions

Factors in project success. The AOP owes its success to a number of factors:

- A landowning peasantry which produces for the internal market.
- A strong demand for wood in Haiti, especially for fuel, most of which is already provided by peasants.
- Before undertaking the design of its new project, USAID carefully reviewed past efforts. This led to a project design reflecting the realities of Haitian life.
- A mechanism was found to channel donor funds and technical resources to organizations working directly with the rural population.
- The project stimulated a demand for seedlings rather than merely producing them.
- Emphasis has been placed on the survival and maintenance of seedlings, not merely on distribution or planting.
- The rights of participants to locate, manage and harvest trees on their farms in the manner they find best are emphasized.
- The project uses fast-growing hardwood species and a nursery technology that produces easily transportable and easily planted seedlings.
- Credibility was established through an efficient system which delivered seedlings on the day expected.
- The focus of the project is on a relatively simple idea carried out well, rather than trying to solve all the problems of Haiti's agricultural sector.

Replicability. The use of an intermediary NGO to channel resources from a donor to other NGOs has many potential applications. It enables a large donor agency to support many different types of NGO without the administrative burdens of making many small grants. It also enables several donors to support the same project activities. The arrangement makes it possible for NGOs to receive major donor funds without feeling intimidated by bureaucratic requirements and inflexibility.

The model used in the USAID/PADF project is a means of channelling technical assistance and project ideas as well as funding. The PADF grant has introduced many NGOs to the concepts of farm forestry and helped them avoid past mistakes. The USAID/PADF model also benefits from economies of scale. These advantages could be applied to many other types of development activities.

Many of the principles used in the AOP are now standard for many reforestation projects. A similar project is being implemented in the Dominican Republic. The specific approach to farm forestry is most appropriate where there is a peasant class with some secure access to land but could also be used on government land which had been subdivided into individual lots for long-term lease.

One of the most important aspects of the AOP is appropriate to many types of tree-planting project: the emphasis on creating a demand for seedlings instead of beginning with the seemingly logical step of developing nurseries around the country.

CASE STUDY 11 *The Guesselbodi Experiment: Bushland Management in Niger*

JOHN G. HEERMANS

Forester, USAID Forest and Land-Use Planning Project, Niger

Despite much investment in forestry in the Sahel after the drought of 1968–74, results in combating desertification have been poor. Natural forest management is now considered essential. The Guesselbodi experiment in Niger is an attempt to manage 5,000 ha of bushland with respect to local attitudes and traditions while adhering to principles of sustained yield, maintenance of biological diversity and soil conservation. The project is based on popular participation or management by villagers, using the forest to generate the income to assure continuity of the operation.

Natural forest and bushlands are essential to the survival of Sahelien inhabitants. The disappearance of the natural forest and the onset of desertification are a result of the breakdown of traditional land tenure systems, leading to the "tragedy of the commons" whereby resources are used by all but managed by no one. Past efforts in natural forest management have entailed uprooting existing "useless brush" with bulldozers and replacing natural vegetation with species neither adapted to the local ecology nor preferred by the local inhabitants. An alternative is to manage existing native forests and bushlands in a manner consistent with sound ecological practices.

The Forest and Land-Use Planning Project (FLUP) in Niger, funded by USAID, attempts to test intermediate-scale interventions in natural resource management to serve as a model for national-level projects designed to arrest environmental degradation in the Sahel and to exploit rationally the forest resource base. Work began in Guesselbodi in 1981. A management plan was implemented in September 1983, and the intervening period was spent conducting studies, and discussions with local villagers.

Project background

Present condition of the forest. Forty to 60 per cent of the total vegetative cover in Guesselbodi has disappeared in the last 30 years. Overgrazing has induced soil erosion. The upper layer of soil has been washed away by sheet and gully erosion. The lower layer contains practically no organic matter and is crusted, allowing little water penetration. In some areas of the forest, ironstone is often exposed or found near the surface. Land that has degraded to these conditions is barren; even if protected from livestock, vegetation will not regenerate on these soils.

Research as management input. Research support is essential to the success of forest management in the Sahel. A 22 ha parcel was set up by the project planners in 1981 to provide the data required for a management plan. Two major research foci emerged: soil restoration/conservation; and factors related to the production, exploitation and management of the local species that are preferred for use as firewood in Niamey (Niger's capital, 25 km to the west). It was decided that a management plan should be created before all the research on the forest's ecology was completed, since there exists a wealth of information from local villagers and Forest Service personnel.

Vegetation and soil mapping. The forest was divided into ten parcels of approximately 500 ha each, and the entire forest was stratified by major vegetation types. The parcelling allowed concentration of effort on one section at a time and more detailed analysis. All plant species were recorded as to percentage of ground cover and classified according to height. Soil was described by its texture and depth; topography was observed, and the percentage of slope was noted.

Interaction with the local population. The traditional role of the forester in the Sahel has been to enforce the contradictory and repressive Forestry Code. As long as the local forester is perceived by villagers as a paramilitary guard, it will be difficult to integrate villagers into management-related activity. Discussions were carried out in 1981 with the affected villagers to explain the proposed intervention and to gather information about uses of the forest, changes over the past 30 years and priorities and preferences for its use.

Management plan

The basic strategy is to exploit the forest in a cost-effective manner based on popular participation. Projects that depend on uncertain inputs from donors or the national budget have no assurance of continuing over an extended period. Ultimately, Guesselbodi forest should be managed by the local users.

Because of the relatively high price of firewood in Niamey, the forest could both meet the needs of the surrounding population and provide continual employment. The villagers see the immediate, significant benefit as the employment of local people to carry out the labour in the work plan.

Work to date

Each of the ten parcels will be individually treated over a decade. As the system improves, the transfer of responsibility from the project to the villagers will take place. Each stratified zone of the parcel is "treated" according to the conditions of topography, soils and vegetation. The work is carried out by labourers hired from surrounding villages. Approximately 80 labourers work in the forest and 15 in the tree nursery, supervised by trained foremen. The work continues to be supervised by the Nigerien forest agent, a volunteer forester and a technical consultant.

Extension work

A management proposal was presented to the villagers in November 1983. Coloured posters were used to emphasize important aspects. The presentation pointed out that 30 years ago the forest had an abundance of flora and fauna that does not exist today and that the disappearance of these resources has been accompanied by rampant soil erosion. The principal cause of this degradation was identified as increased pressure by people and their herds of animals.

Project staff explained that they had come to help the people restore the forest and to work with them in exploring different possible interventions that will assure them an increased and continuing supply of firewood, pasturage and other forest products. The posters told the villagers: "The success of the endeavour depends on you. We invite all of you to be frank with us and continue to provide us with information and ideas." The remainder of the session was spent discussing hiring, grazing, protection, the rotation system, erosion control, cutting, agroforestry and the work calendar.

Soil conservation

Much of the investment to restore the forest is linked to soil conservation. Techniques vary with the nature of the soil and topography of each site.

Contour walls. Stone and earthen walls 20–30 cm high were constructed on slopes greater than one per cent. Trees were planted from nursery stock or directly seeded behind the contour walls. The areas behind the walls remain moist longer and eventually generate grasses, trees and shrubs, which will protect the watershed and provide primary and secondary forest products. This technique is effective, but its high cost has led to the use of other techniques, described below.

Mulch. Small branches and twigs left from harvesting operations are spread out evenly on the barren soils between the clumps of trees. Mulch increases the moisture-absorption capacity of the soil, improving conditions for grasses, shrubs and trees to regenerate. Termites colonize in the soil beneath ligneous mulch, creating pores that allow rainwater to penetrate the soils.

Micro-catchments. Micro-catchments are individual earth structures which channel surface run-off to planted trees, grasses and crops, increasing survival and growth rates. The low cost of constructing the catchments has made this technique an integral component of the conservation effort.

Silvicultural studies/forest inventory

The sale of fuelwood in Niamey was recognized as a principal management objective. To develop a firewood-cutting policy it was necessary to calculate the commercial standing dry weight of the forest's three main firewood species. This information allowed the management team to estimate projected yearly income from the sale of firewood.

Tree planting

Approximately 70,000 nursery-grown trees are planted annually on the treated parcels, within and between existing stands. Species selection was based on preferences expressed by villagers and on site characteristics. Most species planted presently grow naturally in the forest, but several exotics have been tried. Some agroforestry is permitted in the local people's preferred zones for agriculture.

Range management

A major cause of the soil erosion at Guesselbodi is overgrazing. Barren areas will remain so unless systems are developed to control this growing pressure. Each parcel is to be protected from all grazing animals for three years; people will be allowed to cut hay and gather gum, food and medicines. The re-entry of animals will be controlled by grazing permits. Herdsmen are responsible for keeping animals off the parcel, and forest guards mounted on camels patrol the protected areas.

Long-term management

One of the main goals has been to establish a legal structure which combines the two ideals of popular control and economic independence. In 1984 the project began to develop a forest co-operative comprising nine villages located close to the forest. Five officers were elected as representatives from each village.

A contract has been signed between the government of Niger and the co-operative which accords the co-operative the right to exploit the forest. The Forest Service's role is to direct the restoration and conservation programme, work with the co-operative to establish ecologically sound exploitation policies and assure that forest management policies are adhered to. The sale of firewood-cutting and grazing permits are the responsibility of the co-operative. Proceeds generated by the sale of permits are used to pay for recurrent costs.

Approximately 70 woodcutters are now working in the forest to cut fuelwood that is obligatorily sold to the co-operative. All the wood bought by the co-operative is at present resold to private wood merchants, but the co-operative is discussing the possibility of buying a truck and setting up a retail centre in Niamey.

Based on the results at Guesselbodi, other projects plan to create similar mangement enterprises along the main roads leading to Niamey and around other major urban centres. Eventually, all of the forest products sold in the major urban centres should come from forest enterprises controlled by local populations. We are still beginners in regard to the complex environmental and social questions associated with natural forest management in the Sahel. We cannot rush into the endeavour as in the past. The future of the Sahel lies with the people who live there. "Definitive" solutions may not exist, but as a Hausa proverb says: "One who has patience can cook rocks."

PART 3

Appropriate Technology and Industry

CHAPTER 3

Mass Production or Production by the Masses?

MARILYN CARR

Head of Policy Planning, Intermediate Technology Development Group, UK

Although the majority of people in developing countries depend on agricultural production for their livelihood, the industrial sector has just as important a part to play in support of agriculture and, increasingly, as a direct source of income for masses of poor people. In the past, development strategies have tended to emphasize large-scale, capital-intensive, urban industries based on imported technologies and skills, promoting goods which cannot be afforded by a large majority of the population and creating few employment opportunities. Many such industries have proved to be "white elephants", depending on government subsidies and foreign equipment and expertise for their continued existence. Few have had any major impact in terms of contributing to sustained development.

By focusing only on agricultural production at one end of the spectrum and large-scale urban industry at the other, an important sector of economic activity has been overlooked. This is the small-scale industrial sector which comprises millions of small factories and artisanal enterprises in urban areas and many more millions of household industries in rural areas. These hold the key to a development process in which the majority of people can participate and from which the majority can benefit.

It is useful to note a number of characteristics of the sector. First is its size, particularly in terms of the number of jobs it supplies compared with the large-scale manufacturing sector. As can be seen in Table 2, a high percentage of employment in manufacturing is generated in small-scale enterprises, the bulk in enterprises of less than 10 workers.

Secondly, recent ILO statistics show that 86 per cent of employment in manufacturing in Sierra Leone is in rural areas, as is 70 per cent of that in Bangladesh, 63 per cent in Malaysia and 57 per cent in India (Chuta and Sethuraman, 1984). Almost all of this occurs in cottage or family units and much is part-time, often to supplement other economic activities such as wage labour on farms or subsistence cultivation. Since pressure on the land has increased with population growth, and given the inability of urban areas to provide more than a fraction of the employment opportunities needed, it is hardly surprising that more and more people are turning to rural non-farm activities as a source of income. Growth rates in the proportion of the rural labour force involved in these

Table 2   Distribution of employment in manufacturing, by firm size, 1960s and 1970s

| Date | Country | Firm size | | |
| | | Large-scale | | Small scale |
		more than 50 workers %	10–49 workers %	less than 10 workers %
1971	India	38	20	45
1967	Tanzania	37	7	56
1970	Ghana	15	1	84
1969	Kenya	41	10	49
1974	Sierra Leone	5	5	90
1977	Indonesia	16	7	77
1979	Honduras	24	8	68
1978	Thailand	31	11	58
1974	Philippines	29	5	66
1972	Nigeria	15	26	59
1973	Colombia	35	13	52

Source: Elkan, 1986, p. 10

activities over the last three decades have been very great in Central America and the Caribbean, West Africa and South and South-east Asia, where between a fifth and a quarter of the rural labour force now participates in off-farm activity.

Thirdly, the people involved in small enterprises tend to be working proprietors who are mainly or totally dependent on their work for their livelihood. In the case of most informal sector enterprises and off-farm activity in rural areas, the people involved are very poor, often landless. Women account for a high proportion of the labour force engaged in informal manufacturing; most come from the poorest households.

Fourthly, the small businesses are sparing in their use of capital, draw heavily on local skills and resources and produce basic consumer and producer goods demanded by the bulk of the rural and urban population. Tools and techniques tend to be less complex than in the large-scale industrial sector, and they owe little, if anything, to formal research and development institutes or external assistance agencies.

Fifthly, being small-scale, this type of industrial activity lends itself to forms of organization which are less socially disruptive. Although it may pollute or otherwise affect the environment adversely, its dispersion, lesser need for massive infrastructure and simpler processes are likely to result in less grave environmental consequences. Creating off-farm income-earning opportunities helps to achieve environmental objectives by taking pressure off the land.

Despite small industry's attractions in terms of helping to overcome unemployment, poverty and rural–urban drift, relatively little attention has been given to creating the sort of economic environment in which it can flourish. Medium- and large-scale industries also play an important role in the development process, however. They may be the most efficient way of producing low-cost goods for large numbers of rural people. Examples of this include the centralized production of low-cost farm tools and the mass production of bicycles. Large industries may also be the most efficient way of converting local raw materials into exportable products or of manufacturing products which play an essential part in the development process.

Balanced and sustained development requires that technologies utilized at all levels of industry are appropriate in terms of a country's economic, social and environmental objectives and its resources and circumstances. This in turn depends on the amount of resources devoted to developing such technologies and the commitment of governments and development agencies to promoting their diffusion and sustained use.

Review of the case studies

The seven case studies in this part of the book represent a good cross-section in terms of products and processes, scale of operation, pattern of ownership and extent and nature of involvement of indigenous and external development agencies.

Fishing-boats in South India (Case Study 12)

This project is run by a number of closely linked NGOs which have spent many years working with the artisanal fishing communities of Kerala and Tamil Nadu. It started in the mid-1970s in response to the needs of the fishermen for alternative boatbuilding materials and designs in the face of declining resources of timber used traditionally in their craft. The local organizations (drawing on technical assistance from ITDG) have worked with the fishermen to come up with a range of improved boat designs (made from marine plywood) which meet the needs and preferences of communities along the coast.

The three village-based boatyards which produce these plywood boats have far more orders than they can cope with. The boatyards are owned by the fishermen's societies and are well on their way to being self-financing while keeping boat prices as low as possible.

The problem of declining yields of fish along the coast is ascribed largely to the introduction of the inappropriate techniques of mechanized bottom-trawling and purse-seining. In response to this problem, many artisan fishermen have turned to the use of outboard motors on their boats to enable them to cover greater distances and fish in deeper waters. The new plywood boats are better suited to the use of engines than the traditional craft. The long-term effect of even this lesser level of mechanization needs careful consideration. Fishermen's organizations in other parts of South India are seeking assistance in adapting these new techniques to their own needs.

Micro-hydro in Nepal (Case Study 13)

The micro-hydro project in Nepal has developed in response to a clearly identified rural need to relieve time constraints on the processing of traditional crops. It began with the efforts of the United Missions to Nepal and a Swiss-government-supported engineering company. Both were interested in finding an appropriate way of driving grain mills in remote areas using water power.

There are now 450 turbines installed in rural areas and nine companies producing and installing them. Uptake of the technology has been facilitated by the decision of the Agricultural Development Bank of Nepal (ADBN) to switch its loans from diesel mills to water-mills, and successful operation has been ensured by careful selection of entrepreneurs and sites, along with adequate training and follow-up.

These small hydro schemes provide a viable alternative to larger projects that would be environmentally unsound. They offer the basis for provision of cheap electricity in remote areas, which, used for cooking, would contribute towards an easing of deforestation. It is believed that diffusion could now continue through normal market channels.

Improved charcoal stoves in Kenya (Case Study 14)

This is a joint government of Kenya/indigenous NGO project, started in 1981 as part of the programme for combating the woodfuel problem. It has received external assistance and has drawn on the resources of several Kenyan agencies.

Starting with the traditional metal jiko (already popular for use with charcoal in the urban areas), project staff worked with artisans and prospective users to come up with an improved stove design incorporating a ceramic liner. Although more expensive, this stove offered substantial savings to households in terms of reduced charcoal consumption. By the end of 1985, 180,000 stoves had been sold and were in use in 52,000 households, representing the capture of over 10 per cent of the traditional jiko stove market.

At the national level, savings on fuel costs are estimated at US$ 2 million per annum, an equivalent of 1.5 million tonnes of cut trees. Artisanal metalworkers have been able to benefit through accruing substantial profits. A number of urban-based ceramic factories and rural-based groups of women potters have found a new and profitable source of income in the production of ceramic liners. The involvement of artisans in the project has led the government to recognize the importance of the informal sector. The project is being replicated in other countries in the region.

Usutu forest pulp mill in Swaziland (Case Study 15)

The Usutu Pulp Company is a joint venture of the Commonwealth Development ment Corporation, Courtaulds and the Swazi government. Based on a man-made pine forest covering 52,000 ha of previously little-used land, it produces

180,000 tonnes annually of unbleached Kraft woodpulp, all of which is exported to paper factories in Europe and the Far East. The company has been operating successfully for the last 25 years and is Swaziland's second largest earner of foreign exchange. It provides direct employment to 2,800 people. Although facing difficulties, this project has contributed significantly to the country's need for employment and foreign exchange.

Sorghum processing in Botswana (Case Study 16)

In the mid-1970s various agencies concerned with rural development in Botswana became aware that, although sorghum was the preferred food of the rural Batswana, women were increasingly using imported ready-to-cook sifted maize meal and rice because of the tedious nature of dehulling locally grown sorghum. With support from the International Development Research Centre (IDRC), the Rural Industries Innovation Centre (RIIC) devised a dehuller which could meet the requirements of individual women for a milling service and also form the basis of a small-scale decentralized industry. There are now 25 mills in Botswana which flood the current market.

A variety of circumstances have led to a change in the nature of the industry over its short life. The smallest mills which dealt mainly with individual producers/consumers have run out of customers, while large mills which have turned to commercial milling of bulk supplies of grain have received the greater share of imported stocks. The Ministry of Industry has stepped in to restrict the number of hullers which these commercially oriented firms can install, but the future of the smaller mills is uncertain in the absence of measures to reaffirm the policy of support for decentralized small-scale industries.

In other respects, the project has been largely successful. Sorghum is no longer in danger of being replaced in the diet by imported maize meal and rice. The government is to put 20,000 ha of sorghum into commercial production. Production of dehullers has been handed over to local small-scale industries. And, drawing on lessons learned from Botswana, governments in other countries are being assisted to establish small-scale decentralized sorghum-processing industries.

Light engineering in Ghana (Case Study 17)

The Technology Consultancy Centre (TCC) has fostered the growth and development of a light engineering industry which now supplies thousands of Ghana's small farmers and agro-processing firms. Established in 1972 within Ghana's University of Science and Technology in Kumasi, TCC was intended as a research and development facility for outreach to Ghana's ailing industrial sector. Attention was focused on Kumasi's large informal industrial sector, initially through the establishment of campus-based experimental training and production units for the manufacture of nuts and bolts, soap-making equipment and other light engineering processes, and later through the establishment of off-campus Intermediate Technology Transfer Units (ITTUs) within the informal industrial areas themselves.

TCC now has a staff of 22 people plus 27 employees at its ITTU in Suame, 5 employees at the Tamale ITTU and 22 people in the campus production units. It is estimated to deal with 1,000 clients and direct beneficiaries per year.

Since TCC's clients are involved in the production of machinery, the multiplier effects in terms of output, employment and income in other industries are enormous. Some of TCC's clients are now mini-TCCs themselves. This represents the beginnings of the informal sector's ability to carry out its own technology development and diffusion.

Small- versus large-scale cement manufacture in India (Case Study 18)

This case study looks at the history of the development and diffusion of mini-cement plants (up to 100 tons per day) and examines the implications for the economy and environment of meeting India's demand for cement through the mini-plants, large-scale plants (500 to 3,000 tons per day) and imports. The mini-cement project has developed largely outside the realm of development assistance. The most successful diffusion agent to date has been an Indian entrepreneur.

In the five years since they have been commercially available, 60 mini-cement plants have been installed in India, and at least another 50 are on order. They provide jobs for 6,000 people. Mini-plants are owned by small entrepreneurs who tend to be working proprietors. They require relatively unskilled workers, whereas large-scale plants require highly qualified staff. Diffusion has been encouraged by current government policy, which allows mini-plants to sell all of their output at a higher market price.

Mini-plants make more efficient use of resources than large-scale plants, although they are less efficient in their use of energy. Environmentally, there is little to choose between them. Despite their advantages, mini-plants are having few resources invested in their further development and may well be overtaken by large-scale processes which are becoming more efficient. There is, however, a need for mini-plants in remote areas of India and also in other countries which have lesser skills, less rigid quality controls and remote markets near to suitable deposits of raw materials.

Lessons learned

All of the projects have had a significant impact at the national or state level.

In Kenya 52,000 poor urban households are saving on fuel costs through the use of improved charcoal stoves. In South India over 2,000 fishermen now have access to improved boats which do not utilize dwindling forest resources to the same extent as traditional craft. The diffusion of improved mills in Botswana and Nepal has relieved thousands of women and children of the task of milling. Countless farmers, artisans and poor consumers in Ghana have benefited from the increased range of producer goods available from revitalized light engineering industries. In all these cases, valuable employment has also been created. The larger-scale industry projects in India and Swaziland have also brought employment and related benefits and, in Swaziland, foreign exchange earnings.

This is an impressive array of accomplishments which indicate the scope for reaching large numbers of people through appropriate industrial technologies. But have the right people benefited and in what way? What are the chances of replicating successful projects elsewhere?

What is appropriate?

The success of a project in contributing towards sustainable development must be analysed within the context of the objectives it was seeking to achieve and the relationship of these to the overall development objectives of the country.

Social objectives. In many small-scale industry projects, attempts are made to encourage small-scale, decentralized, self-employment or co-operative/group ownership. Production of ceramic stoves by rural women's groups has been encouraged in the Kenya project. Co-operative ownership of boatyards has been promoted in South India. The Botswana project favoured small-scale decentralized service milling. Attempts are being made to affect the distribution of benefits from micro-hydro plants in Nepal through co-operative ownership.

Results have not always been encouraging. The Kenya stoves project has run into a problem commonly experienced of deciding between the relative importance of income for rural poor producers versus the faster, more reliable production through larger factories in Nairobi. In Botswana the absence of a regulatory government policy has resulted in most of the country's sorghum being processed by three large commercial firms, so that the original objective of establishing a network of profitable small mills has not been met. In Nepal attempts to introduce co-operative ownership are being hampered by the lack of an official programme of support for co-operatives.

Socially appropriate forms of ownership are even more difficult to achieve in the medium- and large-scale sector. The case study on mini-cement shows that technologies can be scaled down to the level where they are manageable by a working proprietor rather than by a faceless company. This would seem to be of dubious value to employees, however, if they lose the legal protection afforded to their better-paid colleagues in large-scale factories.

Financial objectives. The projects have been rather more successful in meeting financial objectives, although difficulties have been (or are likely to be) experienced in sustaining viability. One problem relates to assured supply of raw materials. In Botswana many small mills stopped operating when supplies of sorghum dried up. Another problem relates to changing market conditions. The sustained viability of the Usutu Company seems doubtful if world demand and prices for unbleached Kraft woodpulp continue to decline. Yet another problem relates to the inability of technology to keep pace with that used by competitors, as in the case of mini-cement in India. A different problem is evident with the boatyards in South India, torn between keeping the prices of boats low to assist fishermen and raising prices to ensure long-term viability and increase workers' wages.

Environmental objectives. Some projects have resulted in negative as well as positive effects, and others have managed to minimize environmental damage only at the expense of reduced financial viability. The introduction of improved boats in South India has had a positive effect in terms of saving wood and preserving flexibility in boat design to suit varying conditions, but the use of boats with outboard motors has a negative effect in terms of increasing the amount of energy needed to catch the same amount of fish, polluting inland waters with kerosene and contributing to overfishing. The Usutu Company in Swaziland is restrained by strict laws relating to river pollution from maximizing profits through the processing of wood into higher-value products.

Some projects have a significant positive effect on the environment. The introduction of sorghum mills in Botswana has increased the country's ability to cope with the post-harvest bottlenecks associated with drought-resistant traditional cereal crops and has resulted in increased production. In Nepal micro-hydro plants are likely to reduce the need for larger-scale hydro investments and may help reduce deforestation. In Kenya the main purpose of the stoves project is to protect the environment through helping combat the woodfuel problem. This project is also conserving in its use of resources through reliance on recycled scrap metal. The small industries promoted by TCC in Ghana utilize scrap metal and offcuts from sawmills which would otherwise be wasted.

Both small and large industries need careful monitoring for environmental effects. They can be equally guilty with respect to resources depletion and pollution. While pollution control and other legislation can have a significant impact on the practices of large-scale industries such as Usutu, this is less effective in the case of dispersed, small-scale industries. Small industries are often less efficient than large industries in their use of energy. Project interventions which aim to develop and diffuse more fuel-efficient technologies for small industries could help to achieve environmental and financial objectives.

Distribution of benefits. The poorest sections of society seem to benefit in greater numbers and in a more direct way from small-industry projects than from larger ones. In the projects covered, women have particularly benefited, sometimes as producers but mainly as consumers of stoves and milling services.

Small industries generally give poorer people greater control over the means of production and require fewer trade-offs between social, economic and environmental objectives than do large-scale industries. Even so, their impact needs careful monitoring to ensure that the best mix of effects is achieved and maintained. Decisions often have to be made between one group of poor people and another. In the Kenya stoves project and the South India boats project, trade-offs are necessary between the earnings of small producers and their employees and the economic well-being of equally poor customers. In Botswana information is required on the impact of the trend towards monopolization of mill ownership so that policy decisions can be made.

Larger-scale industries can, however, provide substantial work opportunities for poor people, especially if attempts are made to develop and adopt labour-intensive technologies.

Technology development and diffusion

In all the small-scale industry projects, implementing agencies devoted a great deal of attention to identifying the needs of potential users and to developing technologies with their needs and circumstances in mind. Only in the case of charcoal stoves in Kenya has there been any attempt to push a new technology on people for reasons not their own. The objective of reducing rates of deforestation originated with the Ministry of Energy rather than with urban households. A demonstration and marketing campaign was necessary before urban households became convinced that the new stoves would also respond to one of their needs, for cash savings.

In the other case studies, technology development has taken place in response to thoroughly researched felt needs, confirming that resources invested at this crucial first stage can save time and effort later in a project's life. There are numerous cases of so-called "appropriate" technologies which have failed to gain acceptance by intended users because no one bothered to find out if they responded to a priority need. Sanitation technologies are a common example, but even small-scale water projects have failed for this reason.

This "user-needs-based" approach has less significance for the larger-scale industry projects, e.g. cement in India and pulp in Swaziland, which are geared more towards meeting national objectives such as earning foreign exchange.

For the main part, agency staff have worked hand in hand with potential users of technologies and have drawn on their experience and knowledge during the development phase. Most design and innovation work has taken place not in a research laboratory but in the village or the informal industry area, with the full involvement of artisans and households. Agencies such as TCC in Ghana which started off by trying to work in a research environment soon sought ways of locating their research operations in the places where people live and work. This approach of learning from and with potential users of research seems to contribute to the success of projects.

The process of technology development cannot be isolated from that of technology diffusion; the same agency needs to see the whole process through. Agencies such as TCC which tried initially to concentrate on technology development and leave diffusion to others have found that the result was a product or process which no one uses on a commercial basis. In the case of mini-cement, the most successful "agency" has been the one which both developed and diffused its variant of the technology.

Technology and training

In all the case studies funds have been invested in developing a technology appropriate to local conditions, rather than simply relying on commercially available alternatives. Funding from development agencies has been used to undertake research into improved stoves, improved boat designs, small-scale sorghum mills, mini-hydro plants and light engineering processes. Without this funding, local techology units and centres would be unable to do the research necessary to develop technologies appropriate to the needs of small industries. Such support to local "appropriate" R&D centres is essential, since small industries usually cannot afford substantial R&D themselves.

Larger-scale industries are more likely to find the funds internally to undertake R&D work, and this can be of an appropriate nature (e.g. pollution reducing) given the right circumstances. Large companies can and will adapt technologies to make them more labour-intensive if the price structure so dictates (see e.g. Carr, 1981).

An important characteristic of appropriate technology is its suitability to local manufacture and the ability of local skills and infrastructure to absorb its use and provide for maintenance and repair. The importance of training is thus clear.

In the Kenya stoves project, great care was given to choosing and providing the most appropriate type of training for artisanal producers. In the South India boats project, provision is made for village-level training in boatmaking and engine maintenance and repair. In the micro-hydro project in Nepal, extensive training is available for owners and operators of turbine-powered mills as well as for agency and bank personnel involved. In Ghana, TCC provides on-the-job training.

Indigenous technological capability

An objective of many Third World countries is the building up of an indigenous technological capability which allows technical change to take place in response to changing circumstances without continued dependence on external advice or assistance. Projects in the small-industry sector have contributed to this aspect of sustained development to a much greater extent than those involving large-scale industry.

The boatyards in South India are producing variations on the original improved boat design to meet the needs and circumstances along different parts of the coast. Small commercial companies in Nepal have sprung up in response to the market for water-powered devices and are producing a range of technologies. Many of the small engineering companies assisted by TCC in Ghana have now become agents of product design, testing and diffusion. In all these cases, the transfer of technical skills from expatriates to nationals within projects and then to nationals outside projects has been remarkable.

Other studies tend to confirm the greater technological independence of smaller-scale industries (see e.g. Fransman and King, 1984), although examples can be found of large-scale plants which have evolved from being technologically dependent to the point of developing technology of their own and even selling technical assistance at home and abroad. But because of their greater complexity, many developing countries find it difficult to absorb the technologies associated with large-scale industry.

Importance of the capital goods sector

Reliance on imported technology means that industrial development provides little stimulus to the local capital goods sector. By contrast, reliance on indigenous technology usually provides useful backward linkages to this sector. The demand for small-scale sorghum mills in Botswana, small-scale turbines and mills in Nepal and mini-cement plants in India has given a boost to small-scale capital goods firms. By contrast, there have been no such backward linkages in the case of large-scale cement plants in India or the pulp factory in Swaziland. Local technology institutions such as TCC can have an important role in promoting linkages of this type. A flourishing, small-scale, decentralized capital goods sector can also play a key role in promoting sustainable development.

Agricultural development can act as a powerful stimulus to the capital goods sector both through backward linkages (farm tools) and forward linkages (processing equipment). However, much of the benefit of these linkages will be lost unless measures are taken to restrict unnecessary levels of mechanization and unless attention is focused on encouraging the use of equipment which can easily be produced, maintained and repaired by small decentralized industries located in the rural areas.

Different kinds of farm tools produced by local industries in accord with regional variations and preferences have, it seems, greater chance of success than centralized production which gives insufficient consideration to environmental variations (see e.g. Johnston and Kilby, 1975). In South India decentralized, small-scale boatbuilding is seen as the only way of responding to different fishing conditions. The problem may be that the small foundry and casting knowledge, and moulding, pattern-making and machining skills, needed to manufacture simple, hand-operated machines of agricultural implements do not exist, or have been forgotten or eroded. Agencies such as TCC in Ghana can be invaluable in developing and diffusing the technologies which local small industries need.

Markets, products and quality control

A clearly defined market is advantageous in promoting the diffusion of a new technology. Commercialization of a new product or process is rarely a problem if cash or credit is available to help customers meet a felt need.

Small-scale industry usually involves the production and sale of basic goods and services needed by the masses of poor people in rural and urban areas: food, clothing, shelter, basic consumer durables, milling services, etc. A problem is that the potential customers often have no cash with which to pay for what they need. At the household level, it is generally the man who makes decisions on disposal of any available cash, whereas it is the woman who is more likely to want an improved stove or access to milling services.

Where cash is readily available, or where it can be shown that the new technology will quickly pay for itself through cost or time savings, diffusion has been relatively rapid. Once it was demonstrated that ceramic jikos could pay for themselves within two months, demand from urban households started to rise. In Botswana and Nepal the fact that women's time had more value in activities other than traditional processing of crops created a buoyant demand for milling services. In Ghana time constraints on food production and processing have created an enormous demand for small-scale farming and processing equipment.

Credit has an important role to play. Artisans in Kenya and mill owners in Botswana and Nepal would have been unable to respond to demand without access to credit. Sometimes credit is made available to a project on a revolving loan basis. More often the role of the project implementors is to gear up existing credit mechanisms to provide the needed loans. Developments of this nature give the necessary stimulus to the capital goods sector to invest in and produce the machinery required by new businesses and service industries. Generally, the credit agency acts as a link between the entrepreneur and the capital goods sector, further facilitating backward linkages.

However, although quality of production is normally of a high standard during the demonstration phase of a project, quality can decline once the private sector rushes in to meet a credit-backed demand. In India the boost in demand for plywood boats has resulted in a number of small businesses springing up to fill the gap which the boatyards established by the project agency cannot yet meet. To compete cost-wise, these small firms sell inferior boats which could result in financial losses for fishermen. Ways need to be found of maintaining product quality during the diffusion process without imposing unnecessary restrictions.

Institutions

The agencies involved in the projects cover a wide range: government departments, parastatals, commercial and government banks, indigenous and international NGOs, university departments and research institutes, workers' and employers' unions and organizations, commercial firms, transnational corporations and multilateral and bilateral agencies. Normally, there is a combination of several types of agency involved, with one agency acting as a focus for the project. In many small-scale projects, NGOs have taken the lead role in developing and diffusing the technology. Generally, they have been better suited to work with and in rural communities and the informal urban sector.

University-based technology institutes and formal research institutes can play an important role but only if an effective means is found of commercializing the technologies they develop. If the technologies are aimed at the rural areas or informal sector, this may require drastic action in terms of opening up two-way channels of communication between the institute and technology users. With larger-scale technologies and industries, the problems of commercialization are less severe, since close involvement with potential users is not so important. A method of transfer must still be found, however. In the case of CRI in India this was done by means of licensing private sector firms to manufacture and market its cement manufacturing process. Research centres based in the heart of the communities they seek to serve seem better suited to the task of technology development and diffusion than do isolated and remote research institutes.

Commercial firms have an important role to play as carriers of improved technology and as demonstrators of the viability of these technologies. Parastatals and NGOs normally do not have the same entrepreneurial drive as a commercial company and are less likely to generate private sector interest in investing in a new process.

Overseas agencies – NGOs, bilaterals, multilaterals, private companies – can play a variety of roles in projects varying from unconditional provision of funds to provision of personnel, machinery/equipment or technological information. The case studies indicate that small-industry projects have thrived during their early years on the supply of small but timely and flexible funds from NGO donors. Once into the diffusion stage, however, funding from bilateral or multilateral agencies becomes necessary, and conditions attached to such funding often cause unnecessary problems for local implementing agencies. Complications seem least likely to occur when bilateral/multilateral assistance is confined to the financing of small industries through national credit mechanisms.

Policy considerations

Government policies can have a major impact on the way a project develops and on its ability to survive. Subsidies, taxes and price regulations all help or hinder the diffusion of technology, and policies which subsidize capital and foreign exchange generally promote the use of large-scale capital-intensive technologies (James and Watanabe, 1985).

Specific policy decisons can make the difference between life or death for a project. The small sorghum mills in Botswana would not have taken off without the government's decision to back small mills rather than large ones. Similarly, it is unlikely that mini-cement plants would have sprung up so quickly (if at all) in India without their exemption from charging (low) levy prices on their product.

Projects can also have an effect on policy. The micro-hydro project in Nepal has resulted in a change in government policy which allows electricity to be generated and sold by private firms up to a maximum of 100 kW. It has also resulted in the government bank providing loans for water-mills rather than for diesel-powered mills. The stoves project in Kenya promises to have an even more dramatic effect on policy since it has awakened the interest of the government in the role the informal sector can play in overall development.

Implications for development assistance programmes and policies

Possibilities for expanding or replicating projects

Enabling large numbers of people to benefit from development involves getting beyond the project through expansion or replication. Either the improvement introduced through the project gets taken up through commercial channels and reaches increasing numbers of people without the need for further development assistance; or further development assistance can be secured to repeat the project in another district or country.

In the case of stoves in Kenya, development assistance has helped to replicate the initial Nairobi-based project in other areas of the country and is being used to establish small manufacturing companies which will be able to go on producing stoves at the end of the project's life. Multilateral assistance has been acquired to help replicate the Kenya experience in other countries.

The three boatyards in India are now almost self-financing, and there are plans to establish more within the existing project area.

In Botswana dehullers are being exported to other countries. Development assistance is being used in other countries such as Zimbabwe to help replicate the Botswana project. Micro-hydro and mill complexes are now diffusing rapidly in Nepal with decreasing reliance on development assistance and increased participation of the private commercial sector. A few turbines have been exported to other countries, but it is uncertain whether these could form the basis for replication.

In Ghana, TCC has planned to replicate the successful ITTU at Suame in other districts of the country. TCC has been involved in replicating some of its successful projects in other countries including Mali, Guinea Bissau and Zambia. It has also been involved in trying to promote its own replication in other countries.

Expansion or replication is a more difficult issue in the case of the cement and forestry/pulpwood projects. Mini-cement production has expanded rapidly in India without much reliance on external assistance, although more resources could usefully be deployed on developing this small-scale technology. There has been no attempt to transfer the India "project" elsewhere, although similar small-scale plants are in use in other countries such as China. The Usutu Company is a one-off affair within the Swaziland context, although similar projects have been tried elsewhere.

Some interesting experiences to come out of attempts at expansion and replication are as follows:

It is impossible simply to transfer a technology from one place to another and expect it to work without any adaptation to local conditions. The sorghum mill which was appropriate in Botswana was found too large for the smaller, more dispersed settlements of Zimbabwe. The same was found in the case of transferring improved boat designs over even very short distances along the coast of South India. When a Thai stove was originally transferred to Kenya it was found inappropriate to local conditions and had to be modified before it turned into the new jiko. Technical capacities will always be needed within countries to assist with the adaptation of technologies transferred from other places.

Transfer of knowledge seems a useful instrument in promoting replication. Regional seminars and study visits are helping to promote interest in replicating the Kenya stoves project in other countries. Visits by government officials from Zimbabwe to Botswana were instrumental in transferring the sorghum mill project. Study visits by Nepalese employees of turbine manufacturers to Germany and Switzerland have resulted in their adopting turbine designs. Visits by TCC staff to the UK formed the basis of work on small iron foundries.

Once there is a proven market for a product, there will usually be no shortage of small-scale entrepreneurs coming forward to produce it, providing they have the opportunity to do so. Constraints seem to involve lack of access to the technology, to credit and to raw materials and other inputs. Development agencies can provide the means of overcoming these constraints. The Kenya stoves project has provided for the transfer of technology to the informal sector through training and addressing other constraints such as harassment of artisans working on council land. An unplanned transfer of technology occurred in the South India boats project and the Nepal micro-hydro project, with former employees of project-supported production units leaving with their knowledge of the technology to start up their own production units. TCC has worked hard at overcoming the grave constraints faced by the informal sector in Ghana. Apart from transferring technical know-how, it has assisted with the import of otherwise unavailable tools and equipment. External sources of funds have helped make this possible.

The success of a particular project in a particular place seems to depend largely on the nature of the implementing agency and even on the character of a few individuals within it. In many small-industry projects the main implementing agencies are NGOs with staff who are willing to work in rural areas or urban slums and learn from and innovate with the potential users and beneficiaries of improved technologies. Without the existence of such groups in other areas it seems unlikely that projects could be successfully transferred.

This is possibly one of the most important constraints on expansion or replication and it is difficult to identify what role external agencies or Third World governments can play in overcoming it. Problems often arise when governments try to become directly involved in replicating NGOs' successes. There are, however, some successful examples of replication of institutional models using bilateral or multilateral funding, although such replication is still firmly under the guidance of the originator of the project/institution.

Government policy and donor agency practices play an important role in promoting or constraining the replication of successful projects. Insistence of bilateral donors on tying aid to equipment manufactured in their own countries can prevent the proliferation of local small-scale industrial development. Even more important are the policy environment in a country and the appraisal methods of the donor agencies. Fiscal, monetary and foreign exchange policies tend to discriminate against small-scale industries in favour of the large-scale sector. There are promising signs of change in the development plans of many Third World governments, with more emphasis being given to small industry along with rural development. These changes may be due in part to having examples to point to of what is possible if small-scale industry is allowed to flourish.

There is still a great deal of confusion as to what a favourable policy environment means in practice. Governments could devote more attention to establishing mechanisms for examining the consequences of policy choices for the small industry sector, rather than becoming involved in direct support measures. Without a mechanism to promote shifts of investment from large to small industry, projects such as those in the case studies will remain simply projects.

At the donor level, questions are finally being raised as to the appropriateness of conventional appraisal techniques, and thought is being given to non-economic factors such as the environment. The World Bank (1987) has recently published a paper setting out how project design might ensure that economic and environmental concerns coincide. Bank documents have recommended increased lending to the small-industry sector. Donor assistance of this type can be very beneficial in promoting sustainable development.

The constraints on expanding or replicating small-industry development projects are different to those affecting large-scale projects. In the former case, institutional factors and a lack of support at the policy level are major constraints. Access to markets and ability to absorb new technology are not great problems, since projects tend to be based on local wants and needs, local skills and local technical expertise. In the latter case, the situation is reversed.

Priorities for development agencies and Third World governments

In the past, the involvement of development agencies in the industrial sector has tended to be in support of large-scale plants based on capital-intensive technology. Little thought or effort has been devoted to expanding the range of technologies available in the modern factory sector to include some which are more labour-intensive or more environmentally sound while remaining efficient. Even less attention and support has been given to the technology needs of the small-scale sector.

NGOs, small university-based technology centres and the occasional private company have been the major developers of appropriate industrial technologies. Financial and technical assistance for much of the research work has come from NGOs. However, there is a limit to the capabilities of NGOs and small technology units. They are incapable of handling all the R&D needs of the small-scale sector. Replication of successful projects is also beyond their means. Bilateral/multilateral funding sources and supportive government policies are essential at this stage.

There is a need, then, to change the priorities of bilateral and multilateral agencies, as well as Third World governments, and to change the way assistance is delivered accordingly. Bilateral/multilateral funds could usefully be deployed in:

- support to international NGOs with a proven track record in delivering appropriate assistance to small-industry projects;
- better comparative research of the social, environmental and economic characteristics of small- and large-scale industry;
- R&D funds to investigate appropriate small-scale options in the industrial sector;
- support of exchange visits and seminars/networks to assist with the transfer of knowledge;
- support to Third World governments for research into the impact of economic

policy on small industry/choice of technology and for the establishment of technology choice mechanisms;
- increased lending to the small-industry sector through local institutions.

Such agencies would also need to re-examine their attitude towards transfer of inappropriate technology through their lending programmes and redesign their appraisal techniques to take better account of social and environmental factors. In the case of Third World governments, their role should be one of creating a policy environment conducive to the spread of industrial technologies which are more compatible with sustainable development.

References

Carr, M. (1981), *Economically Appropriate Technologies for Developing Countries*. IT Publications, London.

Chuta, E., and Sethuraman, S.V. (eds) (1984), *Rural Small-Scale Industries and Employment in Africa and Asia*. ILO, Geneva.

Elkan, W. (1986), "Policy for small-scale industry: a critique", Discussion Papers in Economics no. 8701. Brunel University, Uxbridge.

Fransman, M., and King, K. (eds) (1984), *Technological Capacity in the Third World*. Macmillan, London.

James, J., and Watanabe, S. (eds) (1985), *Technology Institutions and Government Policies*. ILO, Geneva.

Johnston, B., and Kilby, P. (1975), *Agriculture and Structural Transformation*. Oxford University Press.

World Bank (1987), "Environment, growth and development", paper for Development Committee Meeting. World Bank, Washington, DC.

CASE STUDY 12 *Kerala Fishing-Boat Project, South India*

JOHN KURIEN
Centre for Development Studies, India

The sandy coastline of South India has long been known for its rich fisheries, skilled fishermen and traditional boatbuilders (see Map 3). This region today accounts for a marine fish landing of 400,000 tonnes, about one-third of India's total. Over half of this is harvested by some 125,000 small-scale artisanal fishermen using numerous diverse types of fishing craft and gear.

Competing and indiscriminate use of forest resources has resulted in a scarcity of wood used for making traditional fishing-boats in the lower south-west coast region. The greatest shortage is for the large-girth mango trees used to make the single-trunk dugout canoes called *vallams*. Light-wood logs for making the

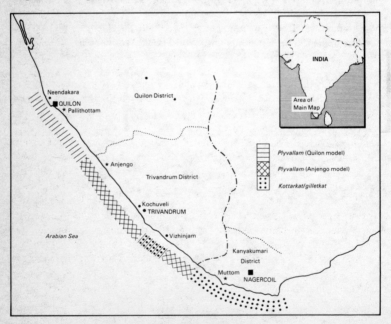

Map 3: Kerala fishing-boat project area, South India

kattumarams are also becoming scarce. The changes at sea are more dramatic. Artisanal fishermen have always used nets and tackle, fabricated and used according to the nature and size of the fish to be caught. With the advent of "planned fisheries development", bottom-trawling and purse-seining have rapidly disrupted the coastal ecosystems.

This ecological crisis has affected the livelihood of the artisanal fishermen, reducing fish harvests and the artisanal fishermen's share of them. With the fishermen population increasing, the situation is aggravated by the growing underemployment of human resources, alternative jobs being scarce.

Project beginnings and take-off

Pierre Gillet and F. M. T. Raj, backed by the Centre for Appropriate Technology (CAT) in Nagercoil and the Muttom Boat Building Centre (MBBC), had long been considering constructing a craft appropriate to the needs of the *kattumaran* fishermen who were experiencing a shortage of lightwood. The new craft had to be light, unsinkable, powered by sail and oars and have a life of six to ten years. It also had to have more carrying space and offer more comfort while fishing.

By mid-1981 they had developed a rough prototype. It caught the imagination of the fishermen, but more work had to be done. Their search for materials, methods and designs had led to two significant contacts: E. W. H. Gifford & Partners (GP) and Jeremy Herklots of the Intermediate Technology Development Group (ITDG), both in the UK. Gifford had been designing small double-hull boats for the tropical fishermen in Africa. Herklots and Gifford had also been working in Sri Lanka on a "stitch-and-glue" technique for flat-bottom boats. In 1981 the four organizations began to build and test in South India double-hull plywood boats fabricated using the stitch-and-glue technique.

The CAT/MBBC idea for the alternative to the *kattumaram* was vastly improved with Gifford's suggestions which made the craft lighter and more stable. ITDG gave financial assistance to help build a prototype. The boat was christened the *kottarkat*. In looks and performance it more than matched the *kattumaram*. The overjoyed fishermen nicknamed it the *plasticmaram*. By the end of 1982 the trickle of cash-down orders from fishermen became a flood.

Prior to the 1983 monsoon MBBC had a large outstanding order for the *kottarkats* which they were hard pressed to meet with the existing facilities and staff. The success of the *kottarkats* being operated by migrant Kanyakumari fishermen opened up possibilities for replacing the *vallams* (dugout canoes) with appropriately designed plywood boats, *plyvallams*. The decline in fish numbers in the inshore areas made the artisanal fishermen consider the possibilities of motorization of their traditional craft, but *kattumarams* proved unable to cope with the vibrations from outboard engines. The "trawler menace" made some sections of the artisanal fishermen see the potential of *kottarkats* fitted with outboard engines.

These needs and expectations of the fishermen were channelled through the

South Indian Federation of Fishermen Societies (SIFFS) and the Fishermen's Welfare Society (FWS). SIFFS, an umbrella body of district-level fishermen federations, saw the potential the new plywood boats offered. It was keen to ensure that the technology and designs remained in the control of fishermen-related organizations rather than falling into the hands of private entrepreneurs. The best way to ensure this was to cater to the growing demand for new boats by setting up more small decentralized boatyards. The fishing village of Anjengo in Trivandrum became the first choice. A boatyard began to function there in early 1983.

The 1983 monsoon took a bad toll. The *kotterkats* and the *plyvallams* developed cracks and leaks. Complaints poured in, and orders were cancelled. But what seemed a complete failure was turned into a new beginning. A thorough repair campaign was undertaken. The additional work helped identify technical faults and paved the way for the stronger models of 1984.

The plywood boat and the outboard engine became an inseparable pair despite GP, ITDG and FCDP/FWS initiatives at demonstrating the advantages of a combination use of sail and engine. An evaluation study was undertaken in 1983 on motorized *kottarkats* compared with motorized and sail-driven *kattumarams*. The *kottarkats* proved a more comfortable platform for fishing and had more space for nets and fish. Being motorized, they were able to go deeper and in different directions at sea. The crew, being less tired, could devote full energy and concentration to fishing.

Fishermen using the motorized *kottarkats* caught ten times more fish than those using the traditional sail-driven *kattumarams*. However, with the much higher depreciation and interest rates applicable to owners of motorized *kottarkats*, only half the owners showed lucrative net returns to their investment. This latter situation could be changed if cheaper bank credit could be made available or subsidies provided, if ownership was made collective and if running expenses were reduced by combining the use of engine and sail.

Plyvallams are much cheaper than *kottarkats*. The immense popularity of the *plyvallam*, and the ability of the FCDP/FWS to convince the nationalized banks about the need and soundness of extending credit to the fishermen, gave a big fillip to boatbuilding operations.

A new industry emerges

Providing appropriate craft design for artisanal fishermen has been the basis for a decentralized, capital-light, skill- and labour-intensive, small-scale rural industry along the coastal belt for boatbuilding and repairs. The three boatyards at Muttom, Anjengo and Pallithotam retain their autonomy, while at the same time maintaining close collaboration, exchange of materials, technical assistance and financial and organizational support. A team approach to production helps workers pick up new skills and gives them a sense of satisfaction when a boat is complete.

As with traditional boatbuilding, the fisherman who places the order visits the yard and watches his boat emerging from the planks. "Standardization" in some mass-production sense is not the goal.

Some of the workers, having picked up the technique and skills, have left the yards and begun small partnerships to build their own plywood boats of similar design. Unfortunately, they tend to use inferior materials. Quality and price will determine how long these small partnerships can continue in business.

SIFFS is opening a second boatyard in Trivandrum and a repair centre to meet the increasing demand. SIFFS' assistance with boatbuilding is likely to be sought in other areas of South India.

Key factors in project performance

Right objective conditions and preparedness to respond. Conditions in the fish economy gave rise to a strong need on the part of the fishermen to acquire new craft designs. The ability to seize the opportunity came from local organizations which had maintained close contact with the fishermen and with each other for several years. They were not just created to implement the boat project. They saw embodied in the venture the ideals of just, participatory and sustainable development.

Foreign organizations and expertise in partnership with local organizations. ITDG and Gifford Partners accepted the local organizations as true partners. The collaboration was not a one-sided technology transfer but a two-way learning process.

Functional flexibility. The "Schumacherism" – the ability to appreciate small things – of ITDG merits special attention. ITDG's flexibility in funding, lack of bureaucratic approach, intimate and responsive monitoring of progress, appreciation of local pressures and problems and willingness to function at the local rhythm of work – these factors, along with the personal qualities of key individuals, contributed immensely to project success.

Feedback without filter. The centrality in the project of organizations like SIFFS ensures that the venture remains within the ambit of the fishermen.

Preserving diversity. The project's success also lies in the willingness of designers to accept diversity of design, rather than sticking rigidly to a standardized design.

Project sustainability

No project has a guarantee of being sustainable in the future. Changing conditions outside a project can send it off the rails, and the boatbuilding venture in South India is no exception. There are four factors to consider.

Lack of control over new raw materials. Some of the raw materials required for the boatbuilding, accounting for half the cost, are manufactured by the large-scale corporate industrial sector in India, whose sole rationale is profits. Continuing price increases could have adverse consequences on the economic sustainability of the boats.

On becoming enslaved to outboard engines. Outboard engines are appropriate for the small-scale fishing industry in South India only by virtue of their size. Everything else about this device makes it a ''millstone'' round the fisherman's neck. This is only now dawning on the fishermen, as they find their enhanced incomes dissipated in fuel and repair costs, not to mention their inability to buy a new engine when the present one wears out. In due course the fisherman will be unable to use his traditional sailing skills. He will be left deskilled and at the mercy of the outboard engine and its foreign manufacturers.

Over-capitalization of small-scale fishing. It is not clear whether unrestricted use of plywood boats and engines, without regard for any form of regulation, will result in a scenario any better than the one created by the trawlers and purse-seiners.

Low prices, fair wages and financial self-sufficiency. An element of conflict exists between the threefold objective of holding down prices of the boats in the interest of fishermen, assuring boatyard workers a fair wage and attaining a degree of financial self-sufficiency for the boatyards.

CASE STUDY 13 *Micro-Hydro Systems Manufacture and Use, Nepal*

DRUMMOND HISLOP
Biomass Energy Services and Technology Ltd

Harnessing water for irrigation and for crop processing is a traditional feature of Nepalese rural life. Several centuries ago, grain milling was mechanized with the development of vertical axis waterwheels (*ghattas*), probably accounting for most mechanized milling in rural Nepal until the last three decades. Since the late 1950s larger commercial mills have been established powered by diesel or electricity. Their capital costs are much higher than those of the *ghattas*, and originally they were accessible only to wealthier farmers and businessmen. But from the 1970s loans from the Agricultural Development Bank of Nepal allowed the establishment of modern mechanized mills in more remote areas and by smaller farmers and entrepreneurs.

The popularity of diesel mills shows that many farmers are prepared to pay for crop processing in cash or kind. Diesel mills are often very small, especially in the hills, but they are more flexible than the traditional *ghatta*; the drive can be switched so that they can process the four main crops of rice, wheat, maize and mustard seed. However, the power of the small diesel mills is still not sufficient to operate more than one machine at a time.

More powerful mills would allow more mechanical crop processing than the traditional *ghatta* and the small diesel; this would reduce the domestic labour burden on women and help to meet the increasing demand for processed grains. The micro-hydro programme is providing two types of modern micro-hydro plant to meet these needs. The most significant in terms of power output and numbers installed is the crossflow turbine, powerful enough to drive three machines at a time to process the four main crops. A second component of the programme is a modern version of the *ghatta*: the Multi-Purpose Processing Unit (MPPU). The MPPU's power can be switched from one milling machine to another, although power is still sufficient to drive only one machine at a time. A significant number of MPPUs have been installed.

Once the early installations of the new turbines and mills were accepted, it became possible in many cases to add small electrification schemes to the new plant. This became the second focus of the programme.

Two organizations conceived and started the programme: United Missions to Nepal (UMN) and Balaju Yantra Shala (BYS). They remain two of the three principal organizations involved. UMN is a private voluntary organization of mission groups and church-related aid agencies. UMN set up the Butwal Training Institute (BTI), concerned initially with apprentice training in its mechanical engineering workshop. As technologies were developed and commercialized, BTI expanded into a holding organization for specialist workshops that in turn became private companies. The mechanical workshop became the Butwal Engineering Works (BEW). These UMN organizations have been important promoters of industrial growth, with manufacturing, training, electricity production and supply, contracting, consultancy and R&D.

BYS is a general engineering company with probably the best equipped engineering workshop in Nepal.

Evolution of the programme and prospects

In the 1960s BYS designed, fabricated and installed a small number of propeller turbines in mills. Maintenance and repair problems quickly arose. BTI received many requests for turbines, or replacements, at a time when it needed to find new marketable products to produce. BTI and Development and Consulting Services (DCS, another UMN offshoot) agreed a proposal for a hydro-power project in the early 1970s. Discussions with mill owners, entrepreneurs and villagers resulted in a development programme for a modern direct-drive turbine, designed to provide enough power to run a rice huller, a grain mill for wheat and maize and an oil expeller for mustard seed at the same time. This meant a power requirement of at least 9 kW, compared to the 3 kW available from small diesels and *ghattas*.

With grant assistance from abroad to start the micro-hydro project, the first scheme was funded by the Nepal Industrial Development Corporation. BEW and DCS then set up a programme called the Small Turbine Mill Project (STMP; UMN micro-hydro activities will be referred to as STMP from now on). The first three schemes were installed in 1977. BYS set up its own crossflow turbine project.

The Multi-Purpose Processing Unit, because of its lower costs relative to those of the crossflow, found rapid favour in some areas. Well over 100 have been installed, mostly with the financial assistance of UNICEF.

The early stages of the programme were concerned, first, with the development of the appropriate technologies. Secondly, although the early mills showed great potential, credit was needed if the programme was to expand beyond the few installations paid for by entrepreneurs. The Agricultural Development Bank of Nepal (ADBN), after evaluating early crossflow installations, ended its loan scheme for diesel mills and switched it to water-mills. Loans are for up to 80 per cent of total costs, for 5–10 years. Additional grants later became available from the government through the ADBN for half the costs of small electrification schemes.

Third was the development of an extension methodology to ensure the integration of the manufacture, delivery, installation and operation of the new plant. Marketing the concept of water-mills was carried out largely by STMP, which published brochures and ran training courses and demonstrations. Once the technology had been demonstrated to potential millers, they quickly recognized the advantages of the new mills. The extension methodology had to overcome the problem of transport in the hill areas. No manufacturer could commit himself to install plant without the assurance that materials, equipment and labour were available on site.

The growing demand for water-mills, matched by the development of an appropriate technology and project procedures, the availability of funding and training and technical support, has stimulated the growth of a significant industry. About 450 new turbines have now been installed, and the number of manufacturers has expanded to about nine. The addition of electricity generation to about 70 mills is extending the scope of the programme and providing important socioeconomic benefits. The programme has demonstrated that in Nepal, at least, it is possible to make financially viable use of locally designed and built micro-hydro systems.

Costs and benefits

Returns to mill owners

STMP has provided typical capital costs for diesel and micro-hydro mills, with estimates of running costs. These are supplemented in Table 3 by indicative costs of MPPUs and low-cost MPPUs from other manufacturers.

Table 3 Comparative costs in Nepali rupees of *ghatta* diesel, turbine, MPPU and low-cost MPPU mills

	Ghatta	*Diesel*	*Crossflow turbine*	*MPPU*	*Low-cost MPPU*
Output (hp)	0.5–1	5	9	4	3
Capital costs	—	46,000	136,000	49,000	40,000
Running costs	—	31,600	1,100	220	20

Although the initial expenditures on turbine equipment require higher outlays on foreign exchange than diesel mills, the use of imported diesel is eliminated.

Costs and benefits to farmers

Time-saving compared with traditional milling. A considerable proportion of women and children's waking hours is taken up by onerous milling. The amount of one household's time saved each year by switching from traditional to mechanical milling appears to range from 800 person-hours, for a mill operating only part-time, to a maximum of 5,000. The time made available may be taken up with improved child and livestock care, more fodder gathering, household chores and longer sleep at night.

Cash savings. The charges for processing wheat, rice, maize and mustard seed are about 30 per cent less on average at water-mills than at diesel mills.

Distribution of benefits

Mills tend to be owned by rich and powerful members of the community, who are likely to grow more wealthy through mill ownership. Recognizing the scope for more equitable distribution of benefits, DCS has been introducing turbine mills under co-operative ownership. Six schemes of up to 10 people and four of up to 100 have been established. However, progress is limited because the legal framework for co-operatives does not yet exist in Nepal.

Environmental benefits

Micro-hydro mill schemes are virtually neutral in environmental impact. Electrification projects have greater potential environmental impact, although in so far as micro-hydro is an alternative to large-scale hydro, the programme is environmentally beneficial. But potentially the most important environmental effects of the programme are those that might result from large-scale use of electric cookers: first, reductions in fuelwood consumption would help reduce the time spent by householders, especially women, gathering fuel; and secondly, in electrified villages they might help to relieve pressure on fast-diminishing wood supplies and buy time for reforestation.

Project sustainability and replication

An indication of sustainability is the degree to which manufacture of the programme's equipment and supply of its services have been taken up by local companies. By this criterion the micro-hydro programme is doing well.

Impact on national policies. The programme has shown that the traditional official Nepalese approach of installing small hydro schemes for electricity generation alone is not as cost-effective as using small-scale hydro resources to meet the demand for processing power as well. Until 1984–5 it was not possible by law to generate and sell electricity privately without a licence. Now, influenced by the programme, the government has changed the regulations, lifting all restrictions on private sales of electricity up to 100 kW. The programme may also have an impact on more general policy issues, particularly on the choice of technology for rural areas, through its links with the ADBN, which now sees itself as a promoter of appropriate technologies.

Key factors in programme performance

Identifying the demand. The conventional approach to hydro projects in rural areas is to assume that the main demand is for electricity for lighting. But while most rural households want electric light, it is not necessarily a major power need, and the result is nearly always uneconomic projects. In contrast, the micro-hydro programme identified a service, mechanical milling, for which there was a large demand, which could be met economically using local hydro resources.

Technology development. The complete system has to be manufactured in Nepal and installed at very isolated sites; it must cope with a wide range of conditions and accept the addition of electrification equipment. To develop equipment that meets these requirements requires a flexible and innovative approach. The programme's success is an indication of the extent to which these qualities were found in STMP and BYS.

Delivering and sustaining the technology. Many projects fail because the conditions under which the technology is transferred to the user are not carefully enough considered. The extension methodology devised by STMP, BYS and the ADBN takes this into account. No stage of the project can begin without completion of the previous stage. Training mill owners and users is an integral component.

Institutional factors. STMP and BYS fulfilled several different functions during the programme: project identification and assessment, technology development, equipment manufacture, funding, extension, installation and evaluation. Secondly, the technical developments for STMP took place within the broader context of the engineering, technical and commercial facilities, skills and training available at BEW, BTI and DSC. BYS turbine development took place within a wider technical background. The emphasis on training and commercialization has been important. Thirdly, UMN and BYS staff displayed considerable personal commitment in the aid business; quality is more important than quantity. Finally, the commitment of the ADBN to rural development and to the provision of finance for the water-mills has been crucial to success.

CASE STUDY 14 *Improved Charcoal Stoves Programme, Kenya*

MONICA OPOLE
KENGO, Kenya

Wood energy accounts for more than three-quarters of Kenya's energy consumption. The demand for firewood is increasing at 3.6 per cent and for charcoal at 6.7 per cent annually. Resources are depleting rapidly, and without drastic action wood could become unavailable as a fuel to many poorer Kenyans.

The improved stoves programme was conceived as a means of using woodfuels more efficiently in order to reduce the resource depletion rate. Unlike many other stove projects it has achieved considerable success, designing, developing, testing and disseminating more than 180,000 units of improved charcoal jikos since its inception in 1981. The success of the programme is mainly due to the adoption of locally available tools, technologies, skills and marketing network. The new ceramic jiko has captured more than 12 per cent of the traditional jiko market.

First stages of the programme

The programme was initiated under the auspices of the Kenyan Ministry of Energy and was part-financed by USAID. The Ministry of Energy, being new and lacking a field extension network, needed to develop collaborative ties quickly with field-operating NGOs. KENGO (Kenya Energy Non-Governmental Organizations' Association) had already organized a national forum for NGOs working in renewable energy in what was then known as the Claystove Working Group, and this group constituted the initial major institution involved in cookstoves development.

Immediate project objectives were to build institutional capability and to develop the entrepreneurial skills needed for planning, evaluating and implementing stove programmes and producing and disseminating improved stoves. A further aim was to monitor and evaluate the impact of improved stoves. The strategy had four main components:

(1) *Applied research and prototype development* – surveys and assessments of existing energy technologies; user characteristics; user patterns; social needs for stoves; formulation of design criteria; prototype design and laboratory testing; field testing and performance monitoring.

(2) *Training, extension and demonstration* – training for trainers, artisans, extension workers and programme managers through seminars or hands-on training workshops.

(3) *Production enterprise development* – technical and material assistance provided to selected artisans, potters and existing stove makers to enable them to set up improved stove production enterprises.

(4) *Monitoring and evaluation* – regular follow-up of field activities and analysis of data collected, to identify any constraints to stove adoption and assess the impact of activities.

The targets originally set for the project included: the introduction of about 5,000 improved stoves in rural and urban poor households; building within the ministry a technical capability to identify, plan, implement and evaluate improved stove programmes; and the demonstration of improved stoves in at least 20 districts in Kenya. Additional targets included the establishment of a network of self-sustaining stove production enterprises.

A field programme was established in Nairobi to test the stoves' energy cooking efficiency, acceptability and durability. The testing proved that the informal sector industry had the capability to absorb the new technology on a self-sustainable basis.

Evolution and production of the KCJ

The Kenya Ceramic Jiko (KCJ) developed over a number of years of testing with consumers and working with informal sector artisans. The model chosen for improvement was the traditional metal jiko, which was cylindrical and had an energy efficiency of about 20 per cent (Figure 1).

Experience in Thailand suggested that the traditional Kenyan metal stove should be selected, rather than new models, because it was easily affordable, had a ready market and had physical features which could be improved upon. Initially the Thai Bucket-shaped ceramic part was placed in the traditional

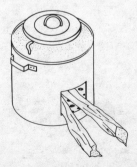

Figure 1: Traditional Kenyan metal stove

stove, but the problem was how to adapt the Thai Bucket liner into metal casings more suitable for Kenyan cooking methods. Five models were produced, and in 1983 Jerri International was commissioned to make 5,000 prototypes of the latest design, later called the Kenya Ceramic Jiko.

The field testing model has a full liner, which closely resembled the Thai Bucket, and a loose grate (Figure 2), both joined to the stove using a mixture of cement and vermiculite. One of the major design features corrected by the field

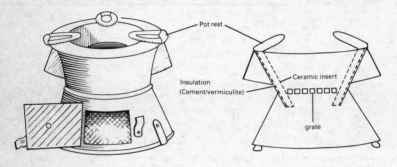

Figure 2: Kenyan stove with full and half-liner bell-bottom cladding

test was the length of the liner; the stove was difficult to light because it had a small air gap. Subsequent models (Figure 3) avoided the full liner. This proved to be a saving for ceramic producers in terms of material, and the reduction in liner size made the stove lighter. It decreased the time taken to light the stove to five minutes.

The jiko industry has been part of the traditional informal sector metalworking industry since around 1920. All KCJ claddings are produced by artisans from scrap metal. The jiko uses material from oil and chemical drums discarded by Nairobi's large-scale industries. Cutting and forming are carried out using the simplest tools.

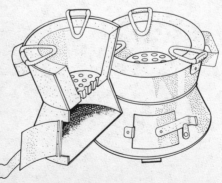

Figure 3: The current Kenya Ceramic Jiko design

The insulative part of the stove is made of local clay mixed with woodash, vermiculite or sand in proportions which decrease the stove weight while increasing the clay's thermal stress and insulating properties. Clay liners are made by a variety of formal and informal sector producers. Assembly simply involves the insertion of the ceramic liner into the metal cladding, using a cement-vermiculite mix between the two to hold them together.

Extension of the programme

By mid-1983 it was evident that initial project targets could not be achieved within a formal government system. It was recommended that KENGO should be subcontracted to carry out the remaining tasks of extending the programme. Extension was implemented by initiating informal, on-site training for cookstove artisans, formal training workshops and seminars for trainers and in-service training at the agroforestry/energy demonstration centres.

Informal on-site training using a mobile stove unit proved more effective and cheaper because the artisans did not have to leave their places of work to attend training sessions. Once shown how to cut the templates, artisans could assemble the stoves without supervision, and only follow-ups were needed to maintain the required standards.

Formal training was effective only for public institutions where trainers went and taught students at village polytechnics on jiko production. Training offered at the agroforestry/energy centres was aimed at creating technical and entrepreneurial skills and the ability to evaluate different cookstove designs.

Extension materials used were posters and booklets. By early 1984 KENGO had started promoting the KCJ technology using television and radio. Public demonstration of working stoves at markets was another effective dissemination method used.

In Nairobi during 1983 traditional metal jikos sold for between KSh 15 and 60 for varying sizes of stoves, while improved jikos of the same sizes were sold for between KSh 75 and 180. Producers were getting five times more profit from selling an improved jiko than from a traditional one. These exorbitant prices were caused by the high demand for the improved stoves and low supply of ceramic inserts. By 1986 the prices of improved stoves had started falling as more producers got into the market. The number of producers throughout the country had increased to 19.

By 1985 official promotion of improved jikos led to an interest in policy changes to legalize, reinstate and encourage the growth of the informal sector, which provided employment opportunities for polytechnic graduates and private enterprise. The institutionalization of the project also resulted in formal agreement to give licences and legal rights for the artisans to occupy city council land previously occupied illegally. This increased the security of people working in this sector, who were formerly evicted from time to time by the council.

Costs and benefits

Costs. Total administrative cost of the stoves programme was about KSh 4.2 million, equivalent to US$281,800. The KENGO project, which follows up the Ministry of Energy programme, proposed to spend KSh 2,485,000 out of a grant of KSh 3.5 m to accelerate production and dissemination of the jiko outside Nairobi. KENGO was to provide about 30 per cent of the total budget.

Economic benefits. Between 50 and 100 new jobs have been created through the programme, in ceramic liner production and stove assembly.

Individual households have been able to benefit greatly from using improved jikos, realizing savings of at least an estimated KSh 32 m (approx. US$2 m) in 1985. A rough estimate suggests that the current adoption rate of about 10 per cent should be saving the nation some KSh 5 m per year.

Ecological benefits. Better use is being made of scrap metal and tree cutting for fuel has been reduced. In 1985 charcoal demand was reduced by over 1.5 million tonnes of cut trees annually. With the development of the ceramic liner technology, efficient firing kilns were also developed that can use waste materials and grass. The quantity of wood used to fire liners is minimal. Carbon dioxide/monoxide levels and toxic fume levels have been reduced by 20 per cent around the stove and kitchen environment.

Key factors in project performance

Reasons for success. The Kenyan jiko programme's success/sustainability and replicability are mainly due to the involvement of local people. Earlier stove programmes had high administrative costs and needed continuous external funding. For each jiko built, a stovemason, local material and a cook were needed. The user had to be shown how to use and maintain the stoves by a trained artisan. These masons were considered aliens because in many cases they did not originate from the same area as the user. The sex of the stovemason was also often a hindrance, because men were not socially accepted to work in kitchens. Stoves built by an "outsider" were bound to fail because they were not properly used or maintained.

The Kenyan experience used a local marketing system, well understood by users and producers. It used existing production methodologies as a base for improving a technology similar to the traditional one. Thus the programme was able to replicate itself without further external funding; and end-users were able to use the traditional method of cooking.

The technology is in high demand in other African countries.

Lessons learned. Lessons learned since the inception of the wood energy programme are as follows:

(1) Government agencies are very important in formulating and providing policy guidance on a new technology, also in legitimizing such technology where there are unclear legislative rules. But they are not as effective at setting up self-sustaining service delivery systems.

(2) Technology design is a very intricate procedure requiring an in-depth understanding of the problems and needs of the target audience. Needs assessment, evaluation of existing designs and an intimate knowledge of the users' environment are paramount.

(3) Training of artisans in a new technology is a time-consuming task, especially if the design deviates from previously known ones.

(4) An effective dissemination strategy needs the following components: a stove designed to users' needs; knowledge of the users' environment; proven field tests demonstrating user acceptability; users' needs to determine the final prototype design; convincing users of positive benefits; ensuring a reliable industry to supply the commodity.

(5) The development and widespread introduction of improved jikos require more resources than previously thought and need to be funded for longer periods if they are to have any substantial impact.

CASE STUDY 15 *Usutu Forest Pulp Mill, Swaziland*

JULIAN EVANS
International Institute for Environment and Development

and DAVID WRIGHT
Intermediate Technology Development Group

The Usutu forest is an area of 52,000 ha of predominantly pine plantations in the highveld of Swaziland. These man-made plantations supply the raw material for the production annually of about 180,000 tonnes of unbleached Kraft woodpulp produced in a mill in the middle of the forest beside the Usutu River. The pulp is Swaziland's second most important export. Manufacture of pulp from this project has continued for 25 years. The enterprise is owned jointly by the Commonwealth Development Corporation and Courtaulds Ltd with holdings by the Swazi government.

Brief history

The Usutu forestry enterprise was initiated by the Colonial (now Common-wealth) Development Corporation (CDC). CDC funded land purchase, and the first plantings took place in 1950. Over the next ten years 42,000 ha were afforested, the largest area of man-made forest in one contiguous block in Africa. Pine grew well under Swaziland conditions.

Initially it was intended that Kraft paper (that used in brown paper bags, cardboard boxes, etc.) would be manufactured for the South African market. However, it was then decided to produce unbleached Kraft pulp for export overseas. A pulp mill was constructed with a designed annual production capacity of 90,000 tonnes and began commercial production in 1962. Capacity subsequently expanded until annual production was double the original design level. The forest area expanded to 52,000 ha. The entire output of unbleached Kraft pulp from the mill is exported, largely to markets in the Far East and Western Europe.

Development of the enterprise

The forest. Afforestation took place on highveld land purchased directly from European settlers and absentee South African farmers. Virtually no Swazi villagers were displaced. Areas of land have also been leased from the Swazi nation. The rough terrain and frequently boulder-strewn ground make much of the area unsuitable for arable farming, while the quality of grazing is not high. Two major forestry-related developments had to be constructed, apart from the mill: accommodation and roads. Present running costs of the forests are not published. However, the delivered cost of pulpwood to the mill is among the lowest in the world.

The pulp mill. In 1959 CDC and Courtaulds decided to form a joint company to construct the pulp mill. When commercial production began the total initial cost of the mill was some £8 m. Not until 1969 did Usutu make any significant profit. The wood pulp business, like that of other commodities, is cyclical. Usutu's earnings and profit record have been similarly volatile. With the increase in production capacity, and with the benefit of new and improved technologies, Usutu has had significant success in reducing its unit costs, but with a rapidly declining world market, the pressure to reduce costs is undiminished.

Benefits

Employment. The company has become Swaziland's biggest private sector employer, providing direct employment to nearly 2,800 people in 1986. The livelihood of more than 20,000 men, women and children depends on Usutu's prosperity. Compared to other companies in related sectors in Swaziland, total remuneration for local employees is high and well ahead of the government minimum.

Training. A formal training centre was established in 1968. The training of Swazi locals for senior management and technical positions has always presented a particular challenge.

Social infrastructure. There are two major townships: at Bunya, adjacent to the plant, principally for the mill workers; and at Mhlambanyati, for administrative and technical staff. These villages, with a number of smaller communities for forest employees, include shops, medical and social facilities and schools.

Economic benefits. The company's earning of foreign exchange are substantial.

Environmental impacts

The man-made forest. The pine plantations achieve high rates of growth. Silvicultural practice is intense, with short rotations, no thinning or large-scale applications of fertilizer and immediate replanting after harvesting. There is some evidence of depletion of nutrients, alteration of soil characteristics and compaction and erosion arising from log extraction on some sites. But the forest has not generally had any significant harmful effects on the soil. The forest cover has reduced risks of erosion and brought into productive use land which formerly yielded little.

Almost the whole of the forest is within the catchment of the Great Usutu River. It is likely that the forest has reduced water yield and this could be seen as an undesirable impact, since some of the crops cultivated depend on irrigation.

The forest provides excellent cover for wildlife. The numbers and variety of animals have increased to include antelope and buck, monkeys, baboons, porcupines, antbears, bushbabies, wart-hogs, guinea fowl, lynx, spring hares, rock rabbits, mongooses, honey badger, cape fox, civet and cervel – animals uncommon in adjacent highveld.

The mill. Conventional thinking in the 1950s was that abundant water supplies and a large river for the disposal of effluent were essential for the production of pulp. Because Swaziland had decided on a law to control the discharge of industrial effluents into rivers, this precluded the establishment of a conventional Kraft mill on the Great Usutu River. The solution adopted was, first, to limit the mill product to unbleached Kraft pulp and, secondly, to adopt a new method of flash drying that involved less clean water than conventional methods.

The limits of water-borne pollutants are reviewed periodically by the Swazi government and are subject to permit. Mill effluents do not appear to result in serious environmental impacts.

Sustainability

Plantation monoculture. Forest monoculture of exotic species is generally regarded as more at risk than mixed, natural woodland. The Usutu experience suggests, however, that large monoculture plantations can be ecologically sustainable. The yields of three successive crops of pines have been studied at Usutu since 1968, and there is no evidence of declining productivity. There have been localized outbreaks of defoliating insects, but so far no pest or disease threatens the enterprise as a whole. Prudent forestry practice will be to maintain observations, research and good forest hygiene to keep risks at a minimum.

Pulp production and marketing. The company has succeeded in sustaining 25 years' production of pulp. The major problem is whether Usutu can continue to sell its single, relatively low-value product profitably. It seems likely that the decline in demand for unbleached pulp will not bottom out before the 1990s. Usutu is now one of only three major producers in the world that have unbleached pulp as their sole product.

The obvious option for Usutu is to upgrade the mill and make higher-value (e.g. semi-bleached) products, but this comes up against the problems of water availability and effluent disposal. There are two possibilities for ensuring sustained operations without causing environmental degradation. The first is to continue with the present product and apply continued efforts to becoming the lowest-cost source of supply in the world. The second possibility lies in the development of a new bleaching technology not dependent on chlorine.

Closely related is the matter of transport. The costs of transport of the pulp to the Far East and Western Europe represent the largest element in the total cost to the purchaser. A further potential point of vulnerability arises from the political situation in Southern Africa.

Replicability

Similar afforestation programmes can be found in Malawi, Zimbabwe, Madagascar and Kenya. Growing pine plantations on tropical and subtropical grasslands is a practicable, successful and sustainable form of industrial forestry development. Less replicable is the pulp mill. The declining market for unbleached pulp has been commented on, and successful pulp mill investments require favourable circumstances. Examples of other successes are balanced by failures.

Why successful?

The forest. A number of factors have contributed to the success of the plantation:

● The original advice on species choice, drawing on experience in South Africa, laid the foundation for a successful forest.
● The single-minded objective of growing solely pulpwood has avoided dissipation of effort and funds.
● Research has contributed to sustained soil fertility, maintenance of productivity and technological improvements that have helped to keep down production costs.
● Two further factors are containment of the plantation resource within 50 km of the mill, and adoption of practices which maximize yield per hectare.

The pulp mill. CDC's invitation to Courtaulds to participate in the design and construction of the mill led directly to the new flash-drying process applied at Usutu. Without this, the mill would not have been possible. The installation of a tall oil plant to treat toxic effluent demonstrates the successful utilization of a previously dangerous waste product. In addition, research and development by Courtaulds and the constant supply of technical personnel from the UK have made a vital contribution to competitiveness.

The whole enterprise. First, continuous successful efforts have been made by Courtaulds to improve the company's sole product, unbleached Kraft pulp, and to extend the range of end-product markets. Secondly, pulp and paper production is costly, and expansion has been the principal means, through economies of scale, of keeping unit costs down. Thirdly, Usutu has been a success because it has enjoyed good management and sound direction. Fourthly, Swaziland has long been a peaceful and stable country, conditions favourable to industrial development.

CASE STUDY 16 *Sorghum Processing, Botswana*

O. G. SCHMIDT

Programme Officer, International Development Research Centre

Shortly after the International Development Research Centre's (IDRC) inception in 1970, its Division of Agriculture, Food and Nutrition Sciences selected the semi-arid tropics and their neglected crops as one of its areas of concentration. Sorghums and millets became a focus of research support. In Africa sorghums and millets are grown primarily by small holder subsistence farmers and mostly consumed by the producer and her/his family. They are well adapted to the semi-arid regions, form the staple food for large rural populations, are still preferred by a substantial percentage of the population, have suffered from policy neglect and are often viewed by the urban élite as a "poor person's crop".

These foods are a logical starting-point for agricultural research, and primary beneficiaries will be the small-scale producer/consumer. Increased production of sorghum and millets will occur if the producers/consumers require increased volumes or if sustained demand for surplus production can be generated. It was soon recognized that a major constraint lay in the difficulty of dehulling the grains prior to grinding them into flour.

Development of dehuller designs

A series of research projects were undertaken in Africa, India and Latin America. The initial focus of these projects was on the development of a simple mechanical dehulling device, suitable to the needs of the producer/consumer of the small grains and grain legumes. More recently the applied research has emphasized introduction of the technology.

The results from these IDRC-supported research projects have culminated in several variants of a basic design, some now on the threshold of widespread use in the semi-arid areas of Africa and Asia. The specific technical designs of dehuller were evolved in relatively close collaboration with the intended beneficiaries.

The hardware technology, informally known as a grain dehuller, is more correctly labelled a dry abrasive disc dehuller. The operational principle is a progressive abrasion of the outer layers of grains or grain legumes. The dehuller consists of a metal shaft on which a number of grinding stones, abrasive discs, are

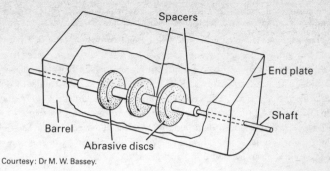

Courtesy: Dr M. W. Bassey.

Figure 4: The principle of the dry abrasive disc dehuller design for sorghum processing, Botswana

evenly spaced about 2 cm apart. This rotor is enclosed by a semicircular sheet metal barrel with a flat top (Figure 4). The barrel is partly filled with grain, and the abrasive discs, spinning at 1,500–2,000 rpm, rub against the freely moving mass of grain. The length of time during which the grain is retained affects how much of the material is removed.

The Botswana experience

Between 1974 and 1975 research into the prevailing food system of Botswana identified two key issues: (1) sorghum was the preferred food of the rural Batswana; and (2) rural food consumption patterns had undergone a significant change over the preceding years. Mainly due to the onerous demands of home dehulling and pulverization by mortar and pestle, women were increasing their purchases of imported ready-to-cook sifted maize meal and rice.

Technology adoption, dissemination and deployment

Between 1975 and 1978 the Botswana Agricultural Marketing Board (BAMB), with support from IDRC, established a processing facility for sorghum at one of its storage depots. The equipment comprised two Canadian-designed dehullers, a large hammer-mill, a flour-sifting unit and weighing and bagging equipment. BAMB was quickly able to demonstrate that urban and rural households liked the flour from decorticated sorghum and were prepared to pay a high premium for this flour over the price of maize flour. By 1978 the factory was under Botswana management, processing and bagging 5–10 tonnes of flour per day. However, this system could not easily deal with small batches brought by individuals seeking a sorghum-milling service.

During 1977 the Rural Industries Innovation Centre (RIIC) participated in a needs assessment survey in Botswana's Southern District. A problem frequently identified by the villagers was the onerous nature of home processing sorghum. RIIC expressed interest in modifying the Canadian-designed dehuller to make it more compatible with the rural need for batch processing. RIIC scaled down and modified the dehuller design. A portion of the bottom surface of the barrel was cut and reattached by hinges. With this "trap door" the dehuller barrel could be emptied at any time, so successive batches could be separated from each other. Thus a customer could obtain a milling service for her batch of sorghum.

Villagers in the vicinity of the RIIC demanded that RIIC make its dehuller available to their needs. The verbal message was reinforced by daily queues of women who had brought batches of sorghum to the mill and refused to leave until their grain had been dehulled and ground. Thus the new RIIC dehuller (Figure 5) was quickly placed into a service milling setting, ably demonstrating the feasibility of service dehulling and grinding.

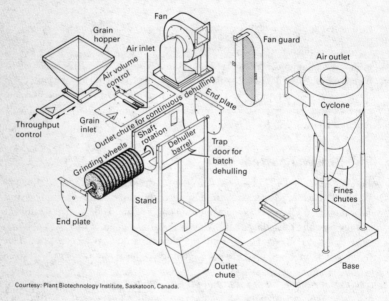

Courtesy: Plant Biotechnology Institute, Saskatoon, Canada.

Figure 5: Exploded drawing of RIIC-style dehuller, Botswana

The small industries branch of the Ministry of Commerce and Industry was eager to see the dehuller deployed in the rural areas. Pressure on RIIC to move to early dissemination was reinforced by a declared intention from the large industry branch within the same ministry. Satisfied that BAMB's installation in Southern Botswana was proving a viable proposition, the branch wished to replicate this factory in the north. At issue was the choice between a relatively centralized sorghum milling industry and many small-scale systems dotted throughout the country. If RIIC could not demonstrate quickly enough that small-scale industrialization was feasible, the ministry intended to opt for the large-scale solution.

RIIC felt compelled to move quickly from its first prototype to the sale of a package containing dehuller (still experimental), hammer-mill and engine. In late 1979 RIIC published a manual in Setswana and English aimed at potential mill owners, and in early 1980 followed this up with a technical operators manual. Several investors were able to obtain credit to buy the equipment.

Sales grew steadily. By 1986, 25 small-scale mills were in operation throughout the country, incorporating 35 dehullers; 11 systems are owned privately, 8 by indigenous development organizations, 5 by co-operative societies and one by BAMB. A mature small-scale milling industry has become established, despite encountering many problems along the way.

The first small-scale mills began as service mills. Soon, however, urban traders began to bring to the mills larger loads for bulk milling. The trader bagged the flour and sold it in his shop. Several of the millers with better management skills and access to operating cash then began to buy bulk supplies of sorghum and to package the flour in paper or plastic bags for sale to shops.

A significant degree of competition arose, and a handful of millers now had the major share of the urban market. Many of the mills saw their turnover begin to decrease. The mill owners' association began to give training and upgrading courses in business management to the ''poorer'' millers.

This evolution of a near-oligopoly dominating the use of the technology was probably hastened by the weather. Continuous drought between 1981 and 1985 drastically reduced Botswana's harvests. BAMB's original role as the residual buyer of local sorghum production, and one of several importers, was changed to that of sole importer. With no access to locally grown grains and controlled access to imported grain, the installations which had remained as service mills saw a complete drying-up of their operations. Their normal customers, all producer/consumers, had no grain to bring to the mill. The commercial millers preferred to sell sorghum flour rather than undehulled grain and were unwilling to sell smaller lots of grain to their service milling colleagues. BAMB's preference for selling grain in bulk lots to buyers with their own transport also strengthened the commercial millers.

Policy issues

The process of dehuller adaptation and introduction was influenced by the conflict between government proponents of large- and small-scale industrialization. RIIC's rapid progression towards selling the milling packages provided the needed ammunition to the small-scale proponents.

In 1984–5 the Botswana Mill Owners' Association (BMOA), seeing the emergence of several dominant commercial millers to the detriment of the economic viability of their service milling colleagues, pointed out that official rural industrialization policy seemed to be honoured more in the breach than the observance. BMOA called for licensing to ensure an equitable utilization of milling capacity. The government announced a licensing policy in 1986, limiting the size of any dehulling/milling establishment.

Key factors in the Botswana experience

The research-for-development process:

- A systematic identification of the key constraints in the food system which impeded the increased production and utilization of the preferred food, sorghum.
- The process of research towards a hardware technology was problem-led, in contrast to an all-too-common solution-led approach.
- The knowledge that there was an entrenched preference for sorghum enhanced the probability of success for the initial transfer of hardware to BAMB.
- Analysis of the initial experiment by BAMB led to the decision to adapt the design to make it more responsive to the needs of rural dwellers. Rurally located service dehulling would be closer to the producer, save family labour and create rural employment.
- RIIC recognized that technology generation alone is not enough; as the technology's "product champion" it persisted until widespread adoption occurred.
- Since the process of technology adaptation was conducted inside the country, an indigenous cadre of personnel developed, ensuring the ability to deliver that technology in a user-compatible way on a sustained basis.

The development process:

- RIIC sought to measure the technology's impact in the rural areas with questions aimed at housewives, farmers and mill owners and operators.
- The mill owners formed an association, initially for group interaction with the manufacturer in order to improve the technology's technical performance.
- The mill owners changed their use of the technology for profit maximization. They also defined new objectives for the mill owners' association to improve their business viability.
- The association (the technology users), rather than RIIC (the technology's initial champion) or the Ministry of Commerce and Industry, has acted to monitor and describe the outcome of intervening with the new technology.
- Government policies, drought and entrepreneurial actions have all contributed to shape the industry to its present form.
- In retrospect, neither RIIC's developmental intentions (rural job creation, a decentralized milling industry) nor those of the small-scale branch of the government ministry have been achieved.
- The nature of the industry's evolution, and drought, may have caused a permanent change in the way sorghum producers view their food. It is possible that sorghum is now considered much more as a cash crop than a subsistence crop. The income from the sale of the crop will be used to buy sorghum flour from the shop or the commercial mill.
- IRDC has observed and participated in the Botswana experience; corporate

learning is taking place within this agency mandated to support Third World research and is affecting its programming strategies.

An expatriate agency and expatriate personnel were critically important in the first few years of the process. Nevertheless, an emphasis on counterpart training and capacity building ensured that the knowledge gained remained in Botswana and was internalized by the citizens who worked on the project.

Costs and benefits

Costs. For Botswana external investments lie in the following range: IDRC, CA$250,000; USAID, approximately US$100,000 (CA$140,000); West Germany's Friedrich Ebert Foundation, in providing core funding to RIIC, the estimated equivalent of CA$100,000. These inputs should be seen as the development costs for creating a viable and useful technology.

The capital required by the milling entrepreneurs, at 1980 prices, for a service mill (engine, hammer-mill, weigh scale and dehuller) and a simple building was equivalent to about US$12,500. Assuming 4–5 employees, the cost per workplace created was about US$3,000.

Benefits. Hours of labour have been saved; a mill operating at the economic break-even level saves 2,000 or more woman- and child-hours daily. Initially, the cost benefit looked to be advantageous, but a fresh study today would provide a gloomy picture for those mills (the majority) which did not switch to commercial milling. Jobs were created; 172 people have found employment in the small-scale milling industry, and during 1979–85 metalworkers were employed by RIIC to manufacture dehullers. Capacity-building has taken place; Batswana and expatriates have participated in and learned from a process of research for development which is transferable to other problems and technologies. Whether the benefits will be sustained, and whether they have accrued as equitably as possible, may not be answerable for several years.

The Botswana experience has been relatively well documented, and the lessons learned are being applied to similar projects in other countries. RIIC has served as the training institution for dehuller familiarization for researchers from Kenya, Senegal, Zimbabwe, Uganda, Malawi and Tanzania. IRDC is supporting applied research on the technology in other countries.

CASE STUDY 17 *Transfer of Sustainable Appropriate Technology, Ghana*

IAN SMILLIE
Development Economist, Consultant, Writer

On independence in 1957 Ghana was well endowed with human and natural resources, although development had been badly skewed towards extractive industries and primary commodities. Kwame Nkrumah, Ghana's first Prime Minister, equated development with industrialization, believing, as many did at the time, that growth could become self-sustaining once it reached "take-off" point. By the 1970s such hopes lay in tatters. Major economic decisions had been made for social or political reasons, often with minimal reference to efficiency or profitability. Output fell, and inflation soared. The "trickle-down" approach had failed. Drought, worsening terms of trade and other factors also played a part. Since 1983 there have been signs of a turn-around, but it was in this climate of chaos and decline that the Technology Consultancy Centre was founded.

The Technology Consultancy Centre

Kumasi is a regional capital of about 350,000 people and home of the University of Science and Technology (UST). Kumasi boasts one of the largest traditional markets in West Africa and one of the biggest open-air informal industrial areas in the world: Suame Magazine, named after the old military depot.

Today there are an estimated 40,000 workers in Suame. A 1971 survey found more than 1,600 owner-operated businesses, of which 500 were involved in vehicle repair or modification and 300 offered welding, carpentry or black-smithing; there were 150 dealers in vehicles and spare parts. Suame acted as a powerful magnet for engineers from UST, and it was decided to create a Technology Consultancy Centre (TCC) aimed at making the university useful to the industrial community. TCC was formally established in 1972 as an autonomous unit within the university. In 1973 TCC received buildings and a small subvention from the university and external assistance from European voluntary organizations. By 1974 it had a functioning machine shop.

The rationale for campus production was that, while it was not difficult for skilled, trained professors to identify a solution to a technical problem, it was another matter to persuade a group or an entrepreneur to adopt the new technology or product. Skill development, dubious markets, lack of equipment or reluctance to invest conspired against the transfer of technology. The units could train craftsmen and managers over a period of time, while product development was completed under production, rather than experimental, conditions. The market could be tested, and entrepreneurs could determine the viability of the activity. The production units were an attempt to avoid what had happened elsewhere: "appropriate" products and technologies that were developed but not transferred.

Clients from government and the private sector began to arrive at TCC requesting assistance. However, most clients wanted TCC to provide them with the missing element in their own production rather than the technology needed to produce it themselves. TCC was also disappointed by the uptake on its advisory activities. Much of its technical advice to clients was ignored.

TCC learned that, for a product or a technology to become successful in the commercial world, it would have to be pursued by an individual or individuals who knew that world and possessed drive and initiative. Groups that came together at the instigation of an external agent were unlikely to have the necessary cohesion or drive. TCC came to the conclusion that technology researched and developed, no matter how appropriate in theory, was worthless unless it could attract agents within society to take and use it productively. Thus transfer of technology gradually came to replace product as the most important aspect of TCC's work.

A change of direction

The people TCC sought to reach were intimidated by the university; most worked in villages or across town in Suame Magazine. The solution: off-campus Intermediate Technology Transfer Units (ITTUs), the first to be established in Suame, a second in the north at Tamale. An ITTU would consist of a group of basic workshops located in an informal industrial area where clients would have regular access and on-the-job training in a realistic production setting.

The acceptance of appropriate technologies had to be considered in developmental terms, which at this time meant production: production of food; of the tools to improve the production of food; of the equipment needed to provide basic human needs such as water, health, clothing and housing; production that would lead to the creation of secure jobs and reasonable incomes. TCC was now in business to encourage appropriate productive enterprise wherever possible.

Despite the identification of interested and potentially competent producers (e.g. of nuts and bolts), none of the shops in Suame had the full range of equipment – lathe, milling machine and drill – necessary to go into production. So TCC took the unprecedented and almost desperate step of selling some of its own machines to potential manufacturers to get production started. Besides TCC's careful selection of clients, the transfer of equipment was probably crucial to success.

TCC then approached international aid agencies with the idea of importing and reselling more machine tools to small-scale entrepreneurs. Proceeds from the sales were then available for other programmes. The aid contributions therefore did double duty: assisting TCC and enabling entrepreneurs to buy machine tools necessary for production.

By now TCC's plans had outstripped the ability of most NGOs to assist with more than specific, small-scale projects. The Canadian International Development Agency (CIDA) and the United States Agency for International Development (USAID) became involved, and their assistance, matched by government contributions, led to the establishment in 1980 of the first ITTU in Suame and the second at Tamale in 1985. The relationship between these two bilateral agencies and TCC was complicated by a series of donor preconditions and lengthy delays, however.

Government support has been an essential ingredient in the annual budget of TCC. In recent years this has averaged 60 per cent of non-capital costs. The balance is met largely from income from sales of ITTU products, equipment rental and consulting fees. This covered an establishment in 1986 of 20 management, technical and support staff, 27 employees at Suame ITTU, 5 at Tamale and 22 at the remaining campus production units. In a typical year, TCC can deal with about 1,000 clients and direct beneficiaries, including roughly 20 new or ongoing machine shops, soap plants and other small enterprises and 300 or 400 farmers and beekeepers.

Technology transfer in the informal sector

For TCC there are four stages of technology: the most primitive stage relies on hand tools that are not designed according to specific principles. The second stage (the first stage of development in mechanical terms) involves hand- or human-powered machines designed in accordance with scientific principles. The third stage relies on scientifically designed machines, powered mechanically; and the fourth, not widespread in Ghana, involves the use and development of scientifically designed automatic machinery.

In Suame most workshops were at stage two when TCC was founded, a survey uncovering a total of only six centre lathes and almost no other machine tools. A survey of only 20 shops in 1984, mostly TCC customers, found 130 machine tools, of which 60 had been provided by TCC. Stage three was well under way – an essential development, because without a local capacity to manufacture plant and machinery there would be little upward mobility from stages one and two in other sectors of the economy.

Ten years after TCC began, a staggering range of machinery for rural industry and food processing was being turned out by TCC clients in Suame and elsewhere. A partial list includes, for agriculture, hoes and cutlasses, gate hinges, fence bolts and nuts, planters, bullock carts and ploughs and slasher blades for tractors. In the woodworking sector there were carpenters' sawbenches, wood-turning lathes and small tools such as hammers and chisels, while new products included broadlooms, warping mills and beehives. There were soap boiling tanks, caustic-soda plants, smokers for beekeepers, charcoal kilns and driers, pyrolisis plants and, for food processing, gari plants, gari presses and corn mills.

Few of the rural enterprises supplied or created would have been possible without the light engineering industry fostered by TCC. Engineering workshops are, in a sense, the real middlemen of appropriate technology, as the following example demonstrates.

SIS Engineering

SIS Engineering began in a small shack in 1972. Two technicians formed a commercial partnership, with two small wood-turning lathes, an electric drill and a universal woodworking machine. They started making school equipment, and by 1973 their product range had expanded to 36 items, including drawing-boards, voltmeters and rulers. SIS purchased a metalworking production lathe in 1974, planning to produce metal jigs and cutters for carpenters, but found it difficult to keep the machine fully occupied.

TCC was looking for the elusive mechanism by which steel bolt and nut manufacture could be transferred from the campus. In 1976, when it decided to sell some of its own equipment to potential producers, SIS was a prime candidate. A capstan lathe was installed in the expectation that SIS would become the first private manufacturer of nuts and bolts. However, the lathe was used for nuts and bolts only half of the time, and labour productivity was low.

Because of repairs SIS had been doing for sawbench operators, they began to manufacture spindles and bearing housings; they were soon fabricating complete sawbenches out of scrap steel. The next step was the production of a simple wood-turning lathe.

These products transformed the neighbourhood within five years. Once a relatively small cluster of carpenters and sawyers turning out basic wooden furniture and fitting, it now stretched for a kilometre, and SIS-made sawbenches reverberated from dawn till dusk. By 1985 SIS had sold 35 machines in Kumasi and as many again to other customers from across Ghana. Some of the sawbenches found their way to Burkina Faso, Nigeria and Ivory Coast, where harder currency was used to buy blades, bearings, tools and motors to feed the growing business in Kumasi. Carpenters discovered that the sawbenches could convert offcuts – previously treated as waste – from the huge government sawmills into useful items. The wood-turning lathes also produced new wooden products hitherto in the hands of a few large capital-intensive firms.

It was not easy for SIS, however. Many customers could not pay, large orders were almost impossible to find, labour turnover was high, and inflation almost impossible. Basic consumables such as cutting tools and welding rods could not be imported without interminable delays. Black-market prices were extortionate.

In 1979 SIS paid off its loan for the capstan lathe purchased from TCC and soon converted the machine into a centre lathe to increase production of bearing housings and spindles for the carpenters. SIS had reached a stage where ideas, techniques and market development were within its own capabilities. TCC assistance was now limited to specific one-off consultancies, a few subcontracts and the essential supply of imported consumables and equipment.

Key factors in project performance

In TCC's experience, the transfer of technology is as important as making the right technology choice. The one does not always follow from the other; the most transferable technology will follow closely on one already known.

The key characteristic of TCC was the role it assumed as an implementing agency: the move to subordinate R&D to the transfer of technology. Analysis of failures to transfer appropriate technology indicates that some research institutions are inadequately linked to the support structures essential to that transfer.

In the absence of appropriate linkages, TCC discovered that training, for example, could not be left to others. It obtained or made much of the equipment necessary for the manufacture of its products. It offered some equipment on time payments and assisted clients with financial planning and credit references. Technical and management assistance became part of the follow-up programme; it helped with bulk orders of raw material and tooling and obtained import licences on behalf of groups of clients.

Client selection. Client selection is of paramount importance. There must be a basic interest in the idea and power to convert the interest into concrete action. Besides access to the technology, there must be knowledge and experience to use it effectively.

Profit. TCC has recognized the importance of profit to the transfer of technology.

Product reliability. TCC learned that, to be adopted, an idea had to be both proven and reliable. Products which advanced beyond the idea stage had to prove themselves under production conditions and in the market-place.

Light engineering. TCC's concentration on light engineering was a key factor. In working with the small-scale machine shops the importance of client development came to the fore, along with the need to provide ancillary services. Much of TCC's ability to do things sprang from its light engineering base. The privately owned engineering workshops it helped to establish in Suame contained roughly ten times the number of machine tools that had existed there ten years earlier. These shops had developed a capacity that ranged from the manufacture of good quality industrial components to finished machines.

Once small workshops like SIS Engineering began to emerge as viable concerns, new products could be developed without great reliance on TCC. By the early 1980s some of the clients had essentially taken over TCC's earlier role, becoming in effect small appropriate technology centres themselves. The importance of this cannot be overestimated.

Staff and continuity. Dr John Powell became TCC's first Director in 1971 and remained in charge until 1986. Because TCC enjoyed the directorship of a single skilled and committed individual over the years, it experienced invaluable continuity. However, at all levels TCC attracted and kept individuals of talent and dedication.

Flexibility. TCC ranks among the most successful technology institutions in the world. But if its success were easily replicable, there would be clones throughout Africa. Each of TCC's clients is unique, and the formula developed by TCC has probably required adaptation and change with each of them. Above all, it is probably TCC's flexibility, its willingness and ability to grow with opportunities, which accounts for its success.

CASE STUDY 18 *Small versus Large in the Indian Cement Industry*

SANJAY SINHA

Director of Economic Development Associates, Lucknow, India

Cement is an essential ingredient in the process of economic development, required for the facilitation of virtually every type of economic activity. It is primarily an intermediate good, commanding considerable attention in development. In India the shortage of cement was for many years (especially in the 1970s) a constraint on all types of development and building activity. The availability and price of cement remain a major issue in the political economy of the country.

Historical context

The vertical shaft kiln (VSK) for mini-scale cement production is a development of the nineteenth-century lime kiln. In the 1930s interest in the VSK revived, and new designs suitable for continuous rather than batch operation were developed. Serious experiments with VSK technology commenced in India in the mid-1960s. Faced with the problem of transporting cement to inaccessible areas, the Ministry of Defence decided to sponsor the development of a 25–30 tpd (tonnes per day) mini-cement plant.

This pilot plant was later transferred to the Cement Research Institute of India (CRI). At the same time, research on VSKs continued at the Regional Research Laboratory at Jorhat, with the emphasis on smaller-capacity kilns down to 1 tonne of cement per day. Patents were handed to the National Research Development Corporation for commercial exploitation.

Interest in the Defence Ministry VSK design was revived in the late 1970s by M. K. Garg under the aegis of the Appropriate Technology Development Association, Lucknow (ATDA).

Another parallel development was initiated by a private entrepreneur, D. P. Saboo. The first experiment, conducted in Saboo's garden in 1981, used a 200-litre drum lined with fire bricks as a kiln. Success led to the setting up of a 10 tpd experimental plant. Within six months the plant had started to pay a return on a commercial basis, leading to a decision to set up a larger production facility.

Against a background of acute cement shortage and preferential policy treatment for mini-cement plants, demand for this production facility blossomed between 1982 and 1984. Rationalization of the controlled price structure in the late 1970s led to an acceleration in new investment in the industry and the commissioning of the first VSK plant in 1981. In 1982 the partial decontrol of cement was announced, with mini-cement plants being fully exempted from price control.

The liberty to sell cement on the open market roughly doubles the ex-works price realization, and between the commissioning of the first VSK plant and 1986 nearly 60 plants became operational in India.

Dissemination

Of the four "developers" of mini-cement technology in India, only the ATDA is yet to begin dissemination. The others have employed various dissemination methods with varying success. Saboo, the most successful, has concentrated on very small units, though he is now offering 50 and 100 tpd plants as well. By 1985, 28 Saboo-built plants were reported to be in production, with another 22 on order.

The CRI has taken the alternative route of licensing a number of machinery manufacturers to undertake dissemination. The leading licensee had commissioned 13 plants by 1986. An additional 14 plants based on the CRI's design were reported to have started production.

Investment costs for mini-cement plants range from $0.5 million for a 20 tpd Saboo VSK plant to £2.0 million for a CRI 100 tpd plant. This is very low compared with a capital cost of $85 million (or $85 per tonne of installed annual capacity) for a 3,000 tpd large-scale plant, and this naturally affects the investor profile. The typical investor in the small-scale VSK plant is a medium- or large-town entrepreneur/trader able to exploit local market conditions and with a preference for tight proprietorial control. Large-scale plants tend to be established by large companies with professional management structures and widespread public shareholding. Roughly 17 per cent of all capacity is owned and operated by government-owned companies.

Resource allocation and utilization

A high level of investor confidence implied by a high demand for mini-cement plants raises questions about the relative efficiency of utilization of resources allocated – a prime consideration in the sustainability of effort.

At market prices mini-cement plants (MCPs) are able to produce cement and transport it to the retailer at costs competitive with those incurred by the large sector. This is because MCPs tend to be situated closer to their markets.

MCPs have a much higher rate of return than large-scale plants due to various factors including lower average capital costs and shorter gestation periods.

From a social viewpoint, numerous market distortions – particularly subsidies implicit in public monopoly supplies and infrastructure provisions – have to be allowed for before a valid conclusion on the efficiency of resource allocation can be reached. For the purpose of calculation, the cost of cement at the point of retail sale rather than ex-factory has been considered, because of the significant resources expended in transportation. On this basis, the resource cost of cement produced by a 100 tpd mini-plant amounts to Rs 860 and that by a large plant to Rs 920 per tonne. The difference of Rs 60 per tonne is attributable entirely to the transport of cement over long distances by large plants.

Under present conditions MCPs are able to supply cement on a cost-competitive basis relative to the large sector. At market prices an efficient 100 tpd MCP even enjoys a small cost advantage over an efficient large-scale plant. At accounting or "efficiency" prices, however, the costs are not significantly different.

Capital resources. The unit capital cost of VSK plants is significantly lower than that of even modern dry-process rotary kiln plants.

Labour. The substantially higher labour costs of the large sector are related to a comparatively high requirement of skilled labour as well as to the operation of the Cement Wage Board. While minimum wages paid by the large sector were around Rs 1,000 in 1984, those paid by mini-plants were Rs 300–350 per month. The employment potential of VSKs is significantly higher than that of large plants. The large sector employs roughly 110,000 people compared to 60,000 already employed in small plants.

Management. Deficiencies in maintenance leading to high repair costs of machinery, waste of production and high administrative costs are commonly reported from large-scale plants. These and the need to maintain a large headquarters establishment are mainly responsible for the high residual costs of the large sector.

MCPs appear to enjoy a clear superiority in resource utilization on all counts except energy use.

Ecological considerations

Quarries

Areas with limestone deposits are, by and large, barren and sparsely populated. As a result, quarrying of the industry's main raw material can be undertaken without the glare of public scrutiny of the working conditions of quarry workers or of its effects on water resources, productive land resources and even scenic beauty.

In the Doon valley of northern Uttar Pradesh, however, nature has conspired to shake the cement industry out of any ecological complacency. The area is endowed with a limestone belt so rich that it has 99.5 per cent purity and low silica content. Despite licensing by the state government, uncontrolled quarrying has taken place with a negative impact on water resources, scenic beauty, livestock and habitat. Neither MCPs nor the large-scale sector can be absolved of responsibility for environmental degradation, and similar devastation may result from the industry's operations elsewhere.

Atmospheric emissions

Cement plants are subject to significant atmospheric emmissions. Much of this consists of particulate matter, in this case partially burnt calcium carbonate, carried away with kiln exhaust gases through a tall chimney. Though the level of atmospheric emissions from cement plants exceeds pollution control standards, the overall effect is more an uncomfortable nuisance than an ecological hazard. Again, there is little to choose between mini- and large-scale plants.

Lessons in sustainable development

Resource sustainability

Capital resources allocated to cement production in India are not inefficiently utilized. An abundance of the major raw materials and an efficient machinery manufacturing capability mean that cement production is an economically sustainable activity.

To the extent that VSK plants make better use of capital, material and transport resources, they enhance the sustainability of cement production. Their relative inefficiency in the utilization of energy resources, however, is a major disadvantage in a country where good quality coal is in short supply and power shortages are a chronic problem. Overall, therefore, there is little difference in resource sustainability between the two sectors.

Indigenous capabilities

The negligible import content of VSK machinery compared with the 25 per cent of modern large-scale cement plants not only saves foreign exchange but also implies that the capability to manufacture the former type of machinery is fully indigenized. Coupled with the better local availability of skills and higher labour content of mini-plant operation, this suggests a greater sustainability of VSK technology diffusion. In managerial terms VSK also has an advantage in that the necessary commitment for efficient production of quality output is more likely to be provided by the proprietorial control typical of mini-plants than by the hired management of the large-scale sector. At the same time, the growth of the MCP sector helps disperse production facilities and contributes to the spread of an industrial culture.

In development terms, however, under present conditions the VSK is essentially a static technology. Its use is on the decline internationally, and an atmosphere of doubt about its capabilities exists in India. Little active research is being undertaken to improve its energy or economic efficiency. Large-scale rotary kiln production, on the other hand, is under constant R&D with expanding frontiers and growing technical sophistication. For a country like India with a growing technical capability, investment in large-scale technology represents an investment in technology assimilation and skill development as well as in efficient production. The indigenous capability and dispersion effects of MCPs cannot become a prescription for abandoning large-scale cement production altogether.

The consideration of VSK cement production as an appropriate technology for Indian conditions is constrained by the requirement that all cement produced and sold should conform to the standards of Portland cement. MCPs cannot supply Portland cement at prices significantly below the prevailing market prices determined by the large companies. But if lower standards are acceptable for certain applications, the relative flexibility of VSK operation could be used to supply cheaper cement. MCPs' effect on overall availability is also limited, though in restricted areas of chronic shortage (characterized by long supply lines and difficult transport conditions) they can have a significant effect on availability and price.

Balancing MCPs' resource efficiency against energy inefficiency, their indigenous sustainability and industrial dispersion against technical stagnation, and their locational convenience against (some) pollution, no definite conclusion in their favour emerges. However, in countries with a low reserve of technical and managerial skills, in the short and medium term, the industrial dispersion effects of mini-plants will have a positive developmental effect. If the technical stagnation of VSKs continues, the large-scale plant will emerge as more sustainable in the long run for large, easily accessible markets.

PART 4

Planning Techniques for Sustainable Development

CHAPTER 4

Planning Techniques for Sustainable Development

COLIN P. REES

Senior Environment Specialist, Asian Development Bank

The rapidly evolving Third World calls for environmental planning strategies and techniques that match its dynamic qualities. Such strategies and techniques must provide for adjustments to biophysical, economic, socio-cultural and political changes. Socio-cultural and political changes are frequently ignored, partly as a response to the charge of "meddling in politics" and partly because it is felt they are difficult to measure. Yet if environmental planning is to be effective, these factors must receive greater attention.

Unstable political regimes tend to create institutions and then dissolve them before they acquire sufficient experience and expertise. Environmental planning must emphasize activities that can endure these changes. It is particularly important that environmental planning has the support and sympathy of the people. Issues must be presented so that they may compete successfully for attention and maintain commitment. All too often, environmental issues are considered trivial save for the need to respond to flooding, starvation, pollution incidents and industrial accidents.

Attitudes towards environmental problems often vary from one group of people to another, with the result that environmental planning that assumes homogeneous attitudes may face serious difficulties in implementation. Wherever possible, planning activities should conform to the contours of a nation's diverse cultural patterns.

In many developing countries the public institutional mechanisms required for environmental planning and management are weak. Consequently, environmental planning is best operated as an alliance with powerful and influential sectors such as agriculture and industry.

The conceptual elegance of the techniques of environmental planning should be subordinated to pragmatism and the realities of implementation.

The author wishes to acknowledge the help given by his colleagues at the Asian Development Bank: Keith Johnson, Bindu Lohani, Pieter Smidt, Peter Thomas and Helen Cruda.

Levels of planning in developing countries

In developing countries there are usually four levels of planning and decision-making: national, regional, sectoral and project.

National level. National policies are formulated and passed on to the regional, sectoral and project levels within the national organization of government. Policy objectives and priorities, macroeconomic objectives and finance and monetary considerations are discussed as a prelude to enunciating development programmes. Examples include national development plans and national annual budgets. Both the plans and the budgets are subdivided into regional and sectoral units, each of which may be further divided into project units. Increasingly, development plans review environmental and natural resources conditions and indicate how development might proceed in terms of legislation, environmental planning and management and investment programmes. At the national level, planning techniques for sustainable development have been expressed in the form of national conservation strategies and country environmental profiles.

Regional level. Regional-level planning involves decisions on a number of interrelated projects that typically cover a plan and programme of work. Examples include watershed development, agricultural development, fish and wildlife management and forest management plans. Regional development planning is another example and may involve urban development. With the current vogue for decentralization, sub-regional-level planning is being adopted at the district or village level.

Sectoral level. The sectoral level involves planning and management of development programmes undertaken by a specific ministry at the national or regional level. Such programmes usually entail separate projects distributed geographically over the nation or a region and are scheduled over a number of years. Examples include: a national fisheries development policy and strategy study; a national or regional forestry management sector study; an urban sector profile dealing with strategic issues in urban development. Banks and bilateral agencies have supported in-country sector studies in an attempt to provide a rational basis for their future operations. Some have utilized their experience on a regional basis to guide their overall policies and programmes and furnish information to developing countries and outside agencies.

Project level. Defined as a relatively self-contained group of activities consisting of physical facilities, management and implementation incentives, a project is the most basic level of planning and decision-making. Examples include: construction and operation of an impoundment scheme to provide irrigation water, hydroelectric power and flood control; a forest management scheme to produce forest products; and low-income housing for poverty eradication.

Development funding agencies employ various environmental planning and management techniques at the national, regional, sectoral and project levels. Because impacts on natural systems are perceived and measured more readily at the project level (especially in the short term) than at higher levels of management, planning techniques have been better developed to influence the various decision points in the project cycle than for other planning levels.

Planning techniques for sustainable development

National-level planning

Country environmental profiles. Environmental profiles vary in format, style, statement of national conditions and methodology of preparation. The general objectives include: description of a nation's physical, socio-cultural and economic condition; the status of its resources; major environmental issues and problems; evaluation of legal and institutional aspects of natural resource management; recommendations for action (including projects) to identify new opportunities and solve problems. Such profiles have been completed by the US Agency for International Development for many of the countries of Latin America, the Caribbean and Asia and for some in Africa. An example of this approach is treated in Case Study 21.

National conservation strategies. National conservation strategies help a government define policies, programmes, institutional arrrangements and action plans necessary to ensuring environmentally sound development and the sustainable use of natural resources. The process combines data collection, consultation with governmental and non-governmental interests and negotiations about objectives and appropriate implementation. Case Study 23 exemplifies this technique.

Country strategy studies. Against the background of major environmental and natural resources problems and constraints, country strategy studies include coverage of environmental issues in each development sector, planning and management needs, and development programmes and projects with which to correct/prevent critical damage to environmental and natural resources. This approach has been used by the Asian Development Bank for a number of its member countries.

Regional-level planning

Neither comprehensive planning nor purely sectoral approaches to project planning and design are thought appropriate for developing countries. Comprehensive planning has proven too expensive, time-consuming, detailed and vulnerable; it is also rarely converted into action. Likewise, sectoral planning as a simple grouping of projects often induces conflicts – one sector or interest group competing with another for goods and services. Neither approach is suitable for achieving consistency and efficiency in integrating environmental considerations in the development process. Hence an intermediate approach is being adopted, variously called integrated regional development planning, master planning, economic-cum-environmental studies or ecological profiling. Other approaches to regional-level planning include land-use planning, though it may be applied equally to national and local levels.

Integrated regional development planning. Integrated regional development planning is characterized by: (1) diagnosis of the major problems and potentials of a given area: (2) preparation of a development strategy; (3) formulation of a co-ordinated "package" of infrastructure, production and services. The planning technique has been utilized in South America and Asia, and its efforts to assemble potential projects into investment "packages" is seen as an innovation. Case Study 19 covers this approach. Some countries have taken initiatives wherein all development projects conform with master plans. In others, regional master plans have been drawn up taking into consideration environmental and natural resources potentials.

Ecological profiling. Ecological profiling generates a spatial configuration of all relevant environmental factors. Conclusions and recommendations are offered in terms of critical areas and projects, mitigation measures and guidelines. Since the results are based mostly on qualitative data, the technique is best applied as an early warning system to indicate areas likely to be affected by development activities.

Land-use planning. Land-use planning provides guidance, and sometimes a control, for the sustainable development of natural resources. As part of land-use planning, land capability assessment helps promote an understanding of the relationships between land and the uses to which it is to be put and to present planners with land-use alternatives. To prove effective, the range of land uses considered has to be relevant to the physical and socioeconomic context of the area, and the alternatives must incorporate socioeconomic considerations. Two approaches are elaborated in Case Studies 20 and 22.

Sectoral-level planning

Since socioeconomic sectors are numerous and the problems in each sector vary from country to country, it has not been possible to formulate a model sectoral strategy applicable to all the countries. These strategies also have to accommodate historical, cultural, religious, philosophical, social and economic traditions and perspectives along with scientific and technological advances.

Environment sector reviews. These review current environmental policies and measures, preparing a conceptual framework for future development of environmental policies and recommending measures for implementation. Such a review conducted by the government of Indonesia focused on resources management, integrated watershed management, integrated waste management, environmental management systems and human resource development.

Sector studies. Sector studies (or profiles) undertaken by international funding agencies attempt to assess the performance of given sectors (e.g. urban, fisheries) and to define policy issues. They also establish the need for further policy-oriented studies as input for the formulation of a national policy. These sector studies are becoming a popular planning tool.

Project-level planning

One of the consequences of single-purpose developments, e.g. housing, highways, industrial plants or hydropower projects, is that measures designed to solve one problem often create or exacerbate problems in another functional area, e.g. the stimulation of unplanned secondary development and dislocation of communities induced by highways. Such cross-sectoral interactions offer a major challenge to those conducting environmental planning and management; every effort should be made to ensure that there is a balance of disciplinary influence from the start. Some methods of achieving this are briefly described:

Environmental impact assessment (EIA). Many governments and international agencies have adopted EIA as a planning tool because of its well-defined, integrated procedures. However, due to the diversity of conditions under which economic development is implemented, approaches differ widely in terms of their legal/institutional base, focus and scope. EIA has been used traditionally in analysing the environmental impacts of large projects involving industry, power and infrastructure. EIA has also been employed for strengthening decision-making or altering behaviour of development agencies.

Some developing countries have generated a number of measures including: (1) appropriate guidelines for preparation of EIAs; (2) criteria for screening proposed development projects so that limited funds may be focused on projects likely to pose significant environmental impacts; (3) a preliminary EIA or initial environmental examination to reduce costs and time; (4) environmental focal points in the major implementing agencies of government, a mechanism by which environmental agencies may communicate directly with those executing development projects.

Although it may continue to be the predominant environmental planning technique for some time, EIA operates on a piecemeal, sectoral basis, often precluding a comprehensive and integrated view, e.g. the capacity to consider common waste collection, treatment and disposal systems, multiple use of natural resources, river basin development, etc. Likewise, the degree to which a particular development's exploitation of resources is at variance with overall regional needs may go unappraised. Thus it is often desirable to broaden the approach of EIA when cross-sectoral or regional development is involved. However, this is difficult because the predicted zone of a project's influence may not coincide with the developer's spatial or financial "boundaries".

Rapid assessment studies. The World Health Organization has developed a procedure to provide a preliminary integrated view of the magnitude of the air, water and land pollution in a given region or country and thereby a beginning to effective and comprehensive environmental pollution control planning. It is especially adapted to conditions in developing countries, primarily urban areas and industrial zones (WHO, 1981).

At the local or municipal level, rapid assessment studies have been used in formulating environmental monitoring programmes in a cost-effective way. They also allow quick pollution control action to be taken against the most severe environment-related public health problems. At the provincial or state level they are often used for setting priorities for pollution control programmes and for formulating laws and regulations. At the national level, inventories of pollution from regions or states can be combined to determine the appropriate balance between industrial and economic development and pollution control. They can also be used to formulate policies with regard to environmental protection in national development plans and in allocating resources and setting priorities.

Environmental guidelines. Many guidelines attempt to demonstrate the application of environmental planning techniques during the project cycle. At their best, they help impart information and experience through description of major problems and relationships, procedural steps, checklists, analytical methods and measures of mitigation or control. Over the years guidelines have become geared less to specifying what information is required for decision-making and more to explaining what steps an analyst or planner should follow to accomplish an environmental assessment or to undertake environmental planning and management of development projects.

Priorities and perspectives of developing country governments and donors

Developing country governments

In general, the relative importance accorded environmental problems is low, and the magnitude of such problems remains unmeasured. New policy directions in economic development are rarely subject to environmental screening.

Many of the financial and economic priorities of developing country governments remain inimical to environmental interests. Most are faced with debt burdens, promoting exports, reducing public spending and reforming price systems. Such pressures tend to shorten the time horizon, making it difficult to promote the sustainability of natural resources over the long term. In contrast, the rising concern over resource depletion and environmental degradation is beginning to affect decision-making and encourage a more reflective view.

Investment decisions can greatly affect the capacity to conduct environmental planning and management. Resettlement, irrigation, hydropower or mining schemes induce cross-sectoral impacts which, if not addressed, may impair implementation and operation. The willingness of a sectoral agency to seek advice and the ability of an environmental agency to respond are often in doubt. In many instances, environmental analysis has yet to play a substantive role in the preparation and execution of development programmes and projects; it is often treated as an add-on component.

Often the most critical component of environmental planning is implementation of policies and procedures. Relevant factors are those affecting the operation of the bureaucracy: political clout of environmental agencies, resources allocated to environmental activities, organizational effectiveness, administrative environmental controls, allocation of authority and timing of implementation.

In most developing countries those areas of government charged with integrating environmental considerations into economic development rarely have the power and influence to compete with agriculture, industry, transport or energy departments. Such areas are often inadequately funded or staffed for the assigned tasks. They are rarely consulted at the inception of development planning when decisions are made regarding project design. The organizational effectiveness of environmental agencies may be judged by their modest impact on public use of environmental resources.

Administrative environmental controls such as environmental assessment, land-use planning and environmental quality standards exist in many developing countries. However, because most of these controls are derived from procedures used in developed countries, modifications are required for them to be effective.

Multilateral development banks and bilateral agencies

The different structures and priorities of donors have a significant impact on the potential for environmentally sound development practices, including the choice of planning techniques for sustainable development. There are many competing interests, institutional constraints and implementation problems; any technique must accommodate multiple, sometimes conflicting demands.

Multilateral development banks. Multilateral development banks (MDBs) must ensure that their borrowers are creditworthy and that their loans support economically productive projects. They place a premium on the soundness of economic appraisal and the speed and efficiency of disbursement of funds. Invariably, their borrowers make the final decision on the scope of project appraisal, including location, design and implementation of projects. Because individual projects are often large and technically complex, their preparation and implementation become complex and time-consuming, discouraging the incorporation of special concerns during the project cycle. All these factors influence the choice of projects, the conditions that the banks attach to projects and their capacity to integrate non-economic issues.

The project cycle concept employed by the banks tends to put pressure on their staff to conduct straightforward, clean appraisals and to process the project quickly and efficiently. There is some leverage for environmental planning if it is demonstrated that significant financial and economic costs are at stake; however, such costs may also prove a disincentive for more detailed appraisal. The banks have a limited role in project execution. The borrowers are primarily responsible for construction and implementation, and, should they violate a loan agreement, there is little the banks can do save suspend disbursement of remaining funds.

Bilateral agencies. Bilateral agencies, being responsive if not subordinate to foreign ministries, promote their national interests as well as serving the developmental needs of borrowing governments. They are also influenced by domestic pressures to the extent that they must pursue certain development policies and support particular types of project in selected countries or sectors. Like MDBs, bilateral agencies serve to disburse funding, spending a minimum of time designing projects and paying little attention to long-term financial soundness.

The agencies often have the most elaborate environmental policies and

procedures and sometimes emphasize the importance of environmental planning and management. They often operate in-country and enjoy young,
committed and well-trained environmental staff augmented by support service
arrangements. Some agencies conduct "policy dialogues" with host countries
about the role of environmental and natural resources planning and management in economic development strategies.

Bilateral agencies nevertheless often prove cumbersome and are heavily laden
with policies and strategies. Field staff are few and overworked, and increasingly
the pressure is for "off-the-shelf" projects with a minimum of deviation and
innovation. Like MDBs, the intervention by special interests requiring time-
consuming procedures is met with little enthusiasm. Also like MDBs, they have
no programme concept of sustainable development.

Implications for environmental planning

The great variation in motives, mandates and perspectives of borrowing
governments and donors offers many challenges concerning the selection and use
of planning techniques for sustainable economic development. Conflicting goals
among donors are commonplace, but, since borrowing countries fear collusion
among the donors, there is little incentive for co-ordination. Traditional sectoral
relationships between borrower and donor are thus strengthened, integrative
relationships weakened. None the less donors have attempted to encourage
governments to establish more effective mechanisms for co-ordinating development decisions and many are conducting sectoral policy reviews to strengthen
co-ordination and planning and reduce the fragmentation of resource management decisions. The role of environmental focal points in this and other activities
is crucial.

We may summarize the implications for the selection and use of environmental planning techniques under the headings of time horizon, co-ordination and
integration, accountability and consultation, administration, and institutional
arrangements.

Time horizon. Governments and donors operate within the short term; they
rarely address questions of long-term sustainability. However, increasing
attention to the costs and benefits of natural resources usage encourages the
wider view. Country strategy studies and environmental profiling also promote
the notion of sustainable development at the macro-level and are beginning to
influence the mix of projects.

Co-ordination and integration. Because environmental management cuts across
sectoral responsibilities, problems of co-ordination and integration are frequent,
often generating conflicting goals. Environmental planning usually takes place
sporadically and in isolation. To solve this problem, co-operative arrangements
(e.g. with planning ministries or line agencies) are deliberately pursued by
development agencies at the outset of project preparation and design.

Accountability and consultation. Governments and donors are rarely held
accountable for the environmental results of programmes and projects. Few give
time to monitoring and managing environmental problems during implemen-

tation. There is also a reluctance to allow active participation of po\
affected populations; narrow political interests often prevail.

Administration. Government organizations and donors are subject to pr\
to meet budget deadlines, manage logistics and cope with limited inform\
This compromises their ability to respond to technical needs such as environmen-✳
tal soundness of development projects and programmes. Inadequate resources
and bureaucratic procedures tend to discourage interdisciplinary analysis and
continuity of effort.

Institutional arrangements. Governments and donors lack a framework for
adequate pursuit of environmental planning and management needs. Strengthening requirements, by means of on-the-job technology transfer, are often
attached to bolster experience in project execution and promote self-sufficiency,
but the results are variable.

Suitability and utility of analytical tools presented in the case studies

How have planning tools responded to these challenges (including implementation arrangements)? The case studies in this part of the book are drawn upon to
illustrate some approaches, and their success and failure are judged against some
of the criteria established earlier.

Integrated regional development planning, Ecuador (Case Study 19)

Recognizing the careful preparation required for a regional development study,
the Department of Regional Development of the Organization of American
States (OAS) fielded a preliminary mission to obtain information on the study
area, the government's goals and intended investment levels, the region's general
problems and potentials, and a knowledge of the agencies conducting the study
and implementing its results. Because problems encountered in development
planning invariably require multi-sectoral solutions, an integrated, multidisciplinary approach was adopted. The joint management of the study by national
counterpart agencies and the OAS helped mobilize local participation and
improved the likelihood of implementing the study's recommendations and
technology transfer.

The execution phase of the study culminated in an agreement with the
government stipulating an action plan and interrelated projects, the financial
commitments of the participants and recommendations for an investment
timetable and institutional arrangements. Local agencies and beneficiaries
participated in this process. The OAS accepted that the greatest challenge was
to get development plans implemented under the prevailing financial and
institutional conditions. Measures to ensure that the recommendations were
heeded were applied throughout the study.

The OAS helped ensure that funding for implementation was included in the
appropriate budget and helped the government prepare loan applications for
international financing agencies. The technique sought the involvement of local

farmers in its early phase, allowing timely consultation with the intended beneficiaries.

The role of the environmental management adviser in this project was critical. It is the capacity of the technique to deliver project "packages" along with care over institutional arrangements that separates it from the conventions of other techniques, such as master planning. However, the demands on the adviser are considerable, e.g. trying to keep the integrated "package" from unravelling, the inclusion of recommendations for border integration with Colombia and the application of the study approach to other parts of Ecuador.

In analysing the proposed strategy and projects in terms of their physical, economic, social and institutional feasibility, particular attention has to be given to establishing the functional links between regional planning and national and sectoral planning. This is particularly important if the development plan cannot be phased with a four- or five-year national plan.

Land capability classification based on the world life zone system, Bolivia (Case Study 20)

Land capability classification techniques have been subject to considerable debate. The UN Food and Agriculture Organization, with its now widely used "Framework for Land Evaluation" (1976) and recent *Guidelines for Rural Land Use Planning in Developing Countries* (1986), addresses the overall needs for such planning applicable to all levels of scale.

The technique deployed in this case study has extended the established bioclimatic zonation scheme of Holdridge (1967) to include technological management levels, cultural constraints on regional development, alternative systems of agriculture, improvement of traditional production systems, introduction of new crops/cropping systems and public management objectives for lands needing protection. An impressive array of specialists is deployed, ranging from sociologists and administrators of rural development programmes to land-use technologists and development planners. However, economic and socio-cultural considerations are subordinate to biophysical factors.

The technique has been deployed in Central and South America but has yet to be used to any significant degree in Asia and Africa. A three-week hands-on training programme in applied ecology and land capability classification helped develop the expertise of government technicians; and the ability of a Bolivian-based organization to exchange its own study results and field data with other institutions may have defrayed time and costs. None the less, the technique appears data hungry, and the need to generate a considerable volume of primary data may produce limitations.

The confrontation, described in the case study, over the land capability classification and project plans suggests a lack of consultation. Was this a product of management failure or a failure of the technique? Details about methods of integration, team structure, administration and liaison would have been useful in determining the utility of the technique.

Country environmental profile, Paraguay (Case Study 21)

In this case study, a compendium of useful information on natural resources and their deterioration has been assembled, and awareness of environmental problems has been stimulated. To some extent the issues of land distribution/ reform and social equity were explored. The process recognized that the barriers to solving environmental problems are not technical but social, political or institutional. Further, by analysing the relationship between development and the natural resource base at several planning levels, one of the themes of sustainable development was upheld. A number of important follow-up actions were executed.

However, a number of improvements may be suggested:

(1) Although the proposed actions – reflecting concerns over natural resources and environmental management – are general in nature and require further study for their implementation, more might have been accomplished had project briefs been produced as part of the profile.

(2) In the profile, appropriate institutions are specified for each proposed action, but estimates of their timing, duration and possible funding arrangements are not included. These would be useful to formulating a development strategy and involving the development community.

(3) The proposed actions are the product of a sectoral approach and remain somewhat piecemeal. Further discussion of the intersectoral conflicts affecting the environment and development would have generated greater integration and helped resolve the conflict between environmental advocates and affected parties and the vested interests of development.

(4) The interconnection of the problems of underdevelopment might have sharpened the section on environmental conservation and preservation policy. It might also have questioned top-down traditions in policy formulation with little or no grass-roots participation.

(5) A more finely focused analysis of the state of the environment would have benefited decision-makers.

Rapid rural appraisal, Pakistan (Case Study 22)

Rapid appraisal techniques have been developed in response to the need to analyse development options rapidly and cheaply and ensure that the ensuing recommendations support sustainable development. They involve village-level investigations by multidisciplinary teams, intensive workshop sessions and, most important, interviews with villagers. The development options are classified in terms of biophysical features and socioeconomic factors. Villagers are further involved in project feasibility studies wherein the costs and benefits and the capacity of the villagers to support a permanent management system are appraised.

The techniques employed are similar to land-use planning applied to traditional village farming, some communal village lands and commercial farmers' fields. They have strong appeal for undertaking rural planning but only in so far as the beneficiaries are discrete, small and homogeneous communities able to express their opinions and aspirations with confidence and clarity. Thus the techniques are likely to be increasingly limited in the development planning of sparsely settled and unsettled areas. However, the agroecosystem zoning technique employed is comparable to that of agro-ecological zonation commonly deployed in land resources evaluation and planning. Both have the advantage of linking national plans to local conditions.

Rapid rural planning techniques, still in the experimental stage, hold promise as long as their limitations and linkages to overall rural planning requirements are recognized. In this regard, we should heed the cautionary note of the case study's conclusion: "in general adoption of RRA techniques is, despite their design, constrained by lack of time and the pressure of other tasks in project management".

National conservation strategy, Zambia (Case Study 23)

National conservation strategies (NCSs), like country environmental profiles, started as largely technical, academic exercises. They were seen to lack application and relevance to developing country needs and often incurred suspicion. In response, the NCS and profiles have progressively focused more attention on the administrative and social structures of society and the interrelationships among social groups and resources. Development objectives are now assessed and appraised in relation to human values.

The Zambian NCS deliberately sought to reflect Zambian interests and to involve the people in the process. This was achieved by the establishment of a task force by the Minister of Lands and Natural Resources. The work was prepared by a 30-person technical group, representing the interests of various government, parastatal and private organizations. Early in the study, cross-sectoral interactions were examined. Obtaining consensus on basic policy matters helped identify priority activities.

Because of the sensitivity attached to criticizing Zambia's current five-year plan, it was considered more productive to attempt to incorporate the NCS in the forthcoming five-year plan. In the interim a few natural resource development projects have emerged.

A number of difficulties were encountered, some of which remain unresolved. The short period of seven months curtailed some activities such as detailed evaluations to determine appropriate investment strategies and demonstrating the value of conservation. The grass-roots view might have been strengthened by an appropriately scaled social survey along with the cultivation of selected MPs.

The current lack of a coherent development planning process is cause for concern, for it may balk NCS activities in the short and medium term. Of equal concern is the lack of significant investment to complement NCS activities. Finally, more attention might have been given to the broad costs of environmental degradation. This may have helped rank development options and investment needs.

Success and failure of planning techniques ✳

The diversity of natural and socio-cultural environments, resource endowments, development policies, programmes and projects and institutional structures among the developing countries does not allow for the formulation of a general approach to planning sustainable development. Nevertheless, some common factors appear:

(1) The need to respect human concerns, values and goals. It is vital that the plan has the sympathy of the affected groups.
(2) Ecological, social and economic interactions must be examined and any conflicts resolved to the extent possible; i.e. the technique should be consensus-building.
(3) There should be flexibility to cope with the unexpected, e.g. failure of communication and co-ordination, unplanned decisions.
(4) The whole development process should be engaged (not just the environmental authorities), and strategic ties with the decision-making process assured.
(5) The paramount importance of developing a sound and adequate data base.
(6) An appreciation of the manpower and skills required and the possibility of transferring skills should be judged against administrative strengths and weaknesses.
(7) The time and cost required, and supporting needs, should be gauged against available local expertise and facilities.
(8) Whenever possible the technique should avoid being expatriate-expert-dependent but at the same time assure quality team leadership; the outlook of the expatriate planner may be inimical to the best "fit".
(9) The technique should ensure development acts emerge from the study/technique and that they can be supported by the people and by the government for funding.

Economic development strategies have shifted away from the "trickle-down" approach towards planning strategies that target investment directly to disadvantaged groups and specific problems. If planners appreciate the historical, social and cultural background in which they intervene, this can lead to more acceptable decisions.

Future trends

The changing perceptions and requirements of the donor and borrower have encouraged the exploration of new approaches to the development of environmental and natural resources; these are likely to influence the use of current planning techniques and shape those to come. They include such activities as macroeconomic analysis and information technology, the employment of NGOs and the need for public participation.

Several development agencies, particularly the World Bank (1987) and

United Nations (UN Statistical Office, 1987), in addition to establishing policies and procedures for integrating natural resources issues into individual project analysis, are attempting to engage the broader context. This is in response to the growing awareness that many environmental problems originate not only from individual large-scale development projects but from the interactions and accumulated impacts of a myriad of activities. A nationwide or regional approach is being entertained as a supplement to the project-by-project approach to environmental planning.

Powerful though these and other tools may be in the quest for sustainable development, pricing and regulatory interventions and structural adjustment may prove the most effective devices in influencing resource use. The challenge to the environmental planner will be to find appropriate techniques. Land-use planners will continue to use conventional remote sensing technologies including satellite imagery and aerial photography for general inventory-taking of land resources and associated land uses. Increasing use will be made of information technology as a basis for planning. There will be increasing demand for techniques more suited to assessing and monitoring change.

Donor agencies are likely to see increased use of such technology for general planning purposes. The installation and development of in-country capabilities for natural resource analysis and management are now recognized as crucial to the attainment of sustainable development. To maximize the utility of these techniques, several donor agencies encourage the wider use of land-use planning analysis and mechanisms in reviewing potential loans. The greater deployment of multi-disciplinary teams and the more general use of integrated planning projects may be anticipated.

Systems analysis, using digitized information, is now used in a number of developing countries. One method – integrated planning technology – addresses the complexity of multiple-resource development and provides improved understanding of how resource systems interact to alter the results of a plan or project. Integrated planning technology also provides a workshop environment where participants outline the structure of important portions of a resource system.

As development activity increasingly impinges on the marginal areas of developing countries and tribal settlements or ethnic minorities, the socio-cultural content of environmental planning is likely to become more substantive. Several agencies have sociological guidelines in place which are beginning to influence development projects and programmes. NGOs representing indigenous peoples and conservation interests are expected to play a seminal role. Their intimate knowledge of local conditions, ability to reach the poor and flexible and cost-effective services have encouraged co-operative arrangements with the aid agencies and developing country governments. NGOs in future may be expected to act as consultants or contractors, trainers, executing or co-operating agencies and co-financiers.

The integration of environmental planning in the development process may be facilitated by public participation. Some developing country governments tentatively support informed public involvement by providing better information through the media or ensuring consultation through selected representatives of communities. Other governments support public hearings through access to the courts and local referendums.

References

FAO (1976), "A framework for land evaluation", *Soils Bulletin* 32. UN Food and Agriculture Organization, Rome.

FAO (1986), *Guidelines for Rural Land Use Planning in Developing Countries*. UN Food and Agriculture Organization, Rome.

Holdridge, L. R. (1967), *Life Zone Ecology*. Tropical Science Center, San José, Costa Rica.

United Nations Statistical Office (1987), *Environmental Accounting and the Standard System of National Accounts*. Environment Statistics Section, New York.

World Bank (1987), "Environment, growth and development", paper prepared for the Development Committee at its April meeting.

World Health Organization (1981), *Rapid Assessment of Sources of Air, Water and Land Pollution*, Offset Publication No. 62. WHO, Geneva.

CASE STUDY 19 *Integrated Regional Development Planning, Santiago and Mira River Basins, Ecuador*

RICHARD SAUNIER

Environmental Management Advisor, Department of Regional Development, Organization of American States

The Organization of American States (OAS) attempts to create and/or organize projects into a "unified" development strategy over a piece of landscape; to formulate a development strategy and ideas for projects and programmes that are compatible with one another and with the needs of the affected populations, suitable for the place in terms of its history, culture and economics, within limitations of time, funding and information. Development and development planning are continuing processes, both objects and instruments of change. Integrated regional development planning seeks to make this change positive and palatable. The aim is to improve quality of life for a target population so that the conflicts inherent in the process are reduced to a minimum.

A full discussion of the project described in this case study is given in the book *Integrated Regional Development Planning: Guidelines and Case Studies from OAS Experience* (OAS/USAID, Washington, 1984).

Development planning in the Santiago-Mira river basins (Phase 1)

Background

The Santiago and Mira river basins cover nearly 25,000 sq km along Ecuador's border with Colombia. The region is diverse. One of the three provinces, Esmeraldas, is coastal, while Carchi and Imbabura are primarily Andean. Population of the area is nearly 600,000 and population growth is rapid.

In 1978 Ecuador's National Planning Board, later the National Development Council, asked the OAS to provide technical assistance to study the region and to prepare a development "plan". Costs for all international technical assistance and some operating expenses were borne by the OAS Program of Technical Cooperation, amounting over the three years of the project to nearly $500,000. Costs of an additional $950,000 for in-country travel, national professional and support staff and office space were borne by the Ecuadorian government.

The Santiago-Mira region is a patchwork of contrasting sub-regions: the

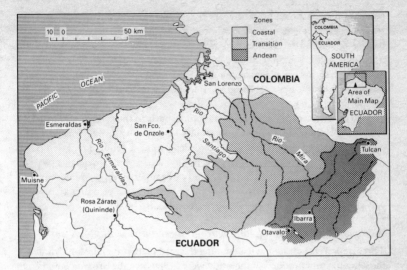

Map 4: Santiago-Mira region, Ecuador

Andean zone, the transition zone and the coastal zone (see Map 4).

The Andean zone has a high population density and is ethnically diverse. Rural settlements are supported by agricultural production. Resources have been over-used; limited water is exploited through a system of groundwater extraction and irrigation. Salinization has become a problem, and run-off carrying the many chemicals used in agriculture threatens the region's lakes. The Andean zone is the most prosperous.

The coastal zone consists of the lower Mira, Santiago and Esmeraldas river basins where lack of connections to the Andean zone hampers development. The port of Esmeraldas has access to Quito but at the time of the study lacked easy access to the north. The northern port of San Lorenzo was isolated from the rest of the region. The coastal zone consists of dry tropical savannah on rolling hills to the south, and lowlands and wet tropical forests to the north. Exploitation of the forest and migrating farmers were impeding forest management. The urban centres of Esmeraldas and San Lorenzo suffered from significant under-employment.

The third sub-region, a sparsely populated *transition zone* between the Andean zone and the coast, consists of steeply sloping forested "piedmont" which appears suitable for hydroelectric development. Data were needed to determine whether such development would serve the whole region well and how it would affect water- and land-use patterns downstream in the river valleys.

Objectives and management structure

The following objectives were identified for the two-year workplan: (1) promote internal regional integration; (2) increase the region's production, employment opportunities, income and social services; (3) define institutional options for a regional development authority; (4) produce a model regional plan or strategy having potential use elsewhere in Ecuador; (5) design development projects using soil, water, flora and fauna in accordance with regional social realities; (6) develop a regional water management plan. An extra-regional goal, included at the request of the Ecuadorian government, was to identify the potential for frontier integration with Colombia.

Two government agencies acted as counterparts to the OAS personnel. The National Planning Board had responsibility for planning seven of the country's eight regions and wanted an integrated development model for use in other regions. The sectoral (water-use) agency's more specific objective was to formulate a national water plan. The study was supervised by an international director, a national director, a co-ordinating committee of representatives of government agencies and an executive commission.

Workplan design/the role of environmental management adviser

Three steps were considered in designing the workplan: principles for identifying the activities and products of the study were developed; the project components were identified, and the components were sequenced. Fourteen study tasks were identified, and the workplan developed so that the tasks would be accomplished through six working groups.

Of particular relevance to sustainable development is the work done on "identification and resolution of potential conflicts". These analyses were conducted during Phase 1. They looked towards the identification and notification of parties that would be affected by the potential development strategy, its projects and programmes. The region's major ecosystems were described, the goods and services available from them were examined, and existing development proposals were reviewed.

The concepts underlying the analyses included the following. Negative environmental impacts are the result of development activities or natural hazardous phenomena which enforce the non-use of goods and services, impoverish or destroy goods and services or intensify hazardous events. All examples of negative "environmental impact" can be described as conflicts between two or more interest groups, the majority of which can be assigned to economic development sectors. These can almost always be identified with existing public agencies. Once potential conflicts are identified, all involved parties must be notified, since only those parties can provide a satisfactory solution to that conflict.

For each ecosystem, potential conflicts between development activities were identified by making a preliminary evaluation of the effect on the goods and services of the more obvious potential development activities and allowing the involved sectors to draw their own conclusions. The effort was not intended to show the value of one proposed activity over others; however, a strategy cannot be put forward with internal conflict still present.

In addition to characterizing the area's environmental units, the environmental management advisers evaluated several large projects that national agencies had proposed for the region. Using a sector-by-sector list, the advisers located proposed and existing development projects on a regional map before assessing how each would affect other development opportunities.

Another method used to uncover potential conflicts between activities was to develop a matrix arraying development sectors along both axes. With respect to each cell in the matrix, the question was asked, ''What will be the effect of activity (x) on activity (y)?'' Identifying and analysing trade-offs early in the planning sequence led to tremendous savings, whether through substituting better alternatives or abandoning projects that would prove unworkable. The idea was to guide investment towards the best all-around development alternatives.

The study's environmental management advisory report summarized the region's opportunities and development constraints and set forth a broad range of recommendations. The report called attention to the economic importance of the estuary at San Lorenzo; a habitat for many coastal fish and a breeding, spawning and nursery area for deep-sea species, it could also supply food for local, regional and national markets. For the humid tropical forests of Esmeraldas the study team recommended that methods be sought for sustained forest production instead of the current method of clear-cutting which allowed later occupation of the deforested lands by agricultural or livestock interests.

The regional development strategy (Phase 2)

Phase 1's 32 sectoral reports were integrated into a synthesis document reviewed by the government. Then during Phase 2 a number of working groups helped to formulate the regional development strategy, which included the water-use plan, institutional arrangements, mining programme, feeder-road programme, agricultural projects, forest industries development programme, forestry projects, agro-industry projects, irrigation projects, housing programme and education plan. A four-year investment plan was developed. The report was submitted to the National Planning Agency for review and forwarded to other national sectoral agencies for use in implementing projects.

The study took three years and involved 129 person-months of OAS specialists and 520 person-months of Ecuadorian counterparts. The final report contained sector assessments, the regional development strategy and 110 project proposals grouped in five programmes: (1) basic government conservation and research services; (2) integrated rural development and colonization; (3) direct production; (4) economic infrastructure; (5) social infrastructure.

Implementation

The project's final report was presented to the Ecuadorian government in May 1981. One year later an OAS staff member assessed the impact of the plan by interviewing officials in the national agencies most closely involved. The results of that assessment follow.

Regional development authority. The understanding, indeed one of the objectives of the project, was that a new development authority would be created for the region. That regional authority has not yet been created although it continues to be promoted by the National Planning Agency. Despite an effort during the project to gain the support of the provincial and municipal authorities for creating it, there is disagreement on where the authority should be located. The three provincial capitals all wanted to be the seat. Negotiations focus on safeguards to ensure that the regional seat would distribute development funds to the other provinces.

Institution-building. Many of the sectoral projects are moving through the process despite budget restrictions, and the study has been an unqualified success as a spur to institution-building. The study was designed to break down workplan preparation into manageable serial tasks leading to an integrated rather than sectoral approach. Other studies of this nature have now been designed in this new way by the counterpart agencies.

Border integration. Progress is being made towards the study's goal of better integrating the border between Colombia and Ecuador. There are several opportunities for the two countries to enjoy economies of scale in the provision of services and the production and marketing of goods.

Environmental management. Ten additional river basins in Ecuador have been analysed using the same methods by national teams. The analyses helped Ecuadorian planners identify misbegotten development proposals before funds were committed.

A seminar was given to the counterpart institutions to explain the methods for determining environmental units, natural goods and services and potential conflicts over their use; this proved very useful. Since the creation of the regional authority is still a strong possibility, a final evaluation of the project's success cannot be made. Meantime, the Santiago-Mira basin study serves as a planning model in several Ecuadorian agencies, and many of the projects proposed by the team are under way.

Lessons Learned

A number of lessons can be learned from this case study regarding planning. Also, a number of points can be made that may help us approach a viable understanding of "environment and development".

(1) The use of the concept of "natural goods and services" as opposed to the less specific "natural resources" is valuable in understanding the dynamics of a region, especially those of land use. Natural systems, when broken down into the numerous goods and services they contain, help identify the interest groups and institutions that must become involved in the development planning process if conflicts are to be avoided.

(2) An integrated development plan such as this, no matter how well executed, can unravel over time. The more politically and economically powerful sectors can begin to implement their projects before the others, and this

tends to disintegrate the development strategy. One way to evade this is to have a "Phase 3" that guides execution of the integrated strategy. This normally means the establishment of a regional development authority. Another way is to have an arrangement with a funding institution that will guide and fund execution of the full strategy. Without the assurance of funds for co-ordinated execution, there is no assurance of "sustainability".

(3) All identified internal conflicts must be resolved before the strategy is presented. Putting forward a strategy which contains incompatible projects leads to frustration. Interest groups who feel themselves trod upon will find ways to obstruct or even bring down development projects seen as harmful to their interests. The disagreement over the regional authority's site illustrates how problems arise if conflicts are not resolved early on.

CASE STUDY 20 *Land Capability Classification Based on the World Life Zone System, Bolivia*

JOSEPH A. TOSI Jr

Tropical Science Center, San José, Costa Rica

In the humanly developed landscape, sustainable productivity of plants and animals depends primarily upon achievement of a proper fit between land utilization and the biological and physical environment. Such a fit exists perfectly in the association or site-specific community of plants and animals which prevails in the unmodified natural ecosystem. Human societies, unlike nature, however, have difficulty adjusting their artificial, economically directed plant communities to fit the environment. Until recently their only recourse was to trial and error methods, which, whilst wasteful of resources and inefficient economically, led over centuries to practical, tradition-perpetuated cropping, grazing and forestry systems, affording the highest sustainable yields possible at a given cultural level of development.

In recent times much rural cultural stability and traditional farming wisdom has become the victim of industrial and population growth, migration and world-wide movement to "modernize" agriculture and human life. Not only has valuable knowledge, including plant and animal genetic material, been lost, but the physical and biological foundations for future land-based productivity and security are now in jeopardy. Fortuitously, an alternative to the trial-and-error method for adapting land use to site qualities is now at hand. The scientific revolution which seems to have got us into trouble also provides the tools for its resolution. This paper describes and gives examples of the application of one of these tools: integrated ecological land-use capability classification.

Land capability classification is customarily portrayed upon maps or photomaps. The methodology greatly increases the accuracy and efficiency of plans for sustainable, resource-conserving, rural development. The overlay comparison of an ecologically integrated land capability map with maps of current land use and vegetational cover indicates where, how and to what degree present land use deviates from true capability – the technically determined use required to achieve the highest permanently sustainable productivity at any given location.

In settled areas these comparisons provide for correction or adjustments to existing patterns of land use and to possible intensification of farming, grazing or forestry. In areas of little or no present human occupancy they serve to establish the feasibility, location and needs of proposed settlement and development, as well as indicating areas unsuitable for economic uses other than wildland protection and management. Correctly applied, they point the way to sustainable development.

Historical overview

Modern land capability classification appears to have its origins in the US Department of Agriculture's (USDA) soil conservation programmes begun during the years of the Great Depression.

Early and later land classification models

In 1962 USDA published its *Agricultural Handbook No. 210* covering "land capability and classification", a soils survey-based system incorporating features developed in the 1930s. This classification was widely adopted and had a tremendous influence among agronomists. The system helps farmers interpret a soils map according to their needs, helps any user of a soils map better understand its meanings and provides for land-use planning on the basis of soil potentialities, use limitations and management problems.

Land capability classification became identified almost exclusively with soils and soils science. Because soils technicians are drawn largely from the field of agronomy, this system contains a strong bias to agricultural land-use regardless of environmental constraints. This bias, enhanced by the development ideology of the green revolution, led to unsubstantiated premises, subjectivity in field evaluations and lack of specificity to culturally determined constraints. Its application to regions ecologically dissimilar to that of its temperate-zone origins, and its widespread misuse, led to grossly over-optimistic predictions of land capability, particularly in less developed regions.

In a few countries of the American tropics, specifically some of those where the "world life zone system of ecological classification" devised by L. R. Holdridge (*Life Zone Ecology*, Tropical Science Center, San José, 1967) has come into application under government auspices, the pedological-agronomic hegemony has been challenged or replaced by a more holistic ecological and socio-cultural methodology. Peru led the way in 1970 with a new and radically different ecologically based system. This was officially adopted in 1972. In 1971 an improved version was prepared for Colombia. Since then a more refined version has been produced in Costa Rica.

Evolution of a specialized land classification institute

Prior to the work in Costa Rica, I participated as an ecological land-use consultant in a USAID-sponsored multidisciplinary environmental assessment of the Chapare region of Bolivia. This region, comprising some 422,000 ha in the wet, forested eastern Andean piedmont and adjacent lowland plain, was then under consideration, and subsequently granted financing, for a major rural development programme focused upon coca eradication. A detailed field map was made of the life zones of the region. Employing that map and existing landform and soils studies, a provisional land capability map was improvised employing the improved Colombian model of the classification.

By analysing the comparative suitability of lands for sustainable human occupancy and socioeconomic development in relation to past and present development activities in the region, this study demonstrated the scope, capabilities and efficiency of the methodology. The analysis showed that both officially held and widely popularized belief in a high agricultural potential for the Chapare were in error. It showed how the ongoing development process might be reoriented to take advantage of the opportunities offered by the ecological circumstances of the region and set up guidelines for such a reorientation.

Two of the Bolivian technicians who had participated as national counterparts in the Chapare exercise, and had been introduced to the concepts and trained in the methodology employed, were sufficiently impressed to seek opportunities for its further application in their country. They convinced USAID in Bolivia to sponsor an intensive short training course in the new system at the end of 1983. Twenty-five of the country's most experienced geologists, geographers, soils technicians, biologists and planners participated. The best of these were later recruited as technical cadre for the new Centro de Investigación y Estudio de la Capacidad de Uso Mayor de la Tierra (CUMAT) in 1984.

CUMAT is a private, non-profit Bolivian institute initially funded by USAID. Today CUMAT contracts with national and international public and private entities in Bolivia to conduct land capability surveys, usually of areas to be, or in the process of being, opened for agricultural settlement, but also of long-settled areas with serious problems of erosion or low productivity.

Life zone ecology and land-use capability

Ecological foundations: the life zone system

As its primary criteria, the integrated ecological land capability classification employs a structural matrix of bio-climatic factors, specifically those which define the life zones within Holdridge's "world life zone system of ecological classification". The latter is a three-level hierarchical system in which bio-climate stands in a primordial and independent position relative to all other site factors. Each life zone is an equally weighted ecological division of the Earth's climatic continuum. At the second level in this hierarchy, each individual life zone encompasses a set of natural ecosystems, termed "associations". While any association is restricted to the limits of a given life zone, its precise nature and geographic distribution correspond to discrete qualitiative characteristics in the overall complex of local site conditions.

While the association is a geographically stable unit as a physical site or habitat, ecosystem variability is introduced locally by short-term changes in the vegetational cover and associated soil and biota due to natural disturbances and those caused by human land-using activities. Recognition of the successive stages (vegetational cover) of each distinctive association is accomplished at this third, most detailed, local level. Some associations, as physical sites, afford numerous options in the way of farming, grazing or forestry for permanently sustainable land use; others have few or none that are "economic" except in the public benefit sense.

Land use is a human-cultural phenomenon. Culture is therefore also a determinant of sustainable land-use options. For example, on a site or sites characterized by a warm, temperate, semi-arid bio-climate, deep, fertile, well-drained alluvial soils afford a clean-tilled cropping option only to peoples possessing the cultural and economic capability for irrigation. Without this technological capacity, land-use capability on these sites is limited to extensive grazing or non-use (protection). Site quality, then, sets the range of options within which choices become further restricted by locational, socio-cultural and economic factors. These last are also broadly "ecological" factors, but they are subordinate to the physical factors.

The ecological land-use capability classification system

The land-use capability classification employed by CUMAT in Bolivia recognizes only five classes of vegetational land use. In descending order of use intensity these are: (1) clean-tilled (or annual) cropping; (2) grazing; (3) untilled (or permanent) cropping; (4) production from managed natural forests (sustained yield forestry); (5) protection (of site under undisturbed natural vegetation). As use intensity diminishes, costs (effort) and returns (productivity) per unit of area worked also diminish. This relationship may be altered in economic terms by relative scarcity or abundance of higher-quality sites nearby.

The higher the use capability class on this scale, the greater the number of ecological options there often are for alternative but less intensive major uses. A site suitable for permanent clean-tillage of annual crops might qualify also for all the less intensive uses below it on the scale. This affords latitude in planning, should current economic or social conditions not be favourable locally in a given time to clean-tillage of field crops. But a site whose highest capability is untilled permanent cropping would, at best, have only forest production and protection as alternatives. Conversely, while a higher-quality agricultural site might afford better physical conditions for forestry than a forest production class site, the option for forestry there would be economically unavailable unless there were no demand for any alternative higher use.

The methodology

Out of a multiplicity of possible ecological factors, only 12 are employed in this system for the determination of major land-use capability. As noted, the first of these is bio-climate measured as life zone. Within each life zone, a series of quantitative values are set for each of 11 topographic, drainage and soils parameters, which function as determinants of capability class limits. These parameters include land gradient, flood hazard and soil depth, texture, fertility and permeability.

The values for each of these parameters are measured directly in the field on individually delineated, ecologically homogeneous landscape units. Land capability is then established by referring the measured values to a field-manual table of values corresponding to the life zone in which the site occurs. Land capability classes are identified, not only as a function of the collective values for these physical parameters, but variably as a function of one of four land management technological levels; these socio-culturally defined levels are termed (1) primitive, (2) traditional, (3) advanced, artesanal, (4) advanced, mechanized.

Application of the system in Bolivia

CUMAT began its activities in 1984 with two pilot studies commissioned by the provincial development corporations of La Paz and Santa Cruz. Each study covered about 50,000 ha.

The first area was located in the climatically moist-to-wet subtropical piedmont and adjacent outwash plains on the eastern foot of the Andes. A base camp was established near the native Indian town of Tumupasa. All CUMAT technicians were assembled there to participate in three weeks' hands-on training in applied ecology and in the land capability classification. Following the initial training period, which initiated the field survey work in Tumupasa, half the technical cadre were transferred to Santa Cruz to begin the companion study.

Study objectives included providing state and private institutions, particularly the development corporations, with a valid instrument for planning sustainable long-term development, and training and enhancing the professional capabilities of CUMAT technicians in the methodologies.

In 1985 COTESU, the Swiss Technical Co-operation Mission, commissioned a major study by CUMAT for the Alto Beni region of La Paz Province. Alto Beni is an area of intense planned and spontaneous colonization. COTESU, already involved there in development programmes, recognized a need for guidance based on sound knowledge of the physical and biological bases for agricultural and forestry development. The Alto Beni project has been projected into a second phase in which CUMAT will provide continuing long-term assistance. Pilot areas of the valley have been selected where advisers from CUMAT will participate in planning and executing plans at the level of the individual farm for communal co-operative settlers' organizations.

CUMAT expanded its staff to undertake several other projects in 1986. A study was undertaken in the area of Altamarani-Rurrenabaque (La Paz Province). The area covers some 81,000 ha and has been proposed as a suitable site for a major agricultural settlement project intended to benefit out-of-work tin miners from the Andean highlands. In July 1986 the departmental government was joined by powerful interests in the national government urging the pursuit of this scheme, for which a $60 million loan was being tendered by the World Bank. A team of foreign experts hired by the World Bank, with CUMAT technicians as counterparts, spent four months developing a senario for this project.

The original field survey by CUMAT, however, turned out results which belie, in large part, the public and official belief that the area can be successfully developed as proposed. Poor soils and poor drainage were determined to be the principal constrains. But the consultants contracted by the World Bank set up an adversary position, belittled or ignored the land capability classification as shown on the maps of the CUMAT survey and submitted a report pressing for the ecologically and economically unrealistic project plan desired by the authorities. CUMAT has submitted a minority report in opposition at some risk to its future as a government agency contractor. Its voice may yet be heard and its counsel taken by the World Bank. CUMAT may propose an alternative development model based upon sustained yield management of the area's rich natural forests.

Assessment

The integrated ecological land capability classification model has become the foundation for, and synonymous with, a national institution in Bolivia. The US Agency for International Development has committed about $1 million to this, much of it for training, offices, materials and equipment. Other institutions have also made substantial contributions, mostly for field operations. Otherwise, virtually all of the incentive and professional talent employed has been of national origin. The system was seized upon as a logical approach to indigenous problem-solving by the Bolivians, who have improved and modified it to fit local conditions. Technical assistance from abroad has come largely from an ecologically specialized, non-government institution, the Tropical Science Center in Costa Rica.

CUMAT's methodology appears to be respected and valued by the agencies which request its reports or its co-operation in the conduct of surveys. Vested political interests, on the other hand, evidence a lack of interest in or opposition to the methods and products whenever these are perceived as alien to their shorter-term interests. The organization is still too young to permit assessment of its programme in terms of effective planned development in the areas studied. However, the fact that CUMAT's services continue to be sought after by other institutions in Bolivia is a favourable sign.

CASE STUDY 21 *Country Environmental Profile, Paraguay*

DENNIS McCAFFREY
Environment and Development Consultant

Since 1977, USAID has been commissioning a series of studies of environmental information for most of the countries in which it works. The first ones (draft of "phase one" profiles) were intended as preliminary works to be followed by more detailed treatments. Phase one profiles tended to be compilations of data available in the United States. By the early 1980s these had been prepared for at least 50 countries.

Before all the phase one profiles were written, preparation of a second phase had begun. Phase two profiles go beyond phase one profiles in two ways; they are performed in the country concerned and state conclusions and recommendations regarding national policies affecting the country's environment. Phase two profiles currently exist for 13 countries, 11 of which are Latin American, plus one for the whole Central American region.

A phase two environmental profile consists of a process that leads to a group of products enabling a nation to evaluate its environment, its needs for environmental management and the means to meet those needs. The process must involve national professionals, sometimes augmented by foreign specialists. The process must fit well into the country's political context. Often this will mean direct involvement by the government as lead agency. In some countries, however, an NGO can take the lead. Both government and non-governmental organizations should participate.

The lead agency should draw people to work on the profile from the broadest technical pool available. Information for the profile should come from a wide range of sectors, using primarily national sources of data. The process brings together people who do not ordinarily work with each other, to discuss information and issues that fall outside, as well as within, their ordinary work. Quality of information is important, data compilation and analysis merely serve as background for the fundamental objectives. These are to examine environmental issues and work towards resolving them satisfactorily. Most of the time the barriers to solving environmental problems are not technical but social, political or institutional.

The products of the environmental profile process will consist of one or more tangible items, such as a book entitled *Environmental Process*, an organized mass of information that supports the book or the restructuring of a government agency to deal with environment. The process also produces some intangible products, which can include increased awareness of environmental problems or changing the attitude of institutions.

Background to the profile of Paraguay

By early 1984 phase two profiles had been prepared for several countries. USAID valued them for development planning, and professionals who had worked with profiles believed they furthered sound environmental planning. The International Institute for Environment and Development (IIED) had participated in the environmental profile process in Ecuador and Belize and had also commissioned two general studies to review phase two profiles. When the opportunity arose to perform a profile in Paraguay, IIED was eager to participate.

As Paraguay developed during the 1960s and 1970s a number of conditions arose that created a favourable climate for purchasing an environmental profile. These included: increased emphasis on planning by the government; construction of several enormous development projects whose operation had noticeable environmental implications; expansion of roads and services into sparsely populated areas, drawing settlers who cleared forests and harvested wildlife that a decade earlier had seemed inexhaustible; increased public awareness of environmental issues.

How the profile of Paraguay was produced

Planning and funding

Generalized planning for the profile occurred in March 1984, when a team from IIED visited Paraguay to confer with USAID representatives, Paraguayan officials and other interested Paraguayans. Principal decisions at this point included designation of the government's Technical Planning Secretariat (TPS) as lead agency and assignment of principal responsibility for the profile to a core staff of Paraguayans, complemented by Paraguayan and, when requested, foreign consultants. Shortly before fieldwork began, more specific planning decisions were made. United States ambassador Arthur H. Davies and USAID/Paraguay mission director Paul Pritz agreed to lend political support to the profile and participate in major decisions on it. Gregorio Raidan of TPS was designated profile director.

TPS would contract 23 Paraguayan technical specialists, and IIED would contract 7 foreign specialists for designated sectors. Each specialist contracted by IIED would work directly with a Paraguayan specialist. Technical specialists would be grouped into teams working together on related sectors. The teams would work serially, beginning with physical sectors and progressing through social to institutional and resource-management sectors.

The profile process would divide into a series of distinct phases:

Phase one would consist of ten weeks of fieldwork lasting to mid-December 1984. This phase would collect and analyse data for more than 20 sectors, resulting in reports for each sector.

Phase two, lasting until April 1985, would entail editing the sectoral reports into several chapters of the profile document. It would also entail writing the chapters that interpreted the data, examined issues and recommended environmental policies.

In *phase three* the profile manuscript would be printed, published and distributed. Projected end date for phase three was June 1985.

Phase four would involve follow-up activities. It would begin as the profile was distributed and continue indefinitely.

Phase five would consist of translating the profile into English, distributing it to an English-speaking audience and conducting follow-up.

An approximate allocation of available funds (US$180,000) among the phases of the profile process was as follows: detailed planning, 5 per cent of funds; fieldwork, data compilation and analysis, 50 per cent; editing, issue identification, recommendations, 15 per cent; printing, distributing Spanish version, 5 per cent; follow up activities, 15 per cent; translating, printing, distributing English version, 10 per cent. (The basic decision phase carried out in March 1984 was funded separately for under US$10,000.)

Methodology

The profile process began by compiling information on a variety of environmental and natural resource topics, plus other subject areas such as demography and economics. The information came largely from government sources and international organizations. At the end of the profile process most of the references remained with TPS, enhancing the agency as a repository of environmental information. Very little original research was done, but consultants spent time in the field checking published data and testing their opinions against field observations. Consultants also interviewed many people to check data and to determine the climate of opinion.

Sectors for which Paraguayan consultants prepared reports, sometimes with outside consultant participation, were: anthropology, sociology, urbanization, public health, environmental education, pollution, environmental law, environmental institutions, national economy, agricultural economy, forestry economy, energy, geology, soils, water resources, forestry, grasslands, fauna, wildlands and protected areas, fisheries. As the facts about particular sectors became known, the profile team began delimiting issues within sectors and across sectoral lines. This exercise unfolded through meetings among profile staff, consultants and people informally involved. The object was to present issues convincingly in the profile document and then to advocate a concerted course of action in national policy.

Editing and writing were done by Gregorio Raidan in consultation with the consultants and others. This method made for a broad sense of identification with the profile by many people. Quality of content received a great deal of attention, as did style of presentation. It was not enough for the profile to be accurate; it had to be readable and had to look inviting to read. For this reason the concluding chapters of the document are in the front, followed by the informational chapters, and great care was taken with the maps, photographs and other illustrations.

Dissemination and follow-up

The publication of the profile in 1985 was greeted as a significant news event in Paraguay. TPS distributed it at three levels: to cabinet members and diplomats; to technical people throughout Paraguay in government, international agencies, universities and the private sector; and to schools, libraries and private organizations. Response was uniformly positive, many people asked for additional copies, and the profile was soon reprinted. IIED published an English version of the report in the USA in 1986.

Two months after the profile's publication, while public interest was at its highest, TPS sponsored a national seminar on it. Nearly 100 technical people attended the seminar, which recommended priority actions for government and the private sector.

In 1986 Gregorio Raidan, on a visit co-ordinated by IIED, brought to Washington proposals for natural resource management for which he was seeking financial and technical support. He made contacts which led to some support, though not always for the proposals on the list.

Also in 1986 a new NGO named Fundación Physis was formed in Paraguay. Many of its founding members participated in the profile, and the Fundación plans to promote and support several of the profile's recommendations, beginning with environmental education.

CASE STUDY 22 *Rapid Rural Appraisal for Sustainable Development, the Northern Areas of Pakistan*

GORDON R. CONWAY
International Institute for Environment and Development

TARIQ HUSAIN and ZAHUR ALAM
Aga Khan Rural Support Programme, Pakistan

M. ALIM MIAN
Soil Survey of Pakistan

There is a paradox in sustainable development. On the one hand, we have to wait a considerable time before we know we have achieved a sustainable development path. On the other, the pressures to alleviate poverty and raise living standards are such that actions have to be taken quickly and often on the basis of incomplete knowledge. The challenge posed is to find ways of analysing situations that are rapid and cheap and ensure recommendations will lead to sustainable development.

The Northern Areas

The area covered by the project described in this case study comprises the upper watershed of the Indus River in Northern Pakistan. It contains a population of approximately 700,000, growing at 3.5 per cent per annum, with, on average, 0.08 ha of cultivated land per person. It also contains some of the highest mountains of the world, the Karakorams. The valleys are very narrow, and the region receives extremely low rainfall. Agriculture is thus constrained by lack of water, steep slopes, insufficient soil cover, stones and boulders on the soil surface and poor accessibility. Although productive agriculture has been made possible through the development of irrigation channels, human existence remains precarious. Earthquakes, landslides, mudflows and sudden floods can undo months and years of painstaking work.

The Aga Khan Rural Support Programme

The Aga Khan Rural Support Programme (AKRSP) is a private, non-profit development company which began work in Northern Pakistan in 1983. Funding comes from the Aga Khan Foundation, the UK Overseas Development Administration, Oxfam and elsewhere. Primary objectives are to reduce poverty in the area and develop local capacities to identify and make use of productive opportunities. This is accomplished through the organization of small farmers into broad-based economic coalitions, called village organizations, which then provide the vehicle for physical infrastructure projects, extension training, provision of agricultural inputs and credit and income-generating activities for women. AKRSP is strongly committed to achieving sustainable development firmly rooted in the villages; it takes account of socioeconomic and ecological variations occurring between and within villages.

Project history

The first phase of the programme focused on the development of 256 village-level physical infrastructure projects. These projects provide an entry point for the AKRSP to assist with development. Funding is in the form of grants backed up by technical expertise. The second phase of development focuses on realizing the agricultural potential of the villages through the judicious use of loans made against villagers' savings. Infrastructure projects include the construction of irrigation channels, siltation tanks, access roads and bridges, and their successful development has quickly established the basis of considerable potential for agricultural development.

AKRSP's experiments with approaches to second-phase programming have been influenced by three major considerations. First, unlike village-level infrastructure projects, most household production activities do not lend themselves to identification and appraisal through village consensus. Secondly, opportunities for and constraints on broad-based development vary greatly over the project area. Finally, staff and other resources are scarce and have to be directed at a few high-pay-off activities. The challenge for AKRSP management is to devise a limited number of "menus" for the development of homogeneous groups of villages or farmers and to enable individual farmers to choose from these "menus" according to their priorities.

This task largely falls to the management team and social organizers in dialogue with village organizations. There are seven qualified development specialists in the management team representing agronomy, economics, livestock development, engineering, marketing and women's development. The twelve Social Organizers, mostly graduates in social sciences, are each directly responsible for meeting the development needs of between 20 and 50 villages within one of the valleys. All the programme staff are Pakistan nationals, with the social organizers and some of the management team drawn from the Northern Areas.

Rapid rural appraisal

The task of identifying and prioritizing development opportunities has to be accomplished quickly and cheaply if development momentum is to be maintained. Rapid rural appraisal (RRA) was developed six years ago in response to needs of this kind and may be defined as a systematic but semi-structured activity carried out in the field by a multidisciplinary team and designed to acquire quickly new information on, and new hypotheses about, rural life.

RRA's rationale is that time, manpower and money are often limited but that quick, unsystematic visits to a project area may be misleading. It aims to provide enough structure to observation and analysis to ensure a relatively high degree of accuracy without incurring lengthy or costly studies. RRA is also a response to dissatisfaction with many conventional socioeconomic and agricultural surveys. In addition to being time-consuming and expensive they often do not ask the key questions or obtain the critical data. Above all, RRA is intended as a highly iterative process. Learning takes place in the field as part of a dialogue with the farmers and the other members of the RRA team. RRA is primarily a process of generating and refining hypotheses about rural development.

There is no single, standardized methodology. In each situation this depends on objectives, local conditions, skills and resources. However, a suite of techniques can be used in various combinations to produce appropriate RRA methods. The suite includes secondary data review, direct observation, conceptual tools, semi-structured interviews and analytical workshops.

Conceptual tools consist of a wide variety of simple techniques for summarizing information, e.g. diagrammatic models such as maps, seasonal calendars, flow and bar diagrams and decision trees.

Semi-structured interviewing is a form of guided interview where only some of the questions are predetermined and new questions or lines of questioning arise in response to answers from those interviewed. The information is thus derived from the interaction between the interviewer and interviewee(s). The latter may be groups, e.g. of village leaders, or key informants, e.g. school-teachers or local government officials, or the farmers themselves.

The RRA analytical workshop takes place soon after field visits. It is semi-structured and provides an opportunity for intensive multidisciplinary analysis of the information acquired in the field.

Over the past two years these RRA techniques have been explored by AKRSP staff as means of determining priorities for the next phase of development in the Northern Areas. The outcome has been a series of RRA methods under the headings of agroecosystem zoning, agroecosystem analysis, topical rapid rural appraisal and farming systems survey. They have been developed and refined on a piecemeal basis, and only recently has their interrelationship become apparent. Table 4 summarizes the different methods and their objectives.

An agroecosystem can be defined as an ecological system partly modified by humans for the purpose of food or fibre production. Each agroecosystem has a characteristic behaviour that may be summarized by four interconnected properties: productivity, stability, sustainability and equitability. These four properties are essentially descriptive in nature, but they can be used in a normative fashion, as indicators of performance, in both the design of agricultural innovation and its subsequent evaluation. In agricultural development there is almost inevitably some trade-off between these different

Table 4 Summary of methods of rapid rural appraisal for agricultural development in the northern areas of Pakistan

Method	Objectives
Agroecosystem zoning	Large-scale zoning of valleys to determine general recommendation domains
Village agroecosystem analysis	Exploratory surveys and workshop analyses to characterize the valley zones, identify preliminary key questions, hypotheses and guidelines for development and assess potential innovations and interventions
Topical rapid rural appraisal	Rapid field surveys and workshops to refine key questions and hypotheses, further evaluate alternative innovations and interventions and define specific recommendation domains
Farming systems survey	Semi-formal surveys to answer key questions requiring quantified answers in a systems context and to define specific recommendation domains together with appropriate recommendations

properties. The challenge for RRA is to foresee accurately these trade-offs and ensure they are taken into account.

RRA methods applied

Agroecosystem zoning

The logical first step in agricultural development planning is to determine land-use potential. Various methods of land-use appraisal are available, all of them requiring extensive field surveys and detailed information. It was felt that AKRSP could not wait for a detailed land suitability analysis of its project area. The immediate need was for a characterization of the valleys into zones such that development innovations tested in one part of a zone should be extendable to other parts of the zone and possibly to other similar zones in different valleys. The method is referred to as agroecosystem zoning and is characterized by a rapid, iterative classification process.

An initial secondary data survey suggested that the primary determinants of the zones were likely to be growing period and resource availability. Farmers were interviewed to determine sowing and harvesting dates and the dates of first frosts, etc. Based on the growing periods and the experience of the field survey the Hunza Valley was divided into nine zones. These zones ranged from Gilgit, a relatively lowland zone with two crops per year, a long growing period and market opportunities for its high-value livestock products and timber, to Misgar, the valley's uppermost zone, characterized by a short growing period and a serious labour shortage. At this stage the zoning is crude but it can be further refined as more detailed information is acquired.

Village agroecosystem analysis

The next stage is to investigate and characterize the valley zones further by an agroecosystem analysis (AA) conducted on representative villages. The primary aim of the AA is to determine the preliminary key questions for research and development appropriate to the zone.

Agroecosystem properties (productivity, stability, sustainability, equitability) are assumed to be determined by a limited number of key functional relationships and management decisions. Research workers have to define and answer a limited number of key questions regarding the key relationships or decisions and how they function in determining the system's properties. This is best done by bringing together a wide range of multidisciplinary experience, spanning the natural and social sciences, to carry out a joint analysis. This is furthered by a workshop environment, by a structured but flexible procedure and by an analysis of the village agroecosystem in terms of four basic patterns: space, time, flows and decisions.

The pattern analysis depends on the interactive use by workshop participants of a large number of simple diagrammatic models produced during a brief exploratory RRA of the village. It involves the preparation of maps and transects, seasonal calendars and flow diagrams showing the production and marketing processes. Maps and transects are constructed by noting the landforms, soils, existing vegetation and irrigation possibilities along one or two transects chosen for their good representation of variations within the village agroecosystem (see Figure 6). The transects reflect the zones and provide an opportunity to characterize them in terms of crops and livestock husbanded and the different problems and opportunities encountered.

The principal outcome of the workshop is a set of key questions, working hypotheses and guidelines for development. These emerge during the pattern analysis phase and are further discussed and refined until they are agreed by all participants. Examples of key questions are: How can soil development be speeded up while at the same time providing a higher return on new land? and How can land be used efficiently after reclamation? Each key question leads to a working hypothesis, suggesting a technical or institutional innovation; together they constitute the proposed agenda for development. The final phase of the workshop is to assess these innovations in terms of the system

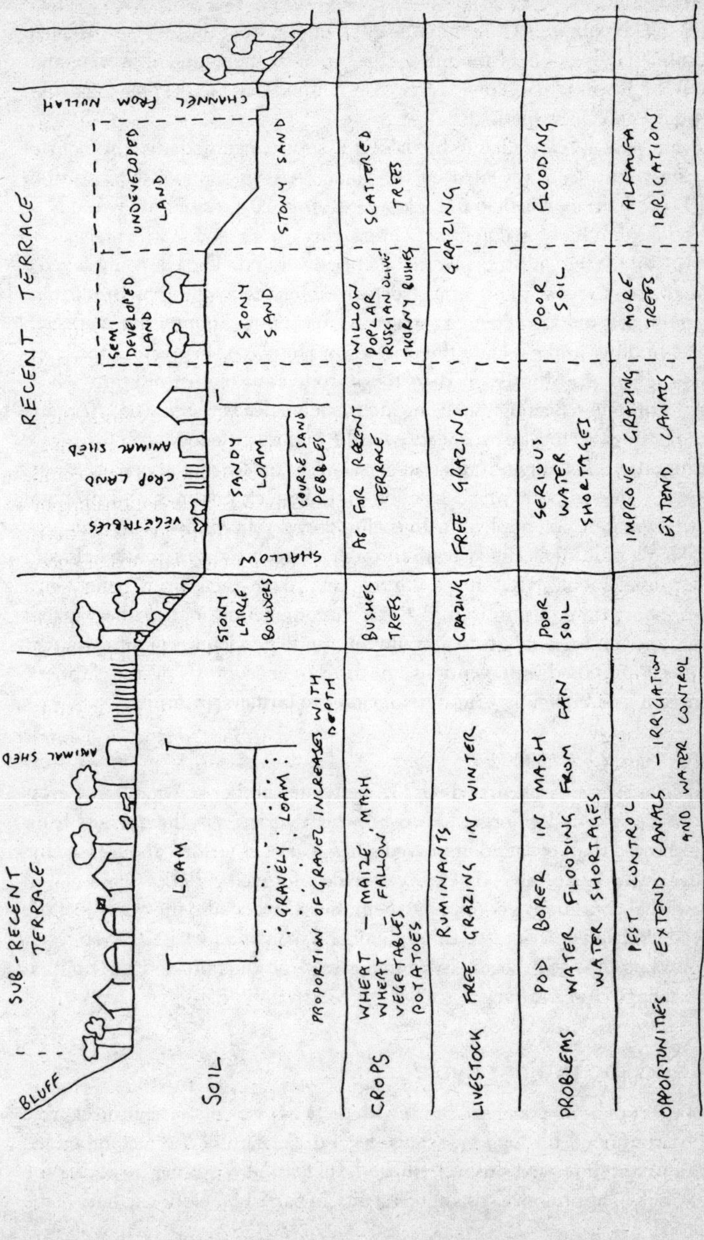

Figure 6: Transect of Rahimabad Terraces

properties and other criteria and rank them in order of priority.

Topical RRA

Some of the key questions and hypotheses emerging from the AA can be acted upon immediately. Others require further investigation, and it is here that topical RRA has its place. Topical RRA is a method that focuses on a particular topic, question or hypothesis.

One such RRA carried out by AKRSP staff concerned the problem of improving winter feed, revealed by the village AAs as a major constraint on livestock production. Participants identified some 20 possible innovations or interventions that had the potential of improving winter feed. Two villages, one at low and one at high altitude, were then briefly visited. The team employed a mixture of direct observation, semi-structured interviewing and the production of diagrammatic models. The next stage was to conduct an intensive workshop to discuss findings and evaluate the original proposals. A surprising conclusion was the highest priority assigned to the introduction of rust-resistant wheat varieties, a finding reflecting the strong interdependence between wheat farming and the livestock sector, for wheat straw is the major cattle fodder in the severe winter months. Since the introduction of rust-resistant wheat varieties increases the attractiveness of both wheat farming and livestock holdings, this proposal offered the greatest potential contribution to farmers' livelihoods.

By taking a multidisciplinary team through an intensive, systematic field and workshop assessment, RRA helps participants revise their prior beliefs in a relatively short time. Using topical RRA in conjunction with agroecosystem concepts, and forcing analysts to account for interdependencies in the system, it helps place proposed interventions in the larger context of the farmers' environment and hopefully brings them closer to farmers' priorities.

Farming systems survey

A semi-formal survey was carried out to investigate another key question: why is there a low level of adoption of improved wheat varieties in the district? Data analysis showed that local and improved wheat varieties yielded about the same grain and straw per hectare – partly because the improved varieties were not well suited to local conditions and management, but also because the quality of the improved seed had deteriorated through mixing with other varieties. As a result of this finding AKRSP began to promote seed production and distribution through village co-operatives.

RRA and the project cycle

Development planning does not finish with these assessments. The project cycle has to be continued through (1) village-level discussions of the recommended innovations and interventions, (2) village-level feasibility studies involving the villagers and (3) appraisal of costs and benefits, in particular of the capacity of the villagers to support the proposed innovation with a permanent management system.

Conclusions

AKRSP is still experimenting with different techniques of analysis in its development planning in Northern Pakistan, ranging from the informal to the formal. These techniques are acknowledged by the project's development specialists as providing clearer insights into development problems and opportunities, and the multidisciplinary aspect helps create a common sense of priorities. In general, adoption of RRA methods is, despite their design, constrained by lack of time and the pressure of other tasks.

AKRSP began with a conscious rejection of a centralized, aggregated approach to research and planning for rural development. Instead, it is exploring incremental iterative approaches which involve village-level learning experiences by multidisciplinary teams, intensive workshops and dialogue with the farmers at all stages in the project cycle. This approach has proved successful in the development of physical infrastructure in the villages and has similar potential in the next phase of agricultural development.

CASE STUDY 23 *National Conservation Strategy, Zambia*

STEPHEN M. J. BASS

Consultant to Conservation Development Centre, International Union for Conservation of Nature and Natural Resources

National conservation strategies: form and function

One of the first attempts to express a theory of conservation as an essential part of the development process was the World Conservation Strategy (WCS). Produced by the International Union for Conservation of Nature and Natural Resources (IUCN), the United Nations Environment Programme (UNEP) and the World Wildlife Fund in 1980, it proposed guidelines for sustainable development developed from the three constituent objectives of conservation: to develop and maintain essential ecological processes; to ensure that exploitation of natural resources is maintained at sustainable levels; to maintain biological diversity. The WCS helped guide conservation authorities towards the urgent task of integrating conservation principles into the development process. Recognizing that the precedent must be set at the national level, the WCS recommended that countries prepare national conservation strategies, involving actors from throughout the development process and not merely the conservation authorities.

A national conservation strategy (NCS) is prepared in order to generate better knowledge of what a country's natural resources are capable of, the consequences of using them and the precautions to be taken to ensure sustainable use. An NCS emphasizes the need for adding the long-term environmental dimension to development planning. In developing countries in particular, governments' priorities are tied to solving immediate problems. The higher authorities are rarely concerned with maintaining the natural resource base upon which longer-term development depends. An environmental profile, no matter how seriously taken by the conservation authorities, is unlikely to change this short-term bias, especially if it is produced by outsiders.

What, then, must an NCS provide to remove this short-term bias and begin tackling the task of integrating conservation and development?

(1) A forum for policy-makers to meet conservation professionals, to expose issues and discuss solutions.
(2) A way of acting on this analysis without sacrificing too many short-term needs.

(3) A way of identifying conservation priorities and of planning and appraising conservation investments for the medium and long term.
(4) A mechanism for attracting funds for this investment.
(5) A consensus on who is responsible for what field of activity regarding natural resources.
(6) The assurance that this process of analysis and consensus building has responded to national needs and is not the product of outsiders.

Most of these requirements were provided satisfactorily in Zambia, but, despite reasonable success so far, further thought needs to go into point (4), funding. The NCS defines many conservation investment potentials for Zambia, and the National Conservation Committee forms a useful co-ordination body. However, there is less co-ordination with respect to conservation among the various aid agencies, and this is retarding progress.

The Zambian government's reasons for preparing an NCS

Zambia's reliance on copper constitutes one of the highest levels of dependence of any country on any one commodity – around 95 per cent of all foreign exchange earnings. Yet the microelectronic revolution has dramatically decreased the world demand for copper, and the world price has plummeted. Lack of long-term planning has caused this overdependence on copper to become a short-term issue. The government is changing the emphasis in development from mining to agriculture as fast as it can. Agriculture is not yet highly developed, and virgin lands will have to be opened up and current farming land intensified; hence the need to know what those lands are capable of producing. Also, since the natural resources upon which agriculture depends are renewable if conserved and destructible if not, there is a need to define ways of ensuring this renewability.

For these reasons Zambia was extremely interested in the principles of the WCS and the possibility of preparing an NCS. Many Zambians were already aware that the natural resource base was coming under enormous pressures from deforestation, soil erosion, degradation of traditional pastures, pollution and poaching of ivory and rhino horn.

The Zambian NCS process

Zambia's President Kaunda has long had an interest in wildlife conservation and has strongly promoted collaboration with international agencies. He invited IUCN to work with the Zambian authorities to prepare an NCS, and the author visited Zambia in 1984 to take part in the NCS formulation.

The NCS was launched as a project of the Ministry of Lands and Natural Resources, with technical assistance from IUCN and funding from the Swedish and Dutch governments. The work was prepared by a 30-strong technical group, representing the interests of government, parastatal and private organizations; it was aided by a secretariat (the author and an officer from the ministry) and prepared under the guidance of a policy-level task force.

NCS formulation was limited to a period of seven months by funding constraints. This was time enough to produce a practical strategy which could be adopted in almost every detail by the Zambian cabinet. However, lack of time and resources has meant that some opportunities for more detailed analysis, which could have resulted in a more effective strategy, have been missed.

Nevertheless, the task force's achievements were significant, reaching consensus on the issues that had retarded progress in sustainable development thus far: establishing the requirements for, and mechanisms to implement, cross-sectoral co-ordination of natural resource management and a conservation co-ordinating body; the need for an environmental component in development planning and how this should evolve; sectoral guidelines on key issues; the need for an NCS to be adopted as a prerequisite to planning longer-term investment in conservation.

For the NCS to be sure of being endorsed, it had to reflect truly Zambian interests and so had to be visibly prepared by Zambians. Thus the first step of preparation was to identify the most suitable local professionals to form the technical group which would prepare background reports on a range of issues. For these reports to be effective, it was essential that the frequent "party-line" analysis of "everything OK but lack of funds" should be avoided. It was therefore established that members of the technical group should have the freedom to be critical.

A key requirement was a conservation co-ordinating body which would unite the weak conservation agencies and enable them to play their part in the development process. An interim National Conservation Committee was formed as a first step before inaugurating a statutory Environment Council. The task force was careful to be as realistic as possible, proposing only the minimum of new bureaucracy. A good organizational set-up is vital to NCS implementation.

In preparing the NCS, the narrowest issues of "conservation for development" ended up by dominating. Opportunities to look at issues such as the contribution of biological diversity to conservation and development were missed. In addition, the definition of conservation priorities had to be pragmatic – achieved through discussions rather than detailed appraisals and costings. At the stage of NCS implementation, however, such detailed evaluations are required in order to determine investment strategies for natural resources.

There were also inadequate time and resources to demonstrate conclusively the value of conservation. However, case studies of existing issues were made. In the next stage of NCS implementation, a project development fund has been set up for the National Conservation Committee to begin activities where these are urgently required or where much can be demonstrated quickly at a low cost. This fund has been used on tree planting, community charcoal stove manufacture, seminars, etc. In retrospect, it is recommended that such a fund be available for the stage of NCS preparation, especially for the demonstration of problems and solutions. Also in retrospect it is recommended that the "standard" NCS project should include the formation of a permanent

Natural Resource Data Bank where such a facility does not already exist.

During the preparation of the Zambian NCS it was considered not politic to analyse the past and current five-year plans and to criticize them for their lack of success in fulfilling conservation objectives. Rather, it was decided that the NCS should "lead" the next five-year plan. A few natural resource development projects have already come out of the Zambia NCS, more quickly than often happens through a five-year plan. In addition, the NCS has been incorporated into the imminent five-year plan.

Media relations were consciously developed throughout the NCS process, as it became clear that the media would be a valuable asset for NCS preparation and implementation.

The Zambian NCS was approved by the Cabinet in July 1985. Ten months had elapsed since the final draft was presented to the Minister of Lands and Natural Resources. The wide representation of interests in its preparation meant that the Cabinet memorandum (prepared by the minister) was not a great surprise to anyone. The NCS did not look like a proposal to satisfy the interests of only one sector. In the meantime the secretariat prepared Natural Resource Development Plan proposals to take up the priorities identified in the NCS. Cabinet approval was necessary to get the NCS adopted as official policy. If the exercise were to be done again, MPs would also be involved. In a stable one-party state such as Zambia this involvement should be considered essential.

Inputs, costs and output of NCS preparation

Inputs and costs. The costs of NCS preparation were low in comparison with other national development planning projects. Seven person-months' consultancy and approximately US$8,000 in travel, stationery, fuel, etc. were covered by the Swedish and Dutch governments and administered by IUCN. The Zambian government contributed staff time and the use of a vehicle and office. For the 12 months of initiating NCS implementation, the Swedish government again provided running costs, two vehicles and a US$10,000 project development fund.

Outputs. The NCS for Zambia contains a range of material from outline recommendations to precise designs. It should guide the work of integrating conservation and development over the next decade at least, with updating every five years. The main strategic elements contained in the NCS document are: (1) guidelines for cross-sectoral conservation action; (2) design of a new conservation co-ordinating body; (3) outline design of an environmental planning process; (4) decentralization; (5) education; (6) rationalizing extension services; (7) emphasizing community participation; (8) extensive manpower training; (9) inventory and research; (10) sectoral guidelines; (11) financial policy; (12) Natural Resource Development Plan. Significant outputs of the NCS process are the consensus achieved on the need for integrating conservation and development and the contacts made between conservation and development interests.

Early stages of NCS implementation

Widespread distribution of a well-presented NCS document is continuing to bring forth new ideas. Background work in preparing a Natural Resource Development Plan is paying off. In addition to its interministerial role, the National Conservation Committee is acting as a lands and natural resources planning unit where none existed before. Funding is beginning to be secured for various proposals. The NCS's consensus and coherence can make it seem a more realistic bet for investment than the five-year plans.

Natural Resource Development Plan

NCSs were once viewed as a way of modifying development proposals. The Zambia NCS has been effective in actually creating development proposals, and the development of projects within the Natural Resource Development Plan is exciting great interest. A useful resource being used in NCS implementation is a loose fund to develop proposals and set up pilot projects, etc., enabling progress to be achieved quickly. US$10,000 have been spent on various initiatives designed either to become sustainable in the short term or to lead to viable project proposals.

Many aid agencies are increasing the proportion of aid allocated to the environment and land development. But such projects have to compete for funds with short-term projects designed to generate foreign exchange, to finance debt repayments and to provide relief from disasters (which often have environmental causes). Project proposals developed so far from the Zambian NCS comprise (1) central activities for NCS implementation, (2) resource development, (3) research for sustainable development and (4) education and manpower for sustainable development.

An environmental planning process

One of the main lessons learned is that what appears to be an exercise in "adding the environmental dimension" exposes many more glaring issues to do with a lack of coherent development planning. Building in an environmental planning process may be extremely difficult if there is no proper development planning procedure to link into, and these issues may balk NCS activities. Setting up the environmental planning procedure in Zambia may therefore be difficult. However, the development planning process is currently being revised, since the recent sadoption of the NCS established a precedent for long-term planning based upon natural resource capabilities.

Persisting obstacles in NCS work

Starting an NCS. Early discussion in a country on whether to produce an NCS must focus on budgets. How much is it going to cost, internally for the country and in terms of technical assistance from outside? In Zambia there was the feeling that, if the stated budgets were too high at the outset, it would be difficult to "sell" the exercise within government. This necessity for an incremental approach to bringing conservation and development together is a common feature in many countries and has been a common experience with many aid agencies. The Zambian NCS was thus undertaken in discrete phases, each phase building confidence and interest in the conservation–development linkage. The NCS is an awareness-raising exercise, but only when it has been completed are the main forces within government necessarily convinced of its importance. Financing NCSs remains a major obstacle.

Lack of finance to implement the NCS. Even when awareness has been developed in a country, the allocation of finances to help inject "sustainability" into the development process is often fraught with difficulties. The debt crisis and population growth are often issues of such magnitude that the management of natural resources for long-term sustainable benefits is often seen as secondary. Thus, even once an NCS has had an initial impact on a country, implementation of its recommendations is rarely straightforward. There is a very real need for additional support to be made available to poorer countries specifically for the management of natural resources for tomorrow's use. This is the major challenge if we are to achieve satisfactory integration of conservation and development.

PART 5

Human and Institutional Development

CHAPTER 5

Human and Institutional Development

DAVID BUTCHER
Resettlement Consultant to the World Bank Energy Department

Three important points should be kept at the forefront of our minds when thinking about human and institutional development. The first is that institutional permanence has little to do with the sustainability of humanity and its environment, since institutions are merely tools to facilitate better organization and should not be sustained for their own sake. Secondly, development assistance, especially in the form of projects, is a fleetingly brief intervention in a very lengthy historical process. Thirdly, when something sustainable is initiated you cannot predict far ahead which future directions it may take or where it will end.

The concept of sustainability is not entirely clear, although most of us have more or less the same understanding of what it means in the context of development assistance. A recent World Bank paper analysing the outcomes of 25 development projects stated that "project sustainability over time was defined as the maintenance of an acceptable flow of benefits from the project's investments after its completion, i.e. after the project ceased to receive Bank financial and technical support" (Cernea, 1986). Although economics are important, there is much more than economics underlying what makes certain courses of action sustainable.

The theme of this chapter, and the group of case studies it encompasses, "human and institutional development", poses similar problems of definition and a lack of an established framework in which ideas, procedures and outcomes can be neatly slotted. We are tilling ground that was newly broken only four or five years ago. Recognition of the importance of institutions has been around a long time. As objects of study, they have been popular with sociologists, political theorists and governments. Institutions tended to appear, grow and atrophy in old age and were sometimes transplanted with varying degrees of success. The present concern by the development community arises from a realization of the importance of institutions and their development as prerequisites to lasting

The author wishes to thank the World Bank for time off to prepare this paper, and Tony Churchill, Bob Saunders and Gwen Butcher for their assistance. The opinions expressed are those of the author and should not be construed as official views of the World Bank.

development. Along with this goes the realization that not only are formal organizations, ministries and parastatals often ill equipped to perform their functions, but there is need to develop lower-level institutions if development assistance is to be useful in its intended purpose.

The case studies

Grameen Bank, Bangladesh, and Small Farmer Development Project, Nepal (Case Study 24)

The Grameen (Village) Bank was started in 1976 as a means of alleviating poverty. The bank provides credit to poor people, who form themselves into groups of five. Collective sense and group pressure are important to the scheme in selection of fundable projects and in ensuring repayment. Income-earning activities funded by the loans include buying a milch cow, a sewing-machine and cloth, a loom, a rickshaw.

When the International Fund for Agricultural Development (IFAD) entered the scene in 1980, the Grameen Bank had provided loans to 6,000 men and women. IFAD provided a $3.4 million loan, with further tranches of $4.23 m and $23.6 m in 1984. NORAD (the Norwegian aid agency) and SIDA (Swedish International Development Authority) have provided $13.8 m and the Ford Foundation a grant of $1.8 m. By 1986 the bank had over 200,000 members and a village staff of 3,200 and had granted over 1.6 million loans. Incomes of members are 50 per cent higher than those of non-members; default rates are very low. The Grameen Bank is now a fully fledged bank in its own right and has a target of 500 branches and 900,000 members. The bank showed its first profit in 1985 and should be able to start paying off its debt to the Bangladesh government by 1995.

Organic Agriculture and Appropriate Technology Centres for the Community (CAOTACOs), Dominican Republic (Case Study 25)

There are two organic and appropriate technology centres, known as CAOTACOs, in the Dominican Republic: one at Loma de Cabrera (1980) and very poor, and the other at Las Matarde Farfan. Incomes in the country are low, and large families are common. The natural resource base is also poor.

The project provides many inputs for rural development, such as credit, agricultural inputs, processing facilities and technical advice on environmental protection, appropriate technology, infrastructure, livestock, housing and health. Although each agriculture and technology centre has a physical centre, Fundación para el Desarrollo Comunitario (FUDECO) which administers the project emphasizes community participation, training at all levels and the formation of small farmers and women's associations. All community-level projects are planned with community participation under community leadership.

FUDECO receives 45 per cent of its funding from Save the Children and the rest from other agencies and the Dominican Presidency. Although FUDECO's present earnings (from swine) are small, it hopes to increase them in future.

The CAOTACOs' achievements include soil conservation, erosion control, increased productivity, improved water supplies for drinking and vegetable production, tree planting, and the introduction of efficient stoves. FUDECO attributes success to proximity to the beneficiaries, decentralization of decision-taking, community participation and staff dedication.

Business Advisory Services, Kenya and Ghana (Case Study 26)

The essence of the assistance provided by the Business Advisory Services Programmes is twofold: to offer short-term help to local enterprises in need of organizational, administrative and basic business skills, and to act as go-between in connecting local groups with sources of finance and the market place. Programmes were set up by Technoserve in Ghana and Kenya.

The majority of time was spent on accounting and control. But Technoserve also considers establishing the credibility and legitimacy of local groups to be important, as well as acting as a "broker and catalyst" (providing an interface with ministries, banks, etc.) and "hand-holding". The projects, funded by USAID, provided 113 services in Ghana and 166 in Kenya between 1981 and 1985 at an estimated cost of $150 per day, compared to an estimated $450 per day for a similar commercial service. Technoserve has followed a similar approach in Zaire, Rwanda and El Salvador.

Integrated Rural Development Programme, Zambia (Case Study 27)

Assisted by the UK Overseas Development Administration (ODA), the Zambia Integrated Rural Development Programme (IRDP) is a pioneering effort to improve living standards by increasing productivity and the provision of services. It is neither an agricultural nor a health *sector* project. IRDP is targeted towards district councils and, in true institutional development style, is modestly trying to help the councils to provide and maintain infrastructure and services. The Zambian government policy of decentralization provided an essential framework within which the project could be pursued.

IRDP has assisted district councils to identify what needs to be done through a combination of what council members say their constituents want and technical and financial appraisal. Other skills imparted include the ability to prioritize needs and to develop a rolling programme within a ten-year time frame. The project approach is now being taken up by other donors in Zambia at the government's behest, and the ODA has started a second project, more accurately called a district development project.

Environmental management development, Indonesia (Case Study 28)

Indonesia is developing a decentralized institutional capacity for environmental management, and several donors have contributed technical assistance and training funds to specific needs. Until 1983, however, there was no mechanism to support the overall framework of developing environmental management. A new, more flexible, structure was needed that could accept Indonesian or donor funds from more than one source, and respond to training needs etc. as they arose. In 1983 CIDA and the Indonesian government created such a structure through the Environmental Manpower (since 1987 Management) Development in Indonesia (EMDI) project.

EMDI is jointly managed by the Indonesian Ministry for Population and Environment and Dalhousie University, Canada. Assistance is available through EMDI to other Indonesian bodies, including NGOs, in line with the decentralized approach to capacity-building. EMDI is a unique type of project, and other countries would benefit from having similar ones.

Implementing environmental programmes (Case Study 29)

Three projects are included in this case study, two involve strengthening national administrations in environmental planning and protection, and the other developing a capability in a multilateral lending institution to ensure the projects it finances are environmentally sound. The three projects involved no capital assistance, only technical and institution-building expertise.

In Hong Kong there was no environmental agency, and an incremental approach was adopted to build up the capability of an initially small unit over a period of eight years, until it was ready to act autonomously.

In 1983 the Indonesian environment ministry embarked on a UN Environment Programme-sponsored project to clean up the Jakarta–Puncak corridor and the adjacent coastal area. Recognizing the scarcity of resources, the project advocated integrating environmental factors into the decision-making process, the widespread use of appropriate technology and obtaining support from communities through a bottom-up approach.

In the case of the Central American Bank for Economic Integration (CABEI), selected individuals in various departments were trained on the job to provide capability in environmental planning. These individuals were trained to produce rapid improvements in projects prior to the establishment of a new department. Environmental Resources Ltd began with the sectoral investment programmes section and then moved down the project cycle path.

In all three projects, emphasis was given to needs for strengthening administration and procedures. Although legislation was considered important, guidelines were reckoned to be of less value.

Sustainability

No project can exist and operate independently, as if the rest of the country did not exist. It forms a subset of activities and relationships within a much wider regional, national and even international system. In the absence of any established methodology for assessing institutional development or sustainability, an attempt is made here to identify important factors which seem to have direct influence on projects. There appear to be two sets of factors influencing a project's success: those external to the project and those which are internal.

External factors

For several years economists have recognized that appropriate pricing policies, realistic exchange rates and political will are essential if a country is to remain solvent and develop. If the maize price in Zambia had not been attractive to farmers in the IRDP areas, they would still be growing it for subsistence only. Similarly the introduction of the foreign currency auction, another form of devaluation, made imports more expensive, and for large-scale commercial farmers in Zambia maize cultivation became unprofitable. However, for farmers using draught oxen, the costs of production increased only slightly, thereby increasing their share of the market.

The general health of the economy is also important in certain cases. The Hong Kong government was in a position to introduce new legislation requiring the public and commercial enterprises to keep to certain standards which meant foregoing some income or profit. In the case of Indonesia, hit by the low oil price in 1983, much less was claimed to have been achieved. The demand for land by "developers" and the need for poor farmers to earn a living make it difficult to ask people to forgo income for an activity without an immediate return. In fact, the success and sustainability of the projects described are only partially connected to the state of the general economy; as Table 5 indicates, there is considerable variation.

Leaving aside Hong Kong, the range of GNP per capita is vast, the Dominican Republic having seven times that of Bangladesh. Yet the CAOTACO projects are not seven times more successful than the Grameen Bank, if at all. The significance of the figures is that it is possible to help the poor in a sustainable project almost regardless of the general level of the economy. This does not mean that changes in the overall national economy will leave ongoing projects unaffected. A highly successful World-Bank-assisted low-income housing project in El Salvador had one of the best loan repayment records of any of its shelter programmes up until 1982, but the subsequent deterioration in the political and economic situation adversely affected cost recovery (Bramber and Deneke, 1984).

Other external factors are also relevant, especially for project design. There would be no point in starting a project to produce maize for the market if there was no road network or market system. Similarly, countries should not embark on ambitious education programmes without first relating course options presented to students to the likely job market.

Although not yet given the same attention as economic and fiscal structural adjustment programmes, the legal framework is extremely important to the creation of an appropriate developmental environment. Laws not only protect the rights of individuals and groups but establish the ground rules within which everyone must operate. The IRDP district councils could not have coun- tenanced raising levies if their right to do so had not existed in law. As the

Table 5 GNP and life expectancy, selected countries

	GNP per capita $	average annual growth	Life expectancy (years)
Low income			
Bangladesh	130	0.6	50
Nepal	160	0.2	47
India	260	1.6	56
Kenya	310	2.1	54
Ghana	350	-1.9	53
Sudan	360	1.2	48
Pakistan	380	2.5	51
Lower middle income			
Zambia	470	-1.3	52
Indonesia	540	4.9	55
El Salvador	710	-0.6	65
Thailand	860	4.2	64
Dominican Rep.	970	3.2	64
Upper middle income			
Hong Kong	6,330	6.2	76

Source: World Bank, 1986.

imposition of a maize levy fell outside the scope of these existing rules, the government of Zambia had first to modify the laws to include the new levy. Laws relating to land and inheritance are often crucially important parameters within which projects must fit. The environmental projects in Hong Kong and Indonesia could not have operated had there been no relevant legal framework. Often an absence of well-formulated laws on land use and landownership inhibits people from investing time, labour and capital in such things as soil conservation.

Although the subject of "common property resources" is relatively new, and not accorded high priority by either aid recipient countries (ARCs) or donors, its relevance will increase as further pressure is put on land. This is because there is a tendency for ARCs and donor organizations to take laws on land, both official and customary, on their face value and as valid and binding for all time. In reality the situation is very different.

The type and form of administrative systems followed in the country as a whole can also affect project implementation dramatically. The introduction of the policy for decentralization by the Zambian government was essential for the IRDP to develop as an institution-building project as it has. Administrative systems take on importance in times of political upheaval and rapid changes of government, providing a form of institutional stability.

In the World Bank review referred to earlier (Cernea, 1986) five sets of factors were identified as having "a decisive bearing" on the sustainability of the projects analysed. These are: (1) institutional build-up and participation of beneficiaries; (2) technological improvements; (3) socioeconomic compatibility; (4) favourable policy environment; (5) recurrent cost financing/recovery. Cernea points out that while there has been increased attention to institutional development, planners have tended to focus attention on public sector management agencies and have left off their agenda the less formal institutions at the grass-roots level. These include such organizations as water users' associations and rotating credit and saving associations. They are the type of institution described in most of the case studies.

Internal factors

The case study projects vary greatly in design, level of operation within the recipient country and what they hope to achieve. Yet all are aimed at improving institutional capability to meet identifiable needs. This brings us to the second common factor, which is that the case studies give great importance to the organization of the recipients. All the authors claim project replicability or sustainability.

Assuming external factors are favourable, there appear to be five internal factors which are prerequisites to project success or sustainability: (1) organization of recipients, beneficiaries and/or project agents; (2) participation of members of the group or organization in group activities; (3) decision-taking on what will be done; (4) payment/cost recovery from those benefiting; (5) sanctions against those who break rules of the group. In addition to these internal factors, there are two others at the core of any development assistance: (6) flow of resources; (7) ideas and innovations or technology. The last two were not included as external factors because, although they originate outside the project, if the project is to work, they must be relevant to people's needs, and that can only be established between the provider and the receiving groups.

The factors mentioned above should not be seen as discrete items, as desirable but not crucial. The factors are all interrelated, always essential and integral to success. As far as a project is concerned they are the basic elements of a viable system which produces results meeting the needs of the people in the system and generating the necessary surpluses to fuel the system to meet further needs.

Organization. Beyond "family", and the rights and obligations between its members, are the broader organizational entities of clan, caste, tribe and nation. In addition there are a plethora of other organizations, to a greater or lesser extent voluntary, which serve the needs of individuals and groups, not always equitably. These organizations range from public administrations, corporate enterprises, armies, religious groups and factories, to clubs, savings groups, secret societies and co-operatives.

The case study projects under review, as well as the Kenya conservation programme (Case Study 7) and the Lampang nutrition programme (Case Study 1), utilize a variety of organizations to receive assistance, as follows:

Grameen Bank – groups of five poor people, with the groups in each village being organized under a "centre chief".

CAOTACOs – community organization, farmers', youths' and women's associations.

IRDP – district council staff; indirectly, district councillors and the wards they represent.

Business advisory services – private and community businesses, community groups, local NGOs, government agencies, an international organization, a transnational NGO.

Environmental management development in Indonesia – provincial governments, university study centres, industry and NGOs.

Environmental Resources Ltd – public sector institutions, multilateral aid donor.

Lampang ANP – village groups.

Kenya conservation – farmers' groups and individual farmers.

These recipient groups vary in type and form and do not in themselves offer a rule or principle to be followed in future projects. For that it is necessary to relate the purpose, level and type of operation of a particular project to the optimum type of receiving organization.

For Environmental Resources Ltd to achieve maximum impact it was best to intervene at the point where the project could influence policy and future legislation but also strengthen administrative procedures and develop the key institution in environmental matters. ERL could thus assist in controlling the behaviour of 5.5 million people in a positive manner. The same principle applied in the Indonesian and CABEI cases.

The Technoserve projects in Kenya and Ghana are the most difficult to analyse, and it is not always clear whether the implementing agency is Technoserve itself or the business advisory services. A wide variety of recipient groups were assisted, from government organizations to other NGOs and small informal groups of women. Had Technoserve concentrated on fewer project types, choosing those with similar group structures in similar lines of business, perhaps its could have achieved more for the money spent.

Both the CAOTACO and the Lampang projects have a similar flavour. Dominican Republic and Thailand are identical in terms of life expectancy and close in GNP per capita and growth rates. Both projects work through community organizations, instil the idea of people paying towards their own betterment and place importance on community groups. The turning of a group from operating as a passive acceptance/rejection device to one that can articulate its needs, prioritize them and suggest its own solutions is the essence of getting a development process started.

The Grameen Bank through its village-level bank workers identifies numbers of poor men and women and suggests they form single-sex groups of unrelated individuals to act as receiving groups. The cohesion of these groups appears strong and is presumably reinforced by the weekly meetings. Project designers realized that there was no way of channelling assistance through the traditional Bangladesh village power structure with any hope of it reaching the poorest.

New groups had to be formed which would bypass the established leade
their cohorts.

The Kenya conservation programme also depends on groups of fa......s
working together. The case study describes how the donor agency, SIDA,
worked through the Ministry of Agriculture in an advisory and institution-
building role. Mention has been made of the systems nature of projects; a whole
series of interrelated activities, relationships and events constantly impinge upon
and affect one another. Where does a project as an entity cease, and where do the
external factors discussed actually become external? The recipient organizations
and groups would in most cases have no reason for existence were it not for the
projects. However, to achieve sustainability, those which have worked through
"permanent" institutions will have the greatest chances of success, even if they
have to create the institution (Grameen Bank) or change and improve its *modus
operandi*. As an ODA study concluded: "project management and implementation should generally be closely associated with if not based in existing
institutions, and proposals for new and separate project management and
implementation organizations should be examined most carefully and critically"
(Moris, 1981). FUDECO and Technoserve must be prepared to integrate their
operations with a "permanent institution", continue their projects indefinitely
or see the benefits gained by people under their projects remain with the select
few or even decline.

There is another type of delivery of assistance to recipients in which a strong
project management unit is established for project implementation. Although
this approach is deemed necessary for large-scale engineering projects, it is
generally unsuitable for assisting the poor in rural development. The project
management unit (PMU) approach is employed when existing institutions and
organizations are considered too weak to implement a project which must go
ahead anyway. There are two schools of thought on the use of PMUs for
agricultural or rural development projects. One considers that the discipline,
technical know-how available and assured markets justify the strong management employed to run the project. Yields can be kept relatively high, corruption
is minimal or non-existent, and farmers or smallholders receive relatively high
incomes. The other view is that dependency on the PMU does nothing to
engender initiative or a sense of responsibility among participants.

Participation. Genuine participation is essential to successful group activity,
which means giving everyone in the group a chance to express their views. While
this is possible in groups formed by people of approximately equal status and
wealth, such as those in the Grameen Bank case, the inclusion of office holders
from the wider society or people with high status can have an inhibiting effect on
the other members and the efficient working of the group. It is inferred that one
reason for forming separate groups in Bangladesh villages for men and women
wishing to join the Grameen Bank programme is to enable the women to speak
their mind, something no woman could normally do in the presence of men other
than her husband.

Participation does not stop at voicing opinion but implies taking decisions and
accepting responsibility for them.

Decision and risks. Decision-taking is at the heart of successful development projects. Decisions to approve the project and supply the funds, to implement the project in a certain way and on where to start the project are all important but are external to the beneficiaries. The individuals in the target group must take all the future decisions or there will be no project. The conditions external to the project must be right. Within the environment of opportunity thus created, people, in groups or as individuals, must perceive the opportunities open to them. Opportunity in this case means a course of action with a foreseeable profitable outcome and a minimum of risk.

On the basis of what people are expected to do, e.g. grow a given crop, for an estimated cost for an estimated return, project appraisal has been developed to a fine art, with considerable quantifiable precision, mainly by economists. To develop the models for analysing projects, economists must use aggregates of expected behaviour by a sufficient number of people. Yet where people are free agents and engage in social, economic, religious and political activities, they are continuously presented with whole ranges of choices. The use of models based on statistics can therefore be useful up to a point but provides no explanation of what causes the underlying behaviour of the people in the population concerned. When models are not based on observed behaviour but on expected or assumed behaviour, they cease to be valid tools of analysis and prediction and become inappropriate for project appraisal.

Projects in which technologists decide which crops people will grow, and how they will grow them, will work only if the people have also decided to grow them. No one can take other people's decisions for them. In the case study projects, people, for better or worse, have taken the crucial decisions. This applies to senior officials in the Hong Kong civil service, the district council staff in the IRDP, the village groups in the CAOTACOs, the members of small business enterprises and farmers' groups in Kenya and the Bangladesh rural poor.

Risk is a factor which influences rural people in Third World countries to a greater extent than is given credit; it is sometimes the reason why seemingly attractive new technologies are not decided upon in a positive manner. There are two essential roles for project personnel acting for the deliverers of assistance. One is to suggest the range of opportunities open to groups and their members, and the other is to play the devil's advocate in getting people to think more carefully through their options before they take decisions which commit them to expense, time and effort.

An agency operative must have extensive relevant knowledge as well as patience, understanding and sympathy for the people who are to be helped. There are a surprisingly large number of people who fit this bill.

Cost recovery. Cost recovery is another prerequisite for sustainability, assuming that what is borrowed must be repaid or the lender goes out of business; and that the provision of infrastructure and services will lead to increased production and incomes, but those directly benefiting should contribute to their upkeep. These are not moral tenets but intrinsic elements of feedback in self-perpetuating systems.

Of the case studies discussed in this chapter the Grameen Bank stands head and shoulders above the others in respect of quantifiable numbers of beneficiaries and quantifiable cost recovery. It alone can be seen as a closed system – lending and recovering with interest, and paying its expenses. The other projects are less tidy; they interact with more variables and are more affected by external factors.

Although it is satisfying to be able to identify whether a project is paying its way or not, there are certain types of project for which this is difficult to ascertain. This does not establish a reason for not supporting such projects in future but indicates that the economists should turn greater attention to this type of problem than most have done up to now. Even though some projects cannot demonstrate direct cost recovery, the economic benefits can be established over time; the necessary analysis could estimate the effects of increased production, employment and incomes and the long-term returns on safeguarding the environment.

Sanctions. Without effective sanctions a project cannot be considered sustainable. The poor and hungry want enough to eat and, having satisfied this basic need, want better shelter. The process does not stop once basic needs are met. New goals are born, and the pressures to meet them are social, not entirely individual greed. While goal-seeking can provide the necessary spur for people to produce, there have to be checks on the extent to which greed, and the means adopted for satisfying it, are permissible. So long as it does not destroy the system of which it forms a part, greed seems to be allowable, but transgressions beyond a given point must be prevented.

The projects under review incorporate sanctions in various forms. In the case of IRDP, ODA will not provide the funds except for projects considered to be economically useful.

The Grameen Bank has built in a type of insurance to cover bad debts and can refuse to make further loans to a defaulter. Within each group it is in the interest of all members that those with loans repay on time, since the rest of the group will not be allowed loans otherwise.

The problem of building-in appropriate sanctions, without donor intervention or the threat of such intervention, is frequently the Achilles' heel of otherwise good projects once the donor withdraws. What will happen if FUDECO withdraws from the CAOTACOs in the Dominican Republic?

Project resources, channels and sectors. Project resources, normally categorized into capital, technical assistance (TA) and training, are intrinsic to development projects. Since they originate from outside the project area, usually from outside the country, they are not considered to be lasting components in what might become a sustainable project. Certain features of these resources nevertheless will have an influence on the project once the donor withdraws.

People-intensive projects, especially those assisting the poor to help themselves, cannot absorb large volumes of capital. When in about 1978 the Bangladesh Small Farmers Project was beginning to make headway, donors expressed a wish to put funds into what was becoming a programme. The Bangladeshi responsible for the projects turned the offers down, as in his estimation the poor people in their groups could absorb only small amounts of cash at a time and remain viable. Clearly it took Dr Yunus (Case Study 24) to develop the concept further before large sums could be utilized in programmes assisting large numbers of people.

The other perceived disadvantage of projects which listen to people, and help them do what they want to do, is that, in addition to not being able to predict exactly what will be funded, the project implementation stage requires too much TA and too much supervision by the donor. This apparent donor suspicion derives from the need to be accountable for public funds.

Where TA is provided, the characters and personalities of the people sent as experts or volunteers is of equal importance to the excellence and relevance of their technical training and experience. Patience, willingness to listen to people and ability to criticize constructively without causing offence are essential attributes of fieldworkers. These qualities, combined with an ability to suppress the urge to do the job or take decisions themselves, are essential in institution building.

In the context of development projects major donors are constrained in the way they transfer money from individual taxpayers in their own country to the people in the ARCs. NGOs manage to do this by transferring resources to an overseas wing or another NGO. Official aid is usually transferred through a ministry of finance in the ARC, and resources are then passed on to whatever ministry is responsible for the sector intended for assistance. For certain types of project the procedure to channel assistance through one ministry or department is benign. The ERL projects in Hong Kong and Indonesia were implemented through the most appropriate organizations in the two countries, an important factor in their success. Similarly, donor funds channelled by the Bangladesh government to the Grameen Bank went to the most appropriate organization, albeit one that was created to fill specific needs not being met by any other commercial bank.

The usual method of channelling project funds by sector is not appropriate for rural development or any other people-intensive project. This is because people do not live in sectors, and attending to one arbitary group of needs while not being able to respond to others can at best be of only limited help. Somehow, funds for the Zambia IRDP are channelled directly to a bank account, which is then drawn against for approved projects in any sector; there is a definite lesson to be learned from the IRDP case.

Ideas, innovations and technology. Besides money, the other important inputs from outside to make projects successful are ideas, innovations and technology. To find the right technology it is first necessary to find out what people want to do, which involves finding out about their goals and aspirations. Having satisfied one goal, or set of goals, people will develop new ones, just as the IRDP district councils first wanted new infrastructure but, having got some, wanted no more, but developed a new goal of wanting to maintain existing infrastructure.

Even in cases where the technology provided is truly appropriate, its application and use often produce new problems. Draught power for tillage enables farmers to plant larger areas of arable crops but increases the labour requirements for weeding, harvesting and processing. Since weeding in many parts of the world is traditionally women's work, wives and other females in the household may be required to greatly increase the time spent on the "man's farm" at the expense of growing subsistence for the family on their own plots, with ensuing bad effects on children's nutrition and women's incomes. Projects should therefore be able to respond to new needs and suggest fresh solutions to problems as they arise. Best of all, local institutions, formal and informal, should be developed to perform this type of service even after the project is "completed".

Lessons learned

Poor rural people can be assisted on a large scale through project interventions. Yet many projects cannot precisely pinpoint who has benefited and by how much or in what way. This does not indicate the projects are unsuccessful but that existing methods of appraisal and evaluation are too limited. There is a need for more thinking on how to appraise projects for institutional development, sustainability and environmental impact.

The case studies indicate the importance of key factors external to the project. Prices, foreign exchange rates, infrastructure and the presence of key institutions and their relative strengths influence decisions on the type and form of projects. Like institutions, projects should be developed in areas where there is genuine need, not just because they are technically feasible.

The channel used as a conduit for aid funds can be restrictive on the range of activities a project can embark upon. Funds channelled through a ministry of agriculture can only be used for activities legitimately carried out by that ministry, but funds placed in a special account can be utilized according to real needs. Just as people-intensive projects should embark only on activities decided upon by the participants, so procedures and mechanisms outside the control of the project, but influencing its chances of success, should be tailored to suit the workings of the project. For donors to complain that this is not policy, or against the rules, would indicate that their policies and rules, and those of the ARC government, need to be changed.

Sustainability is linked to at least five criteria which must mutually support one another as part of an internal project system – the five internal factors, discussed earlier, of beneficiary organization, participation, decision-taking, payment/cost recovery and sanctions. Two additional factors are essential ingredients for the project to get started: the resources provided (quantity, quality and the way they are channelled) and ideas, innovations and technology. In order for a project to develop and grow, it and its impact should also be carefully and sensitively monitored.

An implementing agency working with, or through, an established local institution can have lasting impact after withdrawing from the project. It has also been shown that it is possible to develop a completely new institution to meet the growing demands of people. A further point which emerges is the importance of training, of both agency personnel and the members of participatory groups: not formal training, but training directly related to the operation of a group or institution and how to use whatever technology is required.

Implications for donors

(1) Donors could well take note of the five internal factors deduced to be of critical importance to sustainability and adopt them as headings for project preparation and appraisal, relating each factor to each of the others in a dynamic manner. It is human behaviour which makes things happen; the sum of what individuals do determines the outcome of the group, and the sum of the outcomes by groups equals the statistics by which project success can be measured. It is not feasible to start with the desirable statistics and then expect people to conform their behaviour to them.

(2) Replication of the projects described is possible, but here a word of caution. It is not the activity of individuals and groups which is replicable but the application of the principles which enabled people to do what they did.

(3) Increasing the scale of successful projects can be achieved through additional capital and manpower resources. To provide more than an outside chance that projects will be sustainable, however, it is advisable to work through local institutions and organizations rather than to increase the numbers of expatriates.

(4) Both to replicate and to expand existing projects, donors should give more serious consideration to intensifying their dialogues with ARCs on making laws and regulations more conducive to the sustainability of grass-roots projects. This could go as far as introducing conditionality to achieve the desired results.

(5) Donors should fund only projects appraised with the new methodology indicated in this paper but yet to be developed, which will thus have a strong chance of being sustainable.

(6) Priority should be given to projects assisting rural people in countries carrying out structural adjustment programmes, in order to take advantage of the newly created opportunities.

(7) Donors, especially larger ones, should explore ways and means to channel their funds according to project needs rather than for administrative convenience.

References

Bramber, Michael, and Deneke, Alberto Horth (1984), "Can shelter programmes meet low-income needs? The experience of El Salvador". In Geoffrey K. Payne (ed.), *Low-Cost Housing in the Developing World*. Wiley, Chichester.

Cernea, Michael M. (1986), "Farmer organizations and institution building for sustainable development", paper prepared for the World Bank Expert Group

Meeting on Local Development Innovations, Nagoya, Japan, October; revised version, January 1987.

Moris, J. C. H. (1981), ''A synopsis of reviews of six African rural development projects'', unpublished mimeo. Overseas Development Administration, London, November.

World Bank (1986), *World Development Report*. Oxford University Press.

CASE STUDY 24 *Grameen Bank, Bangladesh, and Small Farmer Development Project, Nepal*

INTERNATIONAL FUND FOR AGRICULTURAL DEVELOPMENT

Poverty not only brings hunger, disease, suffering and a loss of self-respect; it also threatens the environment. The hungry and desperately poor often lack the resources, energy and will to preserve or improve their natural surroundings. Their first concern is survival.

One approach taken by Third World governments and international organizations to improve the quality of the lives of the poorest has been to make credit available to them, particularly in rural areas. This credit would, in theory, help reverse the vicious downward spiral of "low income, low savings, debt, lower income". These efforts have generally been disappointing, benefiting the better-off and failing to reach those most in need. This relative failure has reinforced the common belief that, even when credit is made available, the very poor are unable to take advantage of it. In the last ten years, however, two of the world's poorest nations – Bangladesh and Nepal – have demonstrated that, if credit programmes are carefully devised to meet local needs and aspirations, the poor will respond, with impressive results.

The Grameen Bank, Bangladesh

There has been a rapid expansion of rural credit in a variety of forms in the past few decades: state-owned agricultural development banks, private rural banks, co-operatives and multi-purpose development agencies. These efforts have run into problems. Management costs and overheads are often prohibitively high, because transactions involve small amounts and the clientele are widely dispersed. Income distribution may worsen rather than improve, if the eligibility for credit requires assets and thus eliminates those most in need. Often credit conditions are not responsive to local needs and credit is too little or too late. The poor generally lack banking experience, are ignorant or suspicious of formal institutions and may feel little responsibility to repay an "anonymous" lender.

All of these problems have been eliminated or significantly reduced in the Grameen Bank. A land of lush green fields and a vast network of rivers and streams, Bangladesh is also one of the poorest, most densely populated countries in the world. Over 80 per cent of its almost 100 million rural people live below the absolute poverty line. It is to these, the most destitute that the Grameen Bank has extended loans, enabling them to increase their earning capacity and self-respect and to improve the quality of their lives.

How does it work?

The Grameen Bank is the brain-child of Dr Muhammad Yunus, who, after returning from the United States to take up a position as Professor of Economics at the University of Chittagong, was struck by the appalling poverty. He remembers vividly walking through villages, observing and talking to the people. One woman, working at a decrepit loom in front of her tin shack, spoke to him of the few cents she earned a day weaving, most of which she had to give to the merchant who rented her the loom and to local money-lenders, who charged 50 per cent interest.

Yunus became determined to do something to emancipate his countrymen and women from crushing poverty and debt. In 1976 he persuaded a local commercial bank to set aside some funds for an experimental loan programme. The Grameen Bank was born. The experiment has succeeded largely because its goals are addressed to the needs of the people and because it has a novel system of loans and repayment. Groups of five members are formed at village level. They decide who among the members will get loans, for how much and for what purposes. Weekly meetings inculcate a philosophy of responsibility and social consciousness. There are now over 241,000 members spread throughout almost 5,000 villages. Emphasis is given to reaching women, who comprise 69 per cent of the members.

Decentralized, mobile, highly dedicated staff bring the bank directly to the people. Repeated small loans, at standard commercial rates, are repaid on a weekly schedule. Loans average between Taka (Tk) 1,600 and 1,700 (US$64 to $68); by the end of 1986 a total of Tk 1,364 million had been disbursed. Compulsory individual and group savings are used for personal emergencies and social obligations.

One of the guiding mottos of the bank is: "Take the bank to the people, not the people to the bank." A young man or woman bank assistant or worker goes to a village after a six-month training course and seeks out the most destitute. After an informal talk about the bank and what it stands for, the bank worker begins to form one or more groups of five men or five women, unrelated, who share similar interests and attitudes. Once the group has been identified, the worker meets with them for four more weeks, explaining how the bank works, what it expects of members and what they must expect of themselves. Time is spent answering questions and discussing possible ways to use loans. The group is introduced to the social programme called "Sixteen Decisions" which stresses the importance of discipline, hard work and group unit and outlines a code of conduct aimed at improving home and village living conditions: growing vegetables and fruit in home gardens, using latrines and safe drinking water, investing in housing improvements, sending children to school and refusing to give or receive marriage dowries.

Each of the group members must be approved by the bank worker and the other group members. They then become eligible for their first loans. Initially two of the five receive loans. If repayments have been on schedule, the next two members become eligible, and later the fifth member may borrow. Each group member thus has a personal interest in the success of all the others.

After the group is established, it joins several others in the village to form a centre which elects a centre chief from among its members. The centre chief, who is given additional training, conducts the centre's mandatory weekly meetings and makes recommendations of loans to the bank worker. At these meetings the "banking" work is done publicly: loans are made, repayments and savings collected, loan activities discussed, experiences shared and suggestions made. This continual exchange of ideas at the grass roots reinforces members' efforts and percolates up through the bank's hierarchy.

Credit and savings systems

The criterion for membership and eligibility for loans is ownership of less than half an acre of cultivated land or assets less than the value of one acre. This excludes all but the most destitute. Groups have been allowed to apply for a collective loan for a joint venture since 1982. Loans carry an annual interest rate of 16 per cent and (except those for housing) must be repaid in 52 weekly instalments.

The bank's default rate of less than 3 per cent is very favourable. (In other rural credit programmes default rates of 40–60 per cent are common.) This can be explained by the initial screening and training of group members, reinforced by peer pressure; the close supervision by bank assistants before and after loans are made; the weekly repayment schedule which requires that only a small sum be paid at a time; and the nature of the activities selected for credit.

Loan patterns

Grameen Bank loans finance hundreds of income-generating activities which enable the borrowers to establish small businesses. These can be grouped into three major fields: livestock and fisheries, processing and manufacturing, and trading and shopkeeping. The most popular investment is buying a milch cow or fattening one already owned.

Participation of women has grown dramatically, from 30 per cent in 1980 to 69 per cent in 1986. Loans for collective as opposed to individual enterprises have also increased since 1982. Half of them have been used to improve irrigation for crop production.

Growth and organization of the bank

The steady expansion of the Grameen Bank has not compromised its basic objectives, philosophy or performance. As the bank has grown, its administrative structure has been kept as simple and decentralized as possible. Approximately 90 per cent of the 3,200 full-time staff work in the village branches. A governing board of directors guides overall policy. Under the board is the head office in

Dhaka, one zonal office in each district and branch offices throughout the villages. Distributed more or less evenly over each of the five districts, the branch offices serve neighbouring villages. Branch staff are responsible for screening membership applications, forming and training borrowers' groups, evaluating loan requests, disbursing loans, and collecting payments.

Many of the bank's young workers (both men and women) come from the villages they serve and have a deep commitment to help alleviate the poverty they have seen and shared.

The bank's impact

A study of Grameen Bank members found that over 90 per cent of those surveyed thought their living conditions had improved. Most borrowers had been able to accumulate more "working capital": a milch cow, a paddy husker, a few beehives, materials and tools to build fuel-saving ovens, a large fish net, a bullock cart. A 1985 study found that bank members had about 50 per cent higher income than the target group in villages where there were no bank groups and about 25 per cent higher than target group non-participants in project villages. Loans have been instrumental in generating employment, especially for women. There is a trend among members of a shift away from agricultural wage labour towards better-quality, more remunerative work as independent entrepreneurs.

The Grameen Bank should be able to sustain itself in the business of delivering credit to very large numbers of poor people without being dependent on government or donor subsidies. It showed a profit for 1985 and the first quarter of 1986 and should be able to start paying off its loan from the Bangladesh government by 1995. The Grameen Bank may not be transferable, wholesale, to other parts of the world, but it holds a promise and provides a guide. Based on this, IFAD has initiated several other group-based credit schemes in other countries in Asia and Africa. One of these is the Small Farmer Development Project in Nepal.

Small Farmer Development Project, Nepal

Some 35 years ago the Nepalese government inaugurated its first five-year national development plan. Included were projects to make agricultural credit available to poor farmers. These and subsequent efforts were not very successful. The better-off were getting better off; the poor were getting poorer.

Against a background of rising population, increasing poverty, stagnant agriculture and a deteriorating environment, the Small Farmer Development Project (SFDP) was launched a decade ago. Since it began the project has assisted over 42,000 of the rural poor to increase their income, raise their standard of living and develop self-reliance. It has attracted the support of agencies and has become a model for other rural development programmes in the country.

SFDP covers a cluster of development projects involving a variety of government ministries and institutions. However, all are executed through the

Agricultural Development Bank of Nepal. The bank's branch offices deliver loans and collect payments through fieldworkers called "group organizers".

The SFDP groups. SFDP has focused on the small farmer and the rural poor as key participants in the operation of the programme. The core of the system is the group, 5 to 25 borrowers who identify, plan, put into operation, monitor and evaluate all individual and collective projects.

The process of establishing an SFDP unit begins with a survey of the potential area to be served. Data on topography, climate and natural resources are collected, and patterns of land use, land tenure, basic farm and family structures, general income level and ethnic composition are investigated. Economic and social infrastructures are assessed to ensure they are adequate to support project activities. After this survey, a group organizer visits the villages and conducts household surveys to identify those who would be eligible for and interested in credit. In the early years the criterion was ownership of one hectare or less of land for people in the hills and two and a half hectares or less for those on the plains. Quality of land is supplemented by an income criterion.

The group organizer next forms one or more groups. As often as possible, the group organizer is accompanied by a woman "motivator" who seeks to form women's groups. The groups are relatively informal and autonomous, each setting its own mode of operation. Normally they meet once a month to discuss problems and decide on future activities. Members are of the same sex and usually share the same occupation, interests and caste or ethnic background.

Loans cover an enormous variety of activities; buying and raising livestock, particularly buffalo, are the most popular. The repayment record of SFDP is better than most rural credit programmes in Nepal. In 1985 the default rate was 17.5 per cent, down from 26.6 per cent in 1981.

Other activities. Loans for income-generating enterprises are not the only benefits group members enjoy. Over 5,500 men and women have received training in a wide range of skills. Farmers have learned to improve yields by adopting better techniques of raising wheat, rice or maize or have diversified their production into horticulture, vegetable or sericulture farming, fisheries and beekeeping. Others have gained skills in blacksmithing, carpentry and other agricultural and cottage industries. The project also encourages groups to involve themselves in activities which benefit the community, such as constructing roads and community buildings.

Financing. The first pilot project for SFDP started in 1975. Initial support was provided by FAO. In 1981 an IFAD loan of US$12.5 m and grant of $1.0 m, together with government assistance of $2.6 m, began a phase of rapid extension. In 1986 there were 152 sub-project offices in 50 districts. The total numbers of groups and individual members were 4,554 (3,961 male) and 42,000 (37,000 male) respectively.

Synthesis

The programmes in Bangladesh and Nepal are both directed at the poorest segments of the rural population and have a decentralized organizational structure. Both stress full participation of the poor in deciding how credit will be used; small groups of borrowers, formed and guided by a trained fieldworker, meet regularly to decide on loans. In addition, group members share concerns, hopes and experiences, plan group and community projects and develop a sense of discipline and social consciousness. In both programmes small loans are given to individuals or groups, at regular bank rates, for income-generating enterprises. There is collective responsibility for repayments and emphasis on regular savings, and groups are based on mutual trust rather than family ties or obligations.

The Grameen Bank is a poor people's bank which provides only short-term loans for income-generating enterprises; the SFDP is a development bank giving long-term credit for community development projects as well as short-term loans for economic ventures. The Grameen Bank is a self-contained, independent, full-fledged bank under Bangladesh law, while SFDP, on the other hand, is a cluster of programmes drawing on the services of a number of government agencies.

The administrative apparatus of the Grameen Bank is primarily devoted to economic management; social services are an indirect, "informal" dimension. The Nepal project tends to make less use of the small groups; however, the project provides a wide range of "outside" services through government agencies and programmes. The Grameen Bank has had a strong emphasis on the most vulnerable and neglected of the rural poor – the landless and women – and its loans go almost exclusively to them. In contrast, only 12 per cent of SFDP members are women, while the very poorest are under-represented, largely because the project tends to avoid the most remote areas of the country.

Though their methods may differ, the Grameen Bank and SFDP both work. Each has been able to help large numbers of men and women break poverty's vicious spiral and attain some measure of self-reliance and self-respect.

CASE STUDY 25 *Community Training Centres for Organic Agriculture and Appropriate Technology, Dominican Republic*

HORACIO ORNES
Fundación para el Desarrollo Comunitario

Organic Agriculture and Appropriate Technology Centres for the Community (CAOTACOs) are farm-schools that were conceived in 1979 by the Fundación para el Desarrollo Comunitario (FUDECO) with the objective of stimulating and supporting the self-management development of the rural population in the Dominican Republic. FUDECO, a private, non-profit, voluntary organization, administers the project.

The two CAOTACOs are located in the frontier area of the country – Loma de Cabrera, in the Province of Dajabon, and Las Matas de Farfan, in the

Map 5: CAOTACOs in the Dominican Republic

Province of San Juan de la Maguana (see Map 5). The CAOTACOs were constructed during 1981–3 with support from the Inter-American Foundation, Save the Children Federation (SCF) and the German Agro Action Foundation.

History and chronology

In 1964 efforts were initiated for construction and community infrastructure in the Loma de Cabrera municipality. This work continued with the collaboration of the Dominican government, mainly through the Oficina de Desarrollo de la Comunidad (ODC). Institutions such as Caritas Dominicana, the Dominican church and the Comité de Ciudadanos (Citizens' Committee; a private national institution) participated. At the same time, SCF began working with a programme in Santo Domingo and had a consultant working with ODC.

In 1972 SCF decided to begin working in the community of Hipolito Billini in Loma de Cabrera with participation from the community under the management of the Comité de Ciudadanos. SCF's work began in Hipolito Billini through the sponsorship programme, the children receiving direct cash gifts from sponsors. Community work was also carried out, such as technical and financial assistance to a consumers' co-operative, distribution of plants to farmers, health training courses, family planning, home economics and community leadership.

In 1975 SCF sent two planning consultants to Loma de Cabrera to work directly with the field co-ordinator, and a new concept of community development was defined in the region, establishing a process of self-help and self-sufficiency. This new philosophy responded to political and social changes which favoured the appearance of a more critical attitude towards rural poverty, thus allowing the rural population to develop its organization and making institutions committed to rural development reconsider their approach. International organizations such as SCF adopted a concept of development based on integrated programmes.

Action extended from Hipolito Billini to other locations in the 1970s, thus requiring a formal structure for which an administrative and operational institution was organized in 1976. This was called the Federación de Desarrollo Juvenil Comunitario (FDJC) and was authorized to represent SCF, replacing the Comité de Ciudadanos.

New technicians were contracted, and in 1979 the directorship functions were transferred to Santo Domingo, leaving the office of Loma de Cabrera with an operational role. The agency became a totally national and independent organization, changing its name to Fundación para el Desarrollo Comunitario (Foundation for Community Development: FUDECO). A survey was conducted in order to initiate work in the southern part of the frontier.

Evolution of the project

Present functions. The strategy for creating the CAOTACOs sought to create in the rural population a consciousness that it was possible to obtain better use of the local available resources through technologies adapted to the economic and social characteristics of each community. This philosophy, along with practical work, brought a mutual enrichment between rural communities and FUDECO. This has led to the CAOTACOs assuming multiple functions, transforming them into what they are today: training centres; demonstration, experimental and appropriate technology diffusion centres; channels for resources; instruments for participant planning; integrated models for productive agricultural and industrial activities.

The CAOTACO project includes many components of integrated rural development programmes, e.g. agriculture, livestock raising, supply of inputs, credit, processing of agricultural and livestock products, appropriate technology, environmental protection, infrastructure, housing and health. Although the physical centre is important for a CAOTACO, principles are more important than infrastructure. Principles include use of locally available technologies and constant reinforcement of training.

The project involves two forms of mutually reinforcing technical assistance. CAOTACOs receive students selected by village-based farmers' associations. The benefits of training are then passed on to other farmers in the form of transferred knowledge. Conventional extension is also provided by FUDECO employees. Training and follow-up technical assistance are fully integrated. CAOTACOs also serve as applied research and demonstration centres; methods and technologies are tested, with the help of trainees as a component of their training.

The decision-makers are in close and continuous communication with members of the farmers' associations. Federations of farmers' groups send representatives to the board of directors of their respective CAOTACO. Funding proposals, loan applications and the operations of the CAOTACO are discussed at regular meetings. In sharing decision-making powers with the federations and CAOTACO boards, FUDECO has delegated broad operational responsibilities to the local level but retains an oversight role.

After the failure of a large-scale, nation-wide, public sector programme, the idea of creating these centres was taken up by FUDECO but on a small scale. A more simplified technology was envisaged which would be more appropriate to the practices and habits of the rural areas. There would be a more appropriate mechanism for extension, and beneficiaries would participate via the centre's board of directors. The centres were constructed with financial support from the Inter-American Foundation (FIA), SCF, German Agro Action and the Dominican government.

Present physical structure. Each installation was constructed with appropriate technology in accordance with the cultural and economic condition of the area. It consists of a classroom-dining-room, kitchen, dormitories, fish-ponds, a reproductive pig farm, a mill for grain and animal feed production, a meat, fruit and vegetable processing plant, and vegetable gardens and fruit trees with their own irrigation system.

Management of this organization is based on self-management. Direction is formally in the hands of the board of directors, the majority of whose members are representatives of the farmers' associations and the remainder members of FUDECO. The CAOTACO's board of directors determines priorities and plans activities based on the previous training process, which itself aims to convert beneficiaries into trainers.

Integration has evolved at the CAOTACOs. Each complex comprises an experimental farm for demonstrations and for agricultural production. This provides agricultural products to a plant located in the centre which processes high-quality animal feed for the pig farm, for beneficiaries of the credit loans programme and for the market. The pig farm produces meat to feed programme trainees, provides agriculturalists in the area with reproductive sows and supplies the meat processing plant with developed animals. Organic waste is used as fertilizers and as feed for the fish-ponds. The fish-ponds produce food for the CAOTACO and raw material for the food processing plant, which in turn provides the centre and local inhabitants with processed foods.

The concept of integration not only covers activities physically located in the CAOTACO but also includes activities for the farmers so that they can produce crops that constitute part of the raw material required in the processing industries. The training centre is used to train some of its beneficiaries, as a result of which they experience a change of attitude regarding how best to use the area's local resources.

The CAOTACO is not entirely self-sufficient. It counts on support from FUDECO's field office in the area, which provides agricultural and livestock extensionists, infrastructure technicians and trainers. These staff, with the financial resources for credit loans and the construction of infrastructure, have contributed to an improvement in the living conditions of the farmers and transmitted a new concept of development which is irreversible.

Achievements and reasons for success

Some of the major successes and achievements of the CAOTACO system include:

(1) Democratic participation of the people.
(2) Adaptation of technology appropriate to small-sized parcels of land.
(3) Adaptation to the local small-farmer diet – the "association" of crops that form a balanced diet and, when growing, mutual help in reducing threats of insects and disease.
(4) Utilization of wastes and manures.
(5) Diversification of traditional monocultural production.
(6) Use of the Lorena stove, produced from locally available material, to help conserve firewood.
(7) Soil conservation – use of traditional teams of oxen is easier on the soil than tractors and much more economical; "live and dead barrier" fencing helps keep animals from overgrazing.

(8) Continued promotion of the concept of small-farmer self-determination, although the model used in the Dominican Republic may not be practical in countries where there is less of a hierarchical system or where there are no existing associations to form its basis.

(9) Recruitment and training of personnel who agree with the methodology and have the technical ability to implement it.

(10) Utilization of existing organizations, through agreements, and emphasis on small farm size, *campesino* participation and trust, and a revolving fund that can lead to financial self-organization.

(11) Strategic geographic location in an accessible area, with distribution of the buildings and other features on the campus to make it a compact, self-contained experience that is relevant to the surrounding environment.

(12) Availability and appropriate timing of sufficient funding.

(13) Frequent visitors to the centre from around the world, who get to know the facilities and create added support.

(14) The capacity to correct mistakes, so that they do not damage the community.

(15) Promotion of joint planning and partnership with the beneficiaries, prior to making significant investment decisions.

(16) Utilization of architecture appropriate to the region.

(17) Good communications with local communities through radio, press, etc., to improve their level of knowledge and technical abilities.

(18) A preference for hiring staff from the local area if they are equally qualified as (or better than) other applicants.

CASE STUDY 26 *Business Advisory Services to Small Enterprises and Local NGOs, Kenya and Ghana*

THOMAS W. DICHTER

Technoserve

There are now between 10,000 and 20,000 local NGOs in the developing nations. These new organizations and groups need a great deal of basic help which, increasingly, major bilateral and multilateral development agencies are aware they cannot adequately provide. Disenchanted with "trickle-down", large-scale interventions, these agencies have sought ways to make their programmes benefit poor people more directly. When they tried to create and foster intermediary institutions which could guide the process, the multilateral and bilateral agencies discovered enormous gaps and missing links. Institutions involved tended to be too centralized and politicized and to lack motivated personnel and technical capability.

The experience of Technoserve through its Business Advisory Services Programme in Africa can shed light on this problem. Started in Ghana in 1979 and later extended to Kenya, the Business Advisory Services Programme (BASIG and BASIK respectively) performs two critical functions. First, it offers to local organizations short-term help in fundamental business and organizational skills (e.g. management, book-keeping, accounting systems, administrative structures and review) and other services appropriate to NGOs: review of proposals, project feasibility studies and sourcing of needed technology and equipment. Second, it helps close the gap between local groups and the larger system, including market-place, banks, other institutions and government.

Background, history and chronology

In Technoserve's main line of work – the promotion of and assistance to agricultural community-based enterprises – substantial staff interventions are required. To develop viable and sustainable enterprises is difficult and requires concentrated efforts over time. Such efforts require a staff of technically competent people who remain in their positions for long tenure, capitalizing on their growing experience. As many as four Technoserve staff advisers, working with members of the enterprise who must be trained, spend years getting a project under way. Ideally, such an investment of resources is made in enterprises that have the potential to become economically viable and provide income and jobs to more than just a few people as well as creating backward and forward linkages.

In taking on the Business Advisory Services Programme, Technoserve added short-term interventions to its profile. Yet its staff come from the same pool of professionals (mostly nationals) as Technoserve's other staff project.

After the US Congress's 1973 "New Directions" mandate – stressing grass-roots local-level projects run by NGOs, not USAID itself – USAID underwrote an ambitious programme in Ghana called Farmer Associations and Agribusiness Development (FAAD). One of FAAD's seven NGO contracts went to Technoserve for a project that would help local groups start and run enterprises based on the processing of sugar into syrup. Other grantees (mostly transnational NGOs or affiliates) were having difficulties getting their projects off the ground, some encountering difficulty even completing the initial proposal process. Seeing its grants threatened, USAID asked Technoserve to help rescue its investment.

BASIG was the result. A programme of short-term assistance was designed to cover seven key areas:

- evaluation and assessment of ongoing economic activities;
- feasibility analyses;
- management consulting;
- financial planning;
- support for conferences, seminars, etc., focusing on economic or business related activities;
- identification of technical requirements and sources of information;
- advice in the sourcing of capital goods.

The capacity to undertake these functions for themselves was strikingly absent amongst other FAAD sub-project grantees. The heart of their work was threatened because their administrative and technical support services were inadequate. Eventually such capabilities, the basic nuts and bolts, were admitted as the *sine qua non* of the project. If the books couldn't be kept properly, or the vehicles couldn't be maintained so that field trips could be made, projects would be unlikely even to get off the ground, let alone succeed. Without basic skills and ways to connect with the larger system, no sector of development assistance can move forward or be sustained.

The range of services we performed became very broad – from administrative and managerial advice to legal services, engineering design, locating equipment, acting as a broker for funding, conducting feasibility studies and so on. The commodities we dealt with represented an even broader range. We responded to requests from groups or individuals involved in road construction, fuelwood, lake fishing, shrimping, cocoa, solar energy, tailoring, cane weaving, blacksmithing, sugarcane, rice and pottery. One assignment often led to others.

For the short term, BASIG's work was very positive. The work we did for and with other NGOs had a significant multiplier effect. Another positive result was that, through the BAS kind of assistance, we had a chance to take a thorough look at whether the commitment of a group to a venture was real. In development projects group commitment is hard to judge at the outset, and here was a tool ready-made for that purpose.

In 1981 we added a BAS to our Kenya programme. BASIK was initially a mechanism through which to transfer our project experience and management capabilities to other development entities locally. In Kenya the largest number of BASIK projects involved the provision of book-keeping and accounting systems. Control of money is, in many cases, control of the ultimate outcome of a project, and a crucial missing link in small community efforts at self-help is lack of an accounting system or administrative structure.

For the most part, the BAS programme works well; it has been non-political, non-profit, staffed largely by nationals who are permanent staff members of the Technoserve organization and experienced in their specialism as applied to grass-roots clients. It has been low-cost, in high demand and much used.

Programme services and functions

Between 1979 and 1985 BASIG and BASIK provided services to a total of 242 separate projects/clients (as well as repeat services to those same clients). The clients comprised private enterprise, community-owned enterprise, community groups, local NGO training or educational institutions, local social welfare or development institutions, government bodies, international organizations and transnational NGOs. Services performed (listed earlier) divide up fairly well among the seven key categories for which the BAS concept was originally approved.

However, as already pointed out, besides the services it provides BAS has a second, underlying function. BAS acts as a broker or catalyst to the larger community. It is the agent that links local groups to those structures and institutions, such as banks and ministries, which have traditionally ignored them.

Underlying functions of the BAS programme

Information and knowledge. BAS provides knowledge that is of a critical nature to a group that is either too new, small, unsophisticated or inexperienced to have it on its own. This can mean reporting on conditions, providing commodity expertise, reviewing policy, conducting feasibility or market strategy studies, etc. An aspect of this function could be called "reality therapy"; what groups set out to do is often not feasible, and no comparative advantage (say), in its choice of endeavour or enterprise exists.

Legitimation. Grass-roots groups, groups of poor people, even groups who might be considered middle class, lack credibility in the eyes of authorities. They are not given the benefit of the doubt in the competition for funds or opportunities; what is needed is often simply some aura of respectability, sophistication or credibility. In many developing societies this is a key missing link for those needing access to the mainstream structure.

Acting as bonding agent or guarantor. What is needed may be a guarantee that those who wish to take a chance on a small group with an investment will be taking less of a chance because a respectable agency stands behind that group.

Brokering. Brokering means providing connections – from introductions between group and possible funding source, to finding out how a group can locate a commodity it needs (anything from a waste product to diesel-engine parts), and guidance through the bureaucratic system. Brokering can also cross over into legitimation, since what is needed to grease the wheels of bureaucracy is often knowing who to see and having some legitimacy in their eyes.

Continuity or follow-up. We define continuity as providing to a group the ability to assess its own progress. This is a matter of helping a group connect up with itself and its own stated goals in a more explicit way.

Control. Control probably accounts for most of BASIK's activity. Poor people's relative inability to control their own lives is widely acknowledged, and there are political aspects of the problem that people and organizations can do little about. But there is a surprising degree of control that can be exerted and learned through acquisition of basic skills. Technoserve in Ghana gave assistance to an NGO which was ill equipped to manage its vehicle maintenance programme. Technoserve helped it redesign a programme of vehicle maintenance so that its vehicles could stay on the road, thus enabling it to accomplish its work – an instance of helping a group gain greater control over its resources.

Integration into and access to the modern world-wide economic system

For the poor and uneducated, access to the political and economic system has become an arcane construction of luck, personal clout and knowledge. The operant system in Africa is these days less the tribal seat, which local people can see, know and understand, and increasingly a relatively unknown and far-away set of bureaucracies in towns and cities.

Poor people on the margins of society who try to gain access to the system, acting on their own, have to pay for gifts to officials, for transportation to get to the system and for a scribe to fill out forms. There is also the opportunity cost in lost time that these efforts take. These "transaction costs" can often equal or be greater than the interest that small farmers pay on their loans. Helping others gain access is a critical function of local NGOs, yet many local groups lack the necessary know-how.

These indigenous NGOs need, first, to learn the nuts and bolts of management. Secondly, they need to become brokers for access to the system. Local NGOs and "associative structures" haven't yet been able to learn to play that role for themselves or for others.

Technoserve hoped that the BAS programmes would serve as locaters of potential full-scale enterprise projects. In the first six years of the BASIK programme, seven of the 137 clients assisted became full-scale community-based enterprise projects.

Client dependency and group motivation

In Technoserve's main line of work, dependency is not much of an issue. By carefully selecting farmers' groups with demonstrably strong motivation and commitment, working with them over time to determine their needs and ensuring that the transfer of skills was real and lasting, we developed some keys to reducing dependence on outside assistance. But with BAS we found ourselves filling in gaps with whatever was needed, whether it appeared likely to create dependency or not. Many instances of "dependency" seemed to be unavoidable, and even at times a necessary part of the development process.

A more serious issue than dependency *per se* is whether or not the commitment of the group to the project is strong. In a number of instances, group motivation was weak and signalled how we ourselves had lost sight of one of our own basic principles: the need for strong client motivation and participation.

Programme costs

Has BAS been expensive to operate? The evidence suggests that it has not been, relative to the rest of the portfolio in the two countries. But it is more important to assess cost in terms of the type of service offered and compare our costs with those of a profit-making company offering similar services (in name) to BAS. The total daily rate for such a company in Kenya works out to be about US$450 per day, whereas Technoserve's BAS work, when it was billed at all, used a fee rate of about $150 per day; most of the time we were not paid by the client at all. The key point is not absolute cost, however, but the fact that traditional providers of such services would not take on these clients in the first place, whether they could pay or not.

Lessons learned

(1) The grass-roots African environment has changed in the last decade. The rise of local groups, associative structures and other intermediary organizations and institutions has tremendous potential for development. However, a great many of these groups are not ready for the next steps. What is needed is a disciplined approach to solving problems, for which the seeds exist in the basic techniques of management and financial organization.

(2) If a community project has not become something the community itself is willing to put substantial energy into, it is unlikely that outside technical assistance will take hold in any sustained way. An NGO can get caught up in a cycle of helping to start things going, then rescuing, then restarting, to the point where dependency has been created. One has sometimes to say "no" to requests for assistance, if certain criteria appear to be absent.

(3) Very short or minimal interventions can be remarkably useful for some groups. Yet again, if there is no internal strength in the group to take advantage of the intervention, the impacts of such assistance will be random.

(4) Integration at the small-project (BAS-type) level must be as great as that at the full-project level. Care in selection of the short-term intervention target must be as great as that of main-line long-term assistance projects. Rigour, professionalism and caution all need to be equally applied.

(5) There is a sensible and logical sequence to organizational, and hence also project, development. The lesson can be summed up as "first things first". New, immature, small community groups or enterprises cannot afford to skip the important first definitional stages of their growth and must set up some "nuts and bolts" mechanisms and systems before carrying their mission forward.

(6) Giving advice and assisting in the implementation of those recommendations are two different things and may be hard to reconcile. Technical assistance is most useful when those offering it can stay around to see what happens next.

(7) Accounting and other management skills require an intensive on-the-job training approach. The more unsophisticated the trainee, the more an on-the-job approach makes sense.

(8) The notion of a service centre for business advice can work. If such centres are staffed by a well-run organization which uses well-motivated, trained, permanent, national employees who know how the "systems" work, and the programme is carefully managed, such a programme can work cost-effectively.

Replicability

BAS is an extraordinarily replicable programme. Replicability is built in, almost by definition. Within Technoserve, BAS evolved out of years of staff development and experience in all the areas of service offered under BAS. So BAS is a replication within one NGO of the best skills and services it has to offer. BAS is replicable almost anywhere, regardless of radically different circumstances. The two functions that have been described in this paper are needed everywhere by some entity or other, because they are basic.

Technoserve has successfully replicated the BAS concept (in Zaire and Rwanda) and, since 1984, in El Salvador. The BAS concept adapts well to a different environment. The programme's clientele in El Salvador includes both local NGOs and community groups and enterprises, but the level of sophistication of the clientele is greater than in Africa, and our services have geared to match. In El Salvador the lessons learned from the first days of BAS in Ghana and Kenya were applied; the programme was carefully managed, and project selection criteria were rigorously applied.

CASE STUDY 27 *Integrated Rural Development Programme, Serenje, Mpika and Chinsali, Zambia*

D. R. MELLORS
Rural Development Consultant

The Integrated Rural Development Programme (IRDP) described in this case study, funded by the UK Overseas Development Administration, is now regarded as a model for institutionally sustainable development in Zambia. The programme provides, first, a team of technical co-operation officers acting as development facilitators and, secondly, capital development funds to be used by district institutions to construct and rehabilitate essential infrastructure. Planning, co-ordination and implementation systems were evolved by the district institutions themselves, with the IRDP acting as a catalyst in a flexible "learning by doing", evolutionary approach. Emphasis is on the development of responsibility and autonomy as a precondition for sustainability.

Priority has been given to the support of economically productive infrastructure in the rural areas, with limited expenditure on socially oriented programmes. Increasing attention is paid to the development of local revenue raising in order to sustain the development of districts in the face of national economic decline. Total cost of the programme over the first five years was £4.6 million. The three districts involved have completed over 210 discrete projects – new bridges, roads, houses, depots, health centres, wells, crush pens – which are seen as the means to developing district institutions rather than ends in themselves.

Problems encountered by the programme have resulted from incomplete implementation of the Zambian government's decentralization process, begun in 1980.

Background

Programme area The IRDP covers three districts in Northern Zambia: Mpika and Chinsali in the Northern Province and Serenje in Central Province (see Map 6). The programme area is 81,000 sq km, including large areas of National Park and Forest Reserve. The majority of the agriculture of the area is practised on the upland plateau. Total population is approximately 224,000, with 16 per cent living in three main townships. In the past there was considerable out-migration of labour to the copper mines and Lusaka; but this has stopped, with the trend

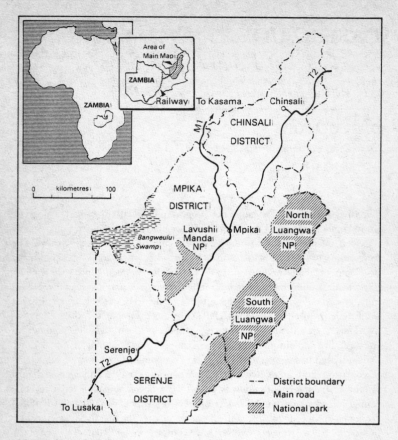

Map 6: Integrated Rural Development Programme, Serenje, Mpika and Chinsali, Zambia

now beginning to reverse as urban economic conditions deteriorate.

One reason for selection of the area for a rural development programme was the construction of the Tanzam railway during the mid-1970s. It was hoped to create a development corridor along the line of rail similar to that along the older railway in Zambia's southern provinces.

Zambian governmental structures. The Zambian Ministry of Agriculture and Water Development has been responsible for IRDP SMC through the period covered by this chapter. (Late in 1986 Phase 2 of the Serenje, Mpika and Chinsali IRDP was transferred to the recently created Ministry of Decentralization.) Fundamental to the approach of IRDP SMC is the policy of decentralized local administration. Under the Local Administration Act 1980 district councils (DCs) became responsible for district development. A DC is a legal body comprising appointed representatives, with a district governor appointed by the

President as chairman and elected representatives (ward councillors) drawn from subdivisions of the district. A DC is served by a secretariat headed by a district executive secretary. When decentralization is complete, all district departmental staff of the line ministries will be responsible administratively to the district executive secretary.

DCs have wide-ranging powers to run almost all development activities within their district. Before they are allowed to take over the running of a key sector such as health or education, they have to demonstrate an ability to manage the sector to the central ministry concerned and the Ministry for Decentralization. No key sectors have yet been handed over to DCs, largely because their staffing and financial resources are not considered adequate. The newly formed DCs and their secretariats were generally ill prepared for the responsibilities conferred on them by the 1980 Act. Posts were left unfilled, many staff were underqualified and there was no strategy for the hand-over of responsibilities from central government.

Rural development programme in Zambia. From an economic history based on copper, Zambia's first awareness of the need for increased agricultural self-sufficiency and the need to reverse rural–urban migration came in the early 1970s. The first rural development programmes suffered from a number of problems: an over-professional approach to planning; planning by outsiders, largely foreigners; implementation by the same outsiders; full control by foreigners; lack of any institutional goal; increased resentment towards the more affluent, externally funded body due to a widening gap between development zones and the areas around them.

In an attempt to overcome these problems, IRDPs were introduced. The objective was to give high priority to the less developed areas with proven potential through a strategy of small-farmer development. By 1981 five IRDPs, including IRDP SMC (Serenje, Mpika, Chinsali) had been established. All had different approaches arising from different local conditions and donor philosophies. With the exception of IRDP SMC, all the programmes were planned and implemented through an autonomous project body, although initially all intended to work with and through local Zambian institutions. These programmes encountered problems of donor dependency.

Early history of IRDP SMC. In October 1978 ODA and a firm of UK-based consultants were invited by the Zambian government to identify possible IRDPs in Serenje, Mpika and Chinsali districts along the new line of rail. The terms of reference envisaged a repetition of the development approach of previous IRDPs, with planning and implementation being largely the responsibility of an autonomous project team. As a result of previous experience with the ODA, its technical co-operation officers (TCOs) had misgivings, notably that the study paid no attention to sustainable development and the means by which the programme was to be implemented and that it did not consider the development of the districts as a whole. The TCO team therefore decided to make the most of the opportunity offered by the 1980 Decentralization Act, with institutionally sustainable development as the fundamental emphasis. This required the development programme to be both planned and implemented by existing local institutions, with the ODA team acting only as external catalyst. The capacity of these institutions, notably the DCs, to undertake such responsibilities was thought to be limited.

Programme evolution and philosophy

Objectives and strategies

Programme objectives could be summarized on two levels:

(1) The ultimate goal of IRDP SMC is the raising of rural welfare in Serenje, Mpika and Chinsali districts.
(2) The immediate objective is to develop district institutions so that they are better able to run and sustain an effective development programme of service provision to the rural population.

The programme hopes to meet these objectives through two closely linked strategies:

(1) The provision of capital funds to enable the construction or rehabilitation of infrastructure, especially economic infrastructure designed to alleviate constraints on services.
(2) The provision of technical assistance through a team of TCOs to develop capacities of the DCs to plan, implement and monitor their own development programme.

The programme

Institution-building. One IRDP expatriate officer was appointed as district representative (DR) to work with the institutions of one district only. There are neither counterparts nor hand-overs, since the role of the DR is to work as a catalyst with the district's departments and organizations. Each district within the programme has its own representative within IRDP. IRDP officers promote an exchange of ideas, expose weaknesses, build confidence and fund approved projects. Crises are not avoided but worked through, even at the risk of failure. IRDP provides support and advice but never takes over responsibility or solves a problem directly. Relationships between DRs and district officials are of critical importance, and mutual trust and patience are essential.

District development plans. Prior to decentralization, planning was little understood by the districts. The planning process now involves each district department drawing up a list of the infrastructure required, in order of priority and with detailed justifications for each proposal. A planning subcommittee approves the submissions and integrates them in accordance with priorities and capacity. Approved priority projects are compiled into a five-year development plan out of which a three-year rolling programme is drawn up. The rolling programme is revised each year, and projects proposed for its first year are compiled as the annual estimate. The annual estimate, with detailed justifications, is presented by the districts to the donors, who agree to fund projects within the programme which meet their criteria.

Funding systems. Funds are deposited quarterly by ODA into a local IRDP bank account. DRs are then responsible for funding each individual approved project, following the submission of detailed planning documents. After approval by the DR, funds are transferred to the DC's development account. The planning document acts as a monitoring document during implementation for checking quantities and costs against estimates. On completion of a project a certificate is submitted by the implementing department, listing quantities and costs incurred.

This funding system (1) allows flexibility on the part of each implementing DC, (2) develops the capacity of DC officers to make realistic estimates, (3) facilitates monitoring, (4) safeguards financial control requirements of donors while giving responsibility to DCs; also (5) funds do not pass through a specific government ministry, thereby becoming confined to a particular sector.

Monitoring. Monitoring of the overall programme is a function of district development co-ordinating committees (DDCCs).

Local revenue raising. Sustainability and autonomy will finally be achieved only when DCs have not only the capability to run and maintain development programmes but also the necessary resources. Rural DCs in Zambia are heavily dependent on central government grants for their revenue needs, and these sources will be reduced by economic constraints on the central budget. Local revenue generation is now seen as essential to the future of DCs and rural service. IRDP SMC councils have been some of the first to tackle this problem and have been strong advocates of the approach. They have drawn up proposals for crop levies in addition to the current local sources which include licences, rents, rates, personal levy and DC-run enterprises.

Training workshops. During the early stages of IRDP SMC no formal training was included. The development of human resources was achieved through a learning-by-doing approach. However, IRDP was introduced to participative training workshops in management and development planning skills, and these workshops have become a significant part of the programme.

Programme costs

IRDP SMC is essentially a technical co-operation project with limited capital funds made available to DCs to finance parts of their development programmes. The capital projects are the means to developing district institutions and not ends in themselves. There are three main sources of funding: (1) capital development funds from ODA; (2) technical co-operation funds from ODA; (3) direct support costs for the programme from the Zambian government. During Phase 1 of IRDP SMC approximately 86 per cent of costs were met by external assistance from sources (1) and (2).

The distribution of development funds by sector within each district varies considerably between DCs. This reflects differences in priority and, more frequently, in implementation capacity. Approximately 20 per cent of funds were expended on social infrastructure – health, water, social development. This was a target limit set at the start of the programme by ODA and coincided with government policy.

The Zambian government supports the programme through the provision of site running costs and in the sense that it pays district staff and the recurrent budgets of the DCs and government departments. During Phase 1 of the programme the government contribution to project running costs included site staff salaries, local spares, fuel, electricity and the provision of vehicles. Under Phase 2, which started in 1986, the contribution has been reduced owing to economic contraints. ODA will now fund most support costs.

Programme benefits

Previous rural development projects have regarded changes in agricultural output, farmer incomes and rural welfare as their major indicators. In the case of IRDP SMC these measures relate to the programme goals and are only indirect indicators. The direct effects of the IRDP are changes in the capability of district institutions and the construction of physical infrastructure.

Subjectively the impact of the institution-building approach of IRDP can be assessed through increased planning and implementation capacity:

Increased planning capacity. At the start of the IRDP, DCs had virtually no experience of planning, and sectoral ministries rarely integrated proposals. District administrations have now gained experience of the whole planning cycle and now review plans and policies annually. DC departments draw up policies, establish priorities, collect data, integrate plans with other departments and carry out economic analysis. They present plans directly to donors and negotiate their own funding. Donors are able to fund projects drawn from a locally produced district plan rather than imposing their own ideas.

Increased implementation capacity. Before 1980 DCs had limited responsibility for project implementation but in some cases acted as agents for the provincial works department. The availability of IRDP funds has enabled DCs to implement projects up to their own organizational capacity. The detailed funding system has greatly improved cost and quantity estimation capabilities. The establishment of DDCCs as a monitoring and co-ordination forum has been fundamental to exposing problems, supervising implementation, co-ordinating use of resources, applying group pressure to member departments and consolidating district identity.

Ecological impact

IRDP SMC has not formulated specific objectives with regard to its impact on the environment. Ecological impact is best considered as an indirect effect of the institution-building input. Having been used to a plentiful supply of land and little intensive farming, DCs are only just starting to perceive the needs of environmental protection. These needs will become much more obvious over the next decade. In 1987, however, the first direct environmental project was funded – an agroforestry/soil conservation pilot project submitted by Mpika DC.

DDCCs offer a forum for the discussion of environmental issues which would not otherwise exist. In strengthening the administrative systems of the districts and promoting the establishment of planning units, IRDP is able to increase awareness of environmental problems including deforestation and soil and wildlife conservation.

The IRDP SMC area contains Zambia's major National Park and three other small parks. The wildlife resources of these parks are invaluable, but there has been heavy poaching, particularly of elephant and rhino. Councils and central government are increasingly realizing the value of these resources, and proposals are being made for the involvement of local councils in collecting and retaining hunting and tourist revenues.

Institutional sustainability and replication

All the working systems of the IRDP programme have been developed with institutional sustainability as the key criterion. Certain factors are essential in promoting sustainability:

Responsibility and autonomy. Responsibility for all aspects of a development programme should be held by local people and institutions. A decentralized government policy is one of the most effective means of facilitating this.

Pressures. People take responsibility from commitment or as a result of pressures, particularly pressures arising from problems perceived as relevant. Under the IRDP programme, pressures depend on: availability of IRDP funds (funds can be used as carrot and stick to exert pressure on DCs and associated staff); the sanction of central government discipline if district institutions are not seen to take up opportunities offered by IRDP; pressure from the DC on its secretariat.

The two major pressures of the present programme are flawed by the fact that they are external. IRDP funds will eventually be withdrawn, and central government discipline is weak. Institutional sustainability can be fully achieved only by internal pressure, which must come from local people through their elected representatives. Latterly IRDP has supported workshops held by the DCs to develop the capabilities of ward councillors.

Local revenue raising in the form of crop levies or rural rates will also generate pressures on the DCs for improved performance. Similarly, DCs will be under pressure to increase their revenue by supporting productive local enterprises.

If the IRDP team were to withdraw from the programme at the present time, the improved level of institutional capability would decline as a result of staff transfers and inadequate local pressures. Infrastructure and maintenance programmes would be cut back owing to insufficient locally raised finance.

Impact on national policy

As the programme progressed and encountered mass staff transfers in the DCs, it became apparent that sustainability depended on the approach becoming more widespread through Zambia. In 1985 the Ministry of Agriculture declared the institution-building IRDP SMC approach to be the "national model" for all area-based development programmes. ODA is also expanding the use of this approach by financing a second phase of IRDP SMC, which began in 1986; and it has established a new District Development Programme for the whole of Central Province in Zambia, which began in 1987.

The fundamentals of the IRDP SMC approach are valid for other countries, i.e. sustainable development of people and institutions rather than short-term development of material resources; an evolutionary process approach rather than a blueprint plan; avoidance of outsider control; working with what already exists rather than imposing outside structures. The detailed working systems that such an approach produces, however, will be radically different in different socio-political environments. The absence of a decentralized system of government would limit local participation and preclude limited autonomy. The absence of basic bureaucratic effectiveness, integrity and commitment would undermine efforts to develop responsibility. In such circumstances the approach might be applied at village or provincial level. Priority should be given to that level at which decisions on planning and funds are made.

CASE STUDY 28 *Environmental Management Development, Indonesia*

Dr ARTHUR HANSON

School for Resource and Environmental Studies, Dalhousie University, Canada

The World Commission on Environment and Development stressed the need to create a philosophy of sustainable development throughout the structure of government within nations. Environmental management should become a responsibility shared between governmental and non-governmental elements within a society. No nation can yet claim a satisfactory level of environmental awareness, planning or management; but progress has been achieved in many countries, including Indonesia.

Indonesia faces tremendous natural resource and environmental management issues in its development. The need for a sustainable, equitable basis of resource and environmental use has long been recognized. Environmental use patterns within Indonesia reflect three trends: (1) population increase from 147 million in 1980 to 165 million in 1985; (2) rapid economic growth; (3) extensive land opening, often under marginal environmental conditions.

Environmental institutional development

Indonesia's environmental institutional structure began to emerge, as in many countries, with the catalytic action of the Stockholm Conference. This process was shaped largely by indigenous thoughts and action. Since the early 1980s a directed effort has been undertaken to ensure simultaneous development of each major component: national and regional government, universities and other educational and training bodies, private sector and NGOs. Each component's objectives and functions are expected to be interactive and to support national needs. Under the 1982 Environmental Management Act, roles and responsibilities are recognized or designated.

Facilitation and co-ordination have been provided by the Ministry for Population and Environment, charged with expanding the level of awareness regarding environmental issues. Its goals are: working with national and local government to create effective planning and management approaches; generating new legislation and regulations on environment and assisting their enforcement; maintaining adequate technical information on environmental problems. The ministry relies on co-operation with other bodies, and the decision to serve environmental management needs through this matrix approach rather than by more monolithic institutional development was influenced by the social and ecological diversity of Indonesia, the relative lack of environmental technical and scientific skills within government and concern over potential for emergence of another large bureaucratic apparatus within an already ponderous administrative system.

Those countries which have placed reliance on a large centralized environmental department find that such units become introverted. The assumption in Indonesia is that environmental management can be successful only if there is widespread awareness and accepted responsibility.

Of the Indonesian government departments most likely to create physical changes in the environment, six require immediate and sustained attention in order to strengthen their environmental capabilities: Agriculture, Forestry, Mining and Energy, Industry, Public Works and Transmigration. The President has assigned the Minister of State for Reform of the State Apparatus the task of ensuring that senior department officials take an active involvement in ensuring that their units properly understand and contribute to environmental management.

The most difficult aspect of environmental issues is the cross-sectoral side. Coastal zone and watershed management, forest land development, industrial hazardous waste disposal, agricultural chemical use and environmental aspects of energy are examples where it is often difficult to obtain relevant sectoral information on which to base decisions, and then to bring sectors together to reach a consensus and act upon it. Environment suffers because either the economic answers are poorly known or described, technical approaches seem unworkable or the inability to provide compliance negates agreement. Sustainable development strategies must be intersectoral, although taking into account sectoral interests.

Foreign donor assistance

A relatively small amount of Indonesia's annual foreign donor assistance is in the form of grants packaged as technical assistance. This assistance is important, not only as direct monetary input, but also for the ideas and advice attached. While all donor-funded projects have their origins within the Indonesian bureaucracy tend to favour ''more of the same'' rather than innovation; however, because projects can draw upon a range of the best Indonesian and foreign technical skills, they provide a potent means for introducing new concepts to the society.

In the field of environmental management, foreign donor assistance is directly channelled into development projects and into appraisal, while far larger sums are committed to sectoral projects which will create changes in environment. There are significant opportunities for enhancing the use of donor assistance to support sustainable development strategies and growing costs of ignoring such opportunities. Meetings concerning environment have been held with donors since 1979, and areas of common interest have emerged:

(1) Environment may be treated as a sector in its own right and may be treated as the focal point for cross-sectoral concerns.
(2) All the elements important to environmental management must be assisted simultaneously.
(3) Natural resource and industrial sectors are of special concern.
(4) Long-term assistance is required for institutional development.
(5) Experimental efforts to apply environmental science and technology in urban and rural development, and to build environmental monitoring and information systems, are needed.

In recent years several projects have been undertaken drawing upon these points. The largest has been funded by the Canadian International Development Agency (CIDA). The UN Development Programme (UNDP), World Bank, UN Environment Programme, bilateral donors such as USAID and the Netherlands and some private foundations have helped in significant ways. Some of these activities are documented below.

Three major themes are now considered: environmental sector reviews; training and education; and environmental management development as a project. Each category provides insight into ways of investing in environment and development.

Environmental sector reviews

Prior to 1983 there had been no external review of performance within the environmental sector. UNDP provided funds for an international team to develop an overview of the activities under way within the Ministry for Population and Environment and relevant activities elsewhere inside and outside government. The review produced several priority issues/policy matters and suggestions for action, many of which have been acted upon through the national five-year plan. A second environmental sector review was to take place during 1987, also sponsored by UNDP.

Training and education

Human resource development is essential to implementing environmental management. One example of donor-assisted efforts is the ongoing effort to upgrade and expand technical skills within the environmental study centre network and, through these university-based units, provide education and training to others, particularly government personnel. This project provides opportunities for environmental centre staff to study environmental issues at an Indonesian university or abroad. The project provides inputs, including buildings, books, journals and field sampling equipment. The Ford Foundation funded programmes at several universities on Java in the 1970s which became institutionalized in the form of graduate programmes and study centres.

EMDI project

Prior to 1983 technical assistance and training funds accessible from donors were for specialized needs; there was no mechanism to support the overall framework of environmental management development. Support of this sort would have to be flexible, and the structure for assistance needed to be open enough to accept Indonesian or donor funds from more than one source. The central point for a grant was to be the Ministry for Population and Environment, but assistance was to be open for regional and sectoral departments, universities, NGOs and private sector training and advisory needs. CIDA decided to fund a project of this nature. The project was set up as an institutional linkage activity and, in the second phase, as a country focus project. From the start, EMDI had the potential to respond in a flexible way to meet emerging needs.

Phase 1 began in late 1983. The title Environmental Manpower Development in Indonesia (EMDI) reflected the concern for education and training. The general objective was "to expand the numbers and capabilities of Indonesian managerial, technical and scientific workers required to implement resource and environmental management in national and regional development". A total of C\$2.5 million was committed by CIDA over a three-year period, along with an equivalent Indonesian in-kind contribution. Activities were to include: a seminar in Canada to introduce Canadian and Indonesian environmental personnel; training and advice in environmental impact assessment; opportunities for graduate studies in Canada; development of linkages between Indonesian and Canadian environmental study centres; assistance for publication development and training; encouragement of linkages with Canadian environmental NGOs. Dalhousie University perceived itself as a manager of Canadian inputs, not the sole source of expertise. Canadians were drawn from a range of backgrounds, an involvement which has been beneficial.

Practical difficulties of initiating this type of project include: (1) overcoming scepticism of those more used to highly focused approaches; (2) management time and costs associated with co-ordination; (3) balancing demands from various parts of the matrix. A serious constraint was the limited inputs set aside specifically for enhancing administrative and management capability within the Ministry for Population and Environment. Another problem, which should have been taken care of at project design stage, was that no funds were earmarked for the preparation of a second phase. A number of EMDI activities had to be slowed in the final year to allow for planning of a second phase.

Phase 2 began in 1987 for a further three years with CIDA funding of C\$6.7 m. The project name was changed to Environmental Management Development in Indonesia to reflect increased emphasis on advisory services and other inputs in support of immediate implementation of the environment and development strategy. It is now possible to be more specific about particular inputs and outputs needed to achieve objectives. The main categories of activities to be undertaken under EMDI Phase 2 are: (1) hazardous substance management, (2) environmental spatial planning, (3) ecosystem management standards, (4) environmental assessment implementation and evaluation, (5) environmental law training and education, (7) environmental education and awareness building, (8) strengthening of environmental study centres, (9) technical advisory group and (10) publication development and international literature transfer. Direct on-the-job skills development and advisory services are used in most of the EMDI components.

Conclusions

The necessity of devising better economic approaches to environment and development has proven a tough topic to bring into focus. Unless the point can be brought home to decision-makers that the issues of resource depletion and environmental protection represent significant losses, or additional burdens on the economy, then environmental management will be constrained. The need for structural shifts in Indonesia's economy as a consequence of introducing sustainable development and environmental planning concepts is far from threatening. There will be true beneficiaries, among them the poorest people, urban *kampung* dwellers, coastal fishermen and families relying on sustainable access to forest products. More work needs to be done on the identification of target groups and the quantification of benefits they may receive.

Entrenched patterns of environmental and resource exploitation involve strong vested interests and a compelling short-term economic rationale. How quickly these patterns can be altered to more sustainable ones is difficult to predict. At best it will be a decade's work to bring about a satisfactory situation in forest land use or coastal zone management. Public, corporate and government attitudes towards environment are gradually shifting, although not at the desired rate and not always consistently. There is a need for continued education efforts and for expanded use of traditional and modern media to spread the message. Belief in environment is linked to a broader set of concerns: harmony with humanity, with nature and with God. This spiritual linkage is essential for the emergence of a national environmental ethic.

Along with attitudinal shifts, there will be a continued evolution of the structure for environmental management. The present system may prove inadequate, and there are several options to modify the existing structure without destroying the matrix approach to management. Donor assistance in support of environmental management, while modest in relation to overall needs and in comparison to other sectors, has been effectively used in Indonesia. Further expansion of assistance will be required over the next decade for full institutional development and to provide for transfer of expertise. On some environmental issues Indonesia can already contribute ideas and expertise to other countries. This regional, and even global, exchange cannot be neglected if environmental management is to transcend national boundaries.

CASE STUDY 29 *Implementing Environmental Programmes – Why It Is Difficult and How to Make It Easier*

Dr ROBIN BIDWELL, Dr JOHN HORBERRY and DAVID GETTMAN

Environmental Resources Ltd, London

In the 16 years since the UN Conference on the Human Environment in Stockholm tremendous progress has been made in sensitizing governments to the importance of the environment. In 1972 only 26 countries in the world had an environment ministry or the equivalent, whereas now about 145 do. Many have passed "framework" legislation, developed broad environment policies and collaborated internationally in assessing problems. The "environmental enlightenment" has become nearly universal.

The adoption of basic goals of environmental protection and natural resource management has posed new problems. First, how does an environmental agency convert its policies into programmes? Unlike policy development, programme development involves identifying tasks, setting priorities for action and acquiring resources. Second, where does the agency find skilled manpower? The skills required are not only technical but include the ability to manage programmes and achieve progress in the face of opposition and shortages of resources. Third, how does the agency implement its programmes? The key to progress is often held by government ministries, and the achievement of environmental goals often requires the reshaping of their activities. Addressing these questions means getting down to hard practicalities, trying to create power and influence within a sometimes entrenched political structure and culture. It means training dozens of people to administer the programme and provide technical support and having a realistic, long-term schedule for programme implementation.

This case study reviews three projects intended to aid the implementation of environmental programmes. Having deduced some of the difficulties that countries face, we have drawn the following general conclusions:

(1) Environmental protection and improvement require management as well as technical skills. Environment agencies have not been paying sufficient attention to this requirement.
(2) Without administration and enforcement, laws, regulations and guidelines are no more than statements of intent.
(3) Short-term expert assistance is often of dubious value. New environment agencies require long-term help.

Hong Kong

Because Hong Kong is industrialized and very small in size, its development pressures conflict sharply with tight natural resource constraints. The Hong Kong government has made an ambitious efforts to implement a comprehensive environmental protection programme, and the experience usefully illustrates the institution-building that should occur, and the issues that may be confronted, in any low resource programme implementation.

In Hong Kong the power to protect the environment was originally in the hands of sectoral executive departments. Powers to control pollution were created whenever the need became apparent, and enforcement powers were conferred on whatever public authority happened to have the appropriate skills and resources. The Hong Kong government's reorganization in 1973 put pollution control in the hands of a Secretary for the Environment, whose small Environment Branch was primarily empowered to formulate policy. Hong Kong also had a semi-independent Environmental Pollution Advisory Committee (EPCOM), which included government officials, technical experts and interested parties from the community. By 1974 EPCOM had become alarmed at the estent of environmental problems and put pressure on the new Secretary for the Environment for something to be done.

The Secretary for the Environment recognized that his Environment Branch had inadequate technical knowledge and little experience of environmental control. He commissioned a specialist consultant project team to research and propose a comprehensive plan for control of the Hong Kong environment. The project team produced a plan which made recommendations in five categories: water, noise, air, solid waste and land-use planning. The plan proposed that all forms of pollution be dealt with by a central control authority, subject to policy control by the Secretary for the Environment. The plan suggested that the authority should follow the "polluter pays" principle but that it could provide short-term subsidies to hard-hit industries. Proposals emphasized the importance of land-use planning.

The establishment of a central control authority was based on the idea that pollution control is not a series of separate problems but largely a single problem. An integrated approach under a single authority can help ensure consistent quality objectives and appropriate and cost-effective methods of control. However, the team stressed that the imposition and enforcement of fixed standards would not be a successful or economic method for achieving environmental improvement. Rather, there was a need for flexibility and sensitivity. The proposed authority could not be simply an administrative body, but, in addition to applying powers of control, would need to develop programmes for environmental improvement, to adapt its controls in response to change and to promote environmentally favourable change. Since Hong Kong could not proceed on all fronts simultaneously, the authority would need to recommend priorities for action to the Secretary for the Environment.

After it was completed in 1977 the plan was generally accepted by the

Secretary for the Environment and EPCOM, and over the past decade progress has been made in implementation. During development of the plan, and subsequently during implementation, a number of critical issues needed to be faced.

First, there was the issue of the proposed *administrative structure*. The project team was concerned that establishing a major new government structure might not be the best institutional method for achieving the programme's aims and that establishing a new authority would be perceived as too expensive. In fact, establishing the new authority did not cost much more than it would have cost to centralize Hong Kong's existing functions. The project team was also aware that the proposal to create a new authority would precipitate power disputes among existing civil departments. This issue was resolved by a gradual approach of institutional development and change. The secretary's policy-making powers were first supplemented by a small Environmental Protection Unit responsible for drafting and enacting new legislation, establishing standards and new programmes and co-ordinating monitoring and enforcement by other departments. The unit gradually developed into an independent agency, the Hong Kong Environmental Protection Authority, which is fast becoming a full-grown government department.

A second issue was finding *qualified personnel* with the necessary management and technical expertise to administer and staff the programme. Staffing for the original unit was particularly important. To establish its authority, the unit would need enough expertise to counter-balance entrenched positions in the various executive departments. To create a better supply of qualified managers, technicians and specialists, the new director of the Environmental Protection Unit encouraged the subsidy of training programmes.

A third issue was the long time it can take to finalize and implement new environmental *legislation*. Although draft legislation was provided by the team in 1975, redrafting and negotiations with interested parties have taken so long that 13 years later the government has still not enacted all the proposed new laws. In the interim the Environmental Protection Authority has learned the importance, when drafting legislation, of seeking early consensus with other branches of government and concerned sectors of the community.

A fourth issue was that the new unit was under considerable *pressure to act* during the early stages. These pressures had the potential to distract the unit from its long-term planning mode and shift it permanently into a "crisis management" mode. From its inception the unit had a broad and long-sighted mission; environmental authorities without such responsibilities will remain hooked on high-profile, short-term crisis management – and slow, unglamorous achievement of real environmental progress will forever be put off into the future.

Indonesia

The UN Environment Programme has a "clearing house" mechanism by which it helps a developing country find a workable approach to its most serious environmental problems and then packages the work to attract bilateral funding. In 1983 UNEP organized a study team to examine implementation problems in Indonesia. The study aimed to propose an administrative framework to help manage development/environment conflicts and to show how Indonesia could take action on critical environmental problems around Jakarta.

The environmental impact of development pressures here was particularly acute. Pressures were resulting in soil erosion and depletion, clearance of natural forest, severe and dangerous water pollution, over-use of groundwater reserves, loss of traditional agriculture and destruction of natural ecosystems. Despite its limited resources, the government of Indonesia had already made progress in creating an administrative framework to address these problems. There was a Ministry of Population and the Environment (MKLH) responsible for policy development and programme co-ordination, which had established a system of liaison with other departments. MKLH saw that there were considerable problems to be overcome in achieving tangible improvement: first, the sheer weight of development pressure; second, the issue of manpower and financial limitations and priorities; third, specific obstacles to "on the ground" environmental control: lack of trained technical advisers, inspectors, field personnel and equipment.

The study team first proposed an "implementation framework" for managing development/environment conflicts. This framework, to be undertaken by strengthening the administrative structure of MKLH, outlined five broad tasks:

(1) Identify programmes to tackle priority problems.
(2) Determine likely effects of options for action and shape actions as appropriate.
(3) Detail resource and training requirements for implementation.
(4) Establish an action plan.
(5) Monitor progress.

The team proposed that MKLH undertake a series of programmes dealing directly with Indonesia's urgent environment problems. These programmes would provide experience of environmental control techniques and land management and would give concerned departments experience in working together under the "implementation framework" and, in the process, help relieve the most serious pressures around Jakarta. The team proposed seven programmes in the Jakarta–Puncak area, which could be replicated elsewhere in Indonesia. UNEP was left to seek bilateral funding.

The study team identified a number of issues to be addressed when trying to implement environmental policies. The first is the *scarcity of resources* needed to carry out programmes. The number of projects that a country like Indonesia can initiate and successfully conclude will be relatively few. The implementation of new environmental programmes should thus (1) make clear the resource needs of proposed actions, (2) set and keep to priorities and (3) only take action which will lead to tangible environmental improvements.

A second issue is the *integration into decision processes* of environmental assessments. Environmental impact assessment (EIA) is an example of information collecting that is not always integrated into decision-making; in many cases, its only consequence is another report on someone's desk. The study team's proposals for Indonesia included a mechanism for integrating EIAs with the government's existing decision structure and provided for monitoring the success of EIAs in influencing project plans.

A third issue – the need for *appropriate technology and management* – is often spoken of but rarely acted upon. Aid agencies are learning that the technical and management solutions of the industrialized world may have only a limited role to play currently in Third World countries. Proposed programmes in Indonesia would help ensure that environmental control procedures were not imposed arbitrarily from without but were allowed to evolve within existing structures. Similarly, the proposed programmes were an acknowledgement that *implementation must be from the bottom up* and needs the support of the people. Community involvement was an important part of each programme.

Central American Bank for Economic Integration

The regional development bank within Central America, the Central American Bank for Economic Integration (CABEI), ran into financial difficulties during the early 1980s. In 1985 USAID proposed a financial assistance package designed to get CABEI back on to its feet. CABEI and USAID agreed that the technical assistance would include setting up an environmental planning function within CABEI. One of the authors (John Horberry, under contract to IIED) was asked to investigate this opportunity and to draw up a programme for its implementation in co-operation with CABEI staff.

The consultant identified the basic issues that should be addressed by any such agency's environmental assessment system: will the proposed project have effects which damage the environment or impair the productivity of natural resources? If there are effects, what is their nature and extent, and are they significant in relation to the project's expected benefits? If the effects are significant, what can be done to mitigate them or to protect against them during project implementation? Tying answers to these questions to the organization's project evaluation cycle requires (1) a focal point for environmental planning in the organization and (2) procedures that identify what action is necessary during the project cycle. Technical guidelines and criteria can then be used to support different tasks or decision points.

The consultant recommended a three-part environmental planning system for CABEI: an environmental focal point in the bank; environmental planning procedures, incorporated into the bank's day-to-day project evaluation routines; and supporting technical guidelines. A programme was proposed for staffing, technical assistance and training, and a starting-point was identified – appointing an environmental specialist to create the focal point. The cost of establishing the environmental specialist post, supported by external consultancies, training inputs and counterpart secondment, was estimated at US$360,000 over two years. Following agreement of the financial package with USAID, an environmental adviser was appointed in 1986. His first tasks were to prepare an environmental policy paper for the bank, and procedures for integrating environmental planning into CABEI's operations.

A number of issues arose during the development of this environmental implementation programme that would seem to apply to others facing a similar task. The first was the difficulty and expense of creating a new department dedicated to "environmental review" and establishing its authority within the existing organization. The consultant suggested starting with a single adviser who would be given authority to influence project decisions. He or she would work with existing officials in initiating the integration of environmental assessment procedures into the project evaluation cycle, contract any needed technicians or specialists, organize in-house training and eventually take on additional staff.

A second issue was that environmental assessment can be costly and needs to be tempered in proportion to the capabilities of the organization's clients – its borrowers from within its member states. Development banks and aid agencies deal with countries that have severe financial constraints, and requirements for environmental information should not be made expensive or burdensome.

The third issue raised is important for all environmental programme implementations. There has been considerable effort on the part of international oganizations and development agencies to prepare environmental guidelines, but less attention has been paid to their integration into the process of environmental planning. *Guidelines should not be the starting-point of an environmental assessment system.* Only after a responsible focal point and procedures are determined should an organization devise guidelines (e.g. on data collection or on analytical methods to aid particular tasks and users) for project reviewers or technical advisory staff.

PART 6

Human Settlements

CHAPTER 6

Human Settlements

Dr YVES CABANNES

Co-ordinator, Habitat Section, Groupe de Récherche et d'Echanges Technologiques, Paris

Trying to give an overview of the human settlements sector at a world-wide level is almost impossible because of the extreme variety of situations each individual country is facing. What do countries like China or India, where over half of the world population is living, have in common with Tuvalu in the Pacific (less than 10,000 people) or Dominica (less than 100,000)?

The world is becoming predominantly urban, and by the year 2000 the majority of the population will live in urban areas. Again the difficulty of a global analysis lies in the extreme variety of situations. What do Latin American countries such as Chile, where 82 per cent of the population live in cities, have in common with Ethiopia, where the recent urban phenomenon represents less than 10 per cent of its inhabitants?

The management of 22 mega-cities of more than 10 million inhabitants, 18 of them in Asia and Latin America, will constitute an unprecedented challenge. However, what is called the urban explosion, with its astounding rates of growth and massive needs, refers to an endless range of individual situations. What does Mexico City with 900,000 additional inhabitants per year have in common with Vientiane, the capital Laos, which faces a slow rate of growth, or with another capital city like Roseau, Dominica, with a relatively high rate of growth but a rise of only 20,000 inhabitants?

This focus on urban explosion does not mean that rural settlements are becoming a secondary issue. Even in countries with a high rate of urban growth, say Kenya, where the urban population originates partially from rural migration, the rural population is still growing; projections suggest rural populations will almost double between 1980 and 2000. Any action which improves living conditions in rural areas or secondary cities will reduce the problem in the capital (by slowing outmigration) and thereby have a double positive effect.

Generally, the most visible aspect of the human settlements issue is the housing deficit. For instance, it is considered that 100 million Latin Americans are in need of shelter, meaning that about 20 million new homes should be built immediately (Ibanez, 1983). In India the deficit could rise to 186 million units by the year 2000.

From a macro- to a grass-roots perspective

This kind of discussion based on hard facts and macrofigures could go on for ever. However, low-income settlements all over the world share much in common, and in this the reality of their inhabitants plays a major role. If one considers development through the life of the poor, one can say that their lack of access to drinking water, sanitation, education and shelter is a constant that knows no national boundaries. Their access to the basic inputs (finance, land, building materials, legal rights) to build and live in a decent home is extremely limited, if it exists at all. The difficulties faced by low-income households are multiple, but two main problems constantly re-emerge: access to land and a decently paid job. Unemployment – or unstable jobs – is a key part of the general question of socioeconomic development.

Meagre income even in the case of jobs. Even for those able to get a declared or non-declared job, the income they get from it is generally so low that it hardly meets their basic needs of food and decent housing. In Addis Ababa a woman carrying wood from the surrounding hills to the *mercato* is paid one *birr* a day (US$0.5), not enough to buy 1 kg of teff, the local cereal used to make *injerrah* bread. In the low-income Chilean settlement of Villa la Concepción, Santiago, a family in the lowest income percentile lives with $1.3 daily; $1 buys 2 kg of bread.

Struggle for land. The struggle to get a land title, the security of tenure or even just a piece of land to live upon is the other major human settlements problem. It seems that in many countries the land situation is getting worse every day for the urban poor. Harassment of squatters and pavement dwellers and orders for the destruction of their modest shelter, on the grounds of illegal occupation of land, are still the daily reality of many urban poor, not only in Asia but in richer countries such as Trinidad. The struggle for legalization or for security of tenure is the reality for low-income earners. Nationalization of land, often considered the number-one measure to solve the problem, does not necessarily mean that access to land is improved.

Limited answers

In 1976 delegates from 132 countries met in Vancouver for the United Nations Conference on Human Settlements and unanimously approved 64 recommendations for government and 3 relating to the means to improve human settlement conditions for their country. The six main recommendations were:

(1) priority to the improvement of living conditions, especially for the destitute.
(2) Support to local initiative.
(3) Pure water and sanitation for all.
(4) Sound standards for housing and services.
(5) Slowing of land speculation.
(6) Development plan based on a realistic development policy.

In 1981 a survey carried out in 17 developing countries representing 60 per cent of the Third World population (China excluded) indicated that only two nations, Tanzania and Tunisia, had started to follow these recommendations (Hardoy and Satterthwaite, 1981); in most cases results were very poor.

In the context of the international financial crisis and the constraints imposed by debt repayments and IMF conditions, human settlements have remained a secondary issue for most governments. Reduction of public expenses, privatization of public services and investments in productive sectors have meant that a very low share of GNP has gone into housing. Even in countries such as Brazil with a well-established financial system for housing, the relative share of investment for this sector has been minimal. A growing number of Third World countries have started to design and implement low-cost housing policies; but, as Silas (1986) reports in the case of Indonesia, "Government housing policy has been two-faced ... 70 times more is being spent on housing higher-income people than on supporting low-income people's own housing initiatives."

Total aid flows going to projects or programmes aimed at directly improving shelter conditions are extremely low. Less than 5 per cent of concessional aid and some 6.5 per cent of official non-concessional aid is allocated to housing, urban and community development, water supply, sanitation, solid waste disposal and the production of building materials. The annual average for such aid for the period 1980–4 was some $3 billion. Annual aid flow going to housing, urban and community-development-related projects represents about one-third of this latter figure, i.e. about $1 billion, less than 2 per cent of official aid received by Third World nations (Cabannes and Satterthwaite, 1985). Apart from the World Bank Group and the USAID Housing Guarantee Programme, which represent the major sources of funds, very little attention is paid today by multilateral and bilateral agencies to the human settlement sector. Despite the growing needs of the sector it does not seem that this trend of minimal involvement will be reversed in the near future. OECD member countries that have important aid programmes, such as Belgium, Sweden, Switzerland and Japan, have no human settlement aid policies and hardly any programmes.

The case study projects

The five case studies in this part of the book were prepared for IIED in collaboration with the Habitat International Council (HIC) NGO Habitat Project. HIC is an international commitee of non-governmental organizations active in the human settlements field, and the project consists of a representative sample of 20 fully documented case histories from developing countries. They demonstrate the potentials of NGOs and community-based organizations (CBO) in the field of habitat.

The Orangi Pilot Project low-cost sanitation programme (Case Study 30), started in 1980, has enabled some 200,000 people in Karachi, Pakistan, to improve their physical environment. The sanitation programme is financed and constructed by the people at about one-sixth of the unit costs of current government agency programmes.

Since 1968 the Centro Cooperativista Uruguayo (Case Study 31) has contributed to the completion of housing for 10,000 families organized in 120 co-operatives. The Complejo Bulevar and Mesa 1 Cases in Montevideo are illustrative examples of the two systems promoted: savings and loan or mutual aid co-operatives. The Uruguayan experience has inspired several Latin American countries.

The case study of the Unión de Palo Alto co-operative (Case Study 32), which binds together some 2,250 members, refers to the long struggle for land and the long experience of a group of squatters who settled on the outskirts of Mexico City. The achievements of this seminal housing co-operative serve as a landmark for other groups and provide a guide for modifying legislation, policies and procedures.

The Chawama upgrading demonstration project (Case Study 33) deals with the socioeconomic and physical upgrading of a squatter settlement in Lusaka, Zambia, where 50,000 inhabitants are living today. It is one of the pioneering programmes initiated by the American Friends Service Committee of Zambia – now HUZA (Human Settlements of Zambia). The NGO intervention, through fostering community participation, enabled co-operation between settlers and authorities in all project activities. HUZA's programme focuses now on promoting income-earning activities, improving nutrition and health and reducing living and housebuilding costs.

Started in 1981 and phased out in 1986, the Integrated Community Development Project, implemented in one of the poorest neighbourhoods of Addis Ababa, Ethiopia (Case Study 34), demonstrates how and to what extent very low-income communities can face and solve their own problems when proper support is provided to them.

Lessons to be learned

Housing is also a people's problem

The first lesson to be learned from the cases is that housing is not only a central government, local authority or private sector question, but, as HUZA states; "urban housing is a people's problem". I would prefer "... *also* a people's problem". *Given a chance*, poor communities hold the key to the solution of their own problems. The direct implication is, first, what kind of opportunity, "chance" or support should be provided to communities? To this question the case studies provide a precise and rich set of answers, which will be developed later on. Secondly, in the words of Turner (OECD, 1986), "centralized housing supply policies, those based on public housing construction, must give way to devolutionary support policies ... governmental involvement would increasingly be focused on legislative/administrative reforms and the provision of basic infrastructure, with maximum reliance on users and local communities for carrying out habitat improvement activities".

Building communities

Improving human settlements from the physical point of view cannot be isolated from *building the community*. Enabling a community to get organized appears the key to facing human settlement problems and obtaining long-term benefits. This broadening of the issue from the mere production of physical outputs to social organization is one of the main conclusions shared by many project promoters. Community development is a must to improve the housing situation of the poor.

Community building can be seen not so much as a prerequisite to a construction programme but as a process which can be initiated through a physical programme. There are three conditions for a housing project to initiate a social change. The first is that the "marginalized" people become subjects (or actors) of this process. The second is that the programme must give to the poor both pride in themselves and social conscience. The third is that the actors adopt the norms, attitudes and values of the social group of which they are part.

Organizing the community – methodology for change

The know-how to organize the community to improve housing conditions and infrastructure is largely shared by all the cases. This might be the real breakthrough in terms of experience gained in this field through the last 20 years. Today a first answer does exist on methods to get a community organized.

Organizations vary according to the socio-political context, the work to be implemented and who is going to do it. For example, in the Orangi Pilot Project (OPP) the first step towards building up a sanitation system was the creation of community organizations based on lanes of 20 to 30 houses. Another system within Orangi was introduced for organizing women through the women's welfare programme, based on a mobile training team, women activists in the lanes and the formation of small groups of neighbours by the activists.

It has been one of the achievements of the support teams to elaborate through experience, on a learning-by-doing basis, a methodology which can be adapted if not reproduced in other contexts. The party framework in Zambia and the *kebele* structure in Ethiopia were the starting-points used to set up *ad hoc* organization and management structures at a programme level. The capacity to adapt or adjust in a flexible way the requirements of a project based on the community to an already existing party structure demonstrates the superiority of NGOs over central government.

Importance of outsiders and leaders

Role of support groups. All the communities concerned have benefited from external support during the development process. These support teams from outside the communities have played a crucial role in enabling people to improve their living conditions. Contrasting examples will illustrate the point. In Kebele 41, Addis Ababa, project staff played a vital role as "animator", flexible and responsible to community needs. The Centro Cooperativista Uruguayo (CCU) has for 25 years provided support services to co-operatives at various levels: legal, social, accountancy, technical. During the implementation phase, the relationship between CCU and the co-operatives has sometimes been rough and tense, but at the end of the process there is a clear wish from co-operatives not to cut the relationship. The Palo Alto case study highlights the multiplicity and the basic role of the "external agents", all NGOs. Thus, independent NGOs, acting as support, advisory or action groups, are the link between the cases. Their role as enabler of the community has gone along with a mediating role with central government and market forces.

The role of "leaders". One ingredient which gives a similarity to the success of the cases is the presence of a charismatic leader who can be an outsider of the community or a real indigenous community leader. Aktar Hammeen Khan, an ex-senior civil servant and social scientist, played a major role in the success of OPP. In Mexico, Palo Alto's union honours Father Escamilla, a Catholic priest who laid the foundations of the Palo Alto Neighbourhood Union in the early 1970s, when they were threatened with expulsion. This does not necessarily mean that such leaders are indispensable, because a methodology can be built from their cumulative experience and practice. Such a methodology reduces the need for a charismatic figure.

The importance of external funding

The leading role of the community, enabled by a support NGO and mobilized at its early stage by a leader or somebody who takes the case as a cause, should not blind us to the crucial role of funding. Two levels have to be differentiated: the funding of the NGOs providing the support to the community, and the funding of the physical and development work that a sanitation programme or an upgrading implies.

In Ethiopia $1.9 million was spent during the lifespan of the project. The larger share originated from Redd Barna (Save the Children, Norway) and the Norwegian government. This allowed for support of the project staff and the whole project cost. In Karachi the second ingredient for the success of OPP is considered to be the Bank of Credit and Commerce International (BCCI), whose foundation covered both the loans and the project team. BCCI is an international bank with headquarters in Luxembourg, launched with Arab capital on the principle of *shasa* (sharing with the poor). In Palo Alto, the support role played by Misereor (a German private organization) has to be acknowledged even if national funds were later made available for credit. The Uruguayan co-operatives' federation has received support from European private organizations, but the credits to the co-operatives were essentially from national sources. For the three areas which were upgraded in Lusaka, a World Bank loan covered nearly half the fund, the Zambian government also nearly half, and the contribution from AFSC (now HUZA) and UNICEF made up the remainder.

Many extremely innovative projects were or are possible thanks to an external source of funding, which provides, at least in the early stages, some degree of independence and also the possibility of covering the expenses of community development work. The decisive role of external funding relates to the question of foreign aid.

Technique, technology and production process

Most experiences show the use of very low-cost technologies, covering a wide technical spectrum: stabilized mud blocks in Zambia, prefabricated concrete elements in Uruguay, light roofing brick panels in Mexico, an alternative sewage system in Pakistan. The decrease in costs is not due to the technical solution *per se* but to the use of alternative production processes. In Orangi the technology allowed for self-help/mutual aid and gave direct control to the inhabitants. The self-help/mutual aid process eliminates the intermediary, which is where the real increase in cost lies. The roofing brick panels used in Mexico allowed the women to participate in construction, adding a component to the labour force. The use of indigenous resources for walls and roof is a step further; the control of the process by the people and the elimination of intermediaries are then extended to the building material production process and not limited to the construction phase (as in Mexico, where the Palo Alto co-operative did not produce the raw materials it used). In the Zambian case, income-generating activities in the building sector are included as a part of the integrated approach. The concern for using indigenous resources, hence reducing the import component, is another positive step in this project.

The necessity to adapt a technical solution to a given problem in a specific social process (community work or women-oriented, etc.) and to a specific economic process (mutual aid, self-help, etc.) is a key to significantly reducing costs and developng appropriate technologies. In general, an appropriate technology is one which permits real control by the users of the production process and/or an alternative production process while considerably reducing profit margins of intermediaries.

Another important issue is suggested by the impressive case of OPP, where an empirical innovative solution, perfectly "non-scientific", proved to adapt itself best to local conditions. Apart from demonstrating the high degree of creativity of an organized community, this solution highlights the untapped resources that lie in the combination of intuition and experience.

Ecology and environment

In all but one of the case studies (the exception being the Chawama upgrading in Zambia) environment-related issues are not a major entry point for action. Environmental issues are implicitly addressed in the Redd Barna and HUZA cases, which are to be complemented through the wide use of energy-efficient stoves aimed at saving fuelwood. However, as yet, insufficient attention has been paid to this element in human settlement programmes. Nevertheless all the cases referred to have improved the surrounding natural environment: a massive sanitation system in Orangi, reclaiming an abandoned quarry in Palo Alto, safer pathways and bridges, and rainwater drainage preventing landslides, in Addis Ababa.

Urban popular settlements often develop in the worst areas of cities: marshes, salted barren lands, steep slopes, stone fields, garbage dumps and cheap land, which tend to be expensive to develop properly. At a great labour cost and through their own effort, poor communities improve these often idle land tracts and add to them a significant economic, social and environmental value. Yet once these lands have acquired a greater value, pressure for eviction or speculation starts, usually at a high social cost.

At a broader scale, the analysis of Orangi raises the question of the contribution of popular settlements to environmental degradation. The solution chosen for the OPP sewage system in Orangi would contribute 5 million gallons of untreated sewage to the sea, adding to marine pollution. On the other hand, all government and private development in Karachi discharges untreated sewage into the sea. Hence, instead of questioning OPP's technological choice, pressure should be put on government agencies to set up treatment plants. As one Orangi resident stated at a meeting with health engineeers, "Why is our sewage any different from yours?"

Implications for development assistance programmes and policies

The difficulties of phasing out

Before examining whether the processes started in the cases have had an impact and are replicable, it is necessary to look into what appears as one of the most difficult moments in the lifetime of a project: phasing out, the moment when the action group (the NGO providing support to the community-based organization) withdraws, leaving the community running on its own. This moment is a crucial one, and the impact of phasing out can be felt at several levels:

(1) The community. The need for a strongly built and democratic community-based organization with a self-management capacity is the key for long-term success.
(2) The government and local authorities. "Local institutionalization" is the other side of the coin. Transferring the management of a school to the Ministry of Education, or the maintenance of a road to the local authority, is difficult to achieve although apparently not impossible.
(3) Transferring the mediating role. External support NGOs have a mediating role with the government that community-based organizations do not have. So one of the major tasks is to facilitate the establishment and maintenance of functional links between community structures and government ministries and authorities.
(4) The impact on maintenance. These elements are not only crucial in terms of development but have direct and immediate impact on the physical aspect of the programme. The delicate issues of maintenance and recovery of loans

contracted by the users are directly related. Many projects which have been promoted from the outside face problems of maintenance; public conveniences might not be working, water supplies stop, etc., meaning that financial and labour efforts are ultimately wasted. Usually lack of awareness and proper community organization and lack of resources and/or commitment from local authorities and government are the main reasons. Among the difficulties indicated by HUZA, two are underlined: the poor maintenance, especially of roads, and the resistance to pay back from the residents even using the local block leader as the collecting agent. In OPP, again, maintenance of the sewer lines is a difficult aspect of the programme and the fact that the people came together to finance and to construct the system did not allow for protection against the maintenance problem. The maintenance question reflects the difficulty of transferring responsibilities and building a self-management capacity.

(5) The level of the market forces. Phasing out from a project also means that all the income-generating activities developed in the lifetime of the project will have to be self-sufficient and confront and survive market forces. Many of these productive activities have difficulty surviving after the end of a human settlement programme, and more attention should be given to this aspect.

Impact of NGO programmes

(1) In very few cases have NGO-supported programmes and actions brought about structural, social and political changes; Palo Alto is among the few. Nevertheless there are cases of NGO staff becoming influential within the state apparatus.

(2) NGO programmes supporting community-based organizations have often been a laboratory to experiment with new approaches and to lobby for policy changes. In that sense, the HUZA programme in Zambia is significant, as the Chawama upgrading project paved the way for the policy of the Third National Development Plan (1979–83).

(3) Another level of replicability is reached when a community-based organization (CBO) decides to expand through popular mobilization in order to force the government to give more attention to low-income earners' needs. Among the most significant popular movements is the national co-ordination of popular urban movements in Mexico, which recently played a leading role in building up a Latin American federation of community-based groups. Mutual support among squatters in Bangkok slums when a group of them are harassed for eviction is gaining weight at the political level. Promises from political parties before Thailand's 1986 general election have been followed by the opening of new communication channels between squatters and the government. In Uruguay support groups and communities defined together a national plan for popular housing which was put through parliament.

(4) Again the role of foreign financial assistance to support the start of innovative programmes or their reproduction has to be underlined.

Limits of replicability and of NGO activities

(1) In many countries and regions the possibilities of development for NGOs and CBOs are extremely limited and their emergence as a necessary part of the *société civile* is still doubtful. Community development as a line of action for addressing the human settlement issue has a long way to go.

(2) In most countries very few projects are developed, and the recognition of their excellence does not mean they are having a massive impact. Many of them are limited in size, institutionally fragile, isolated and unrecognized by governments.

(3) Many support groups do not last long, or simply survive without being able to pass from an extremely committed voluntary organization to a professional institution. Failure stories are plentiful.

(4) Political pressures upon and harassment of institutions giving support to CBOs in the field of human settlements still occur in some political contexts, e.g. in Chile and South Korea.

Implications for development assistance

(1) Growing needs in the field of human settlements, especially in urban areas, are mostly unattended. This sector should receive far higher priority from donor agencies.

(2) Development assistance in the urban areas should (a) promote urban self-reliance and (b) support and develop the opportunities of mega-cities. At the same time there is a need for "rethinking the city of the future" (Swedish Ministry, 1985), along with a parallel implementation of innovative programmes the results of which would feed back into a general strategy.

(3) Most of the Third World cities are built by the lower income group, and poor communities, when given a chance, hold the key to the solution of their own problem. *Development aid should be aimed precisely at giving the poor a chance.* This means supporting settlers in getting organized to face their difficulties and enabling them to have access to the necessary inputs to improve their living conditions.

(4) The case studies advocate support institutions or action groups (advocacy planners, barefoot architects, independent support teams, intermediaries) as the best instruments to help communities get organized and to support them at all necessary levels.

(5) CBOs are far more efficient, better equipped and much cheaper than central government in their role as enablers of the community. These NGOs need (a) to be known, through publicity and increased capacity to disseminate their experience, (b) to be recognized by governments as a professional sector indispensable for the implementation of support housing policies and (c) to be supported politically, institutionally and financially, especially by the donor community.

(6) Development aid in the field of human settlements should be shifted from support to centralized housing policies (i.e. based on public housing

construction) to support (a) governments which are giving way to devolutionary support policies and (b) NGOs, the potential of which has been largely under-utilized and underestimated. Aid should not only be concentrated in major cities, as is the case today, but should also benefit small and intermediate urban centres and rural settlements.

(7) Assistance given to NGOs by foreign agencies in their innovative attempts has generally been successful, and very little of the money spent by the donor community has been misused. Social and economic benefits have been achieved globally.

(8) A claim for wider support to NGOs is not merely based on their higher efficiency and "flexibility". It lies also on the grounds that they reflect better people's aspirations and needs and have strong relations with CBOs. Hopefully, support from governments to these provides a way to structural changes towards a society economically viable, socially equitable and environmentally sustainable.

References

Cabannes, Y., and Satterthwaite, D. (1985), *Financial and Other Assistance Provided to and among Developing Countries for Human Settlements*. United Nations Centre for Human Settlements, Nairobi.

Hardoy, J. E., and Satterthwaite, D. (1981), *Shelter: Need and Response*. Wiley, Chichester.

Ibanez, A. F. (1983), "La Producción del habitat basada en la organización de los pobladores. FUNDASAL". In *Financiamiento del Habitat para Sectores de Bajos Ingresos en America Latina*, Seminario DSE, Berlin.

OECD (1986), *The Role and Comparative Advantages of NGOs and Community-Based Organizations (CBOs) in Urban Development*. Organization for Economic Co-operation and Development, Development Assistance Committee, Paris. Annexe prepared by J. Turner in consultation with HIC NGO Project Steering Group.

Silas, J. (1986), "Banyu Urip: kampung improvement by the people". Subaraya University, Indonesia. Paper prepared for HIC NGO Project.

Swedish Ministry of Housing and Physical Planning (1985), *Rethinking the Third World City*. Report from round-table meeting. Stockholm.

Note

All five case studies that follow were prepared in collaboration with the Habitat International Council NGO Project.

CASE STUDY 30 *Orangi Pilot Projects, Karachi, Pakistan*

ARIF HASAN
Architect and Consultant to the Orangi Pilot Project

The Orangi Pilot Project (OPP) was set up in 1980 as a result of an understanding between Akhtar Hameed Khan, a renowned Pakistani social scientist who is now project director, and Aga Hasan Abadi, president of the Bank of Credit and Commerce International, which provides project funds. Orangi is the largest squatter colony in Karachi. About half of this township falls within the target area of OPP, an area consisting of about 2,000 acres, 3,181 lanes and 43,424 housing units.

Except for a recently installed water supply system through stand-posts, and OPP's low-cost sanitation programme, urban services in this area are non-existent. The most pressing need of the squatter colonies, or *katchi abadis* as they are called, is sanitation, particularly for the disposal of excreta and waste water. OPP's sanitation programme has shown that the unequal political relationship between government agencies and the poor can be changed through a development strategy in which the poor participate and contribute financially.

Orangi Pilot Project sanitation programme

There are two major problems in providing a sanitation system to the squatter colonies. First, local authorities do not have the necessary finances to construct a sewerage system. Where international finance is available, the problem of repayment arises; in any case, international loans can deal with only a small part of an immense problem; there are over 362 squatter colonies in Karachi alone, housing over 4 million people. The cost of urban services developed by the local authorities is five times the cost of labour and materials required for such development. Users in squatter colonies cannot afford to pay these charges in one go, and experience has shown that it is impossible to recover development expenditure from low-income users in instalments.

Before the OPP programme began, the people of Orangi felt that the local bodies should develop their sewerage system free of cost. They were led to believe by their local leadership that the more affluent areas of the city did not pay for the installation of urban services.

With the above factors in mind, the OPP programme aimed from the beginning at discovering alternative sources of finance for development. This could come only from within the community and had to be available before development work was undertaken. An alternative, low-cost method of implementation of development was also necessary. To achieve these objectives OPP needed to study the sociology, technology and economics of the people's solutions to the sanitation problem and see if it could build on them.

Before the programme started, the majority of the people of Orangi used bucket latrines, emptied every fourth or fifth day often into the unpaved lane. The more affluent houses constructed soakpits, which filled up after a few years. Some people had laid sewerage lines from their houses to the nearest natural creek or *nullah*. These lines were usually defective, and one found many parallel lines in one lane. The people had a preference for an underground system; OPP felt that, if the right residents could be organized and trained to use them, an underground sewerage system financed and constructed by the people could be developed.

The first step was the creation of community organizations. The lane, which in Orangi consists of about 20 or 30 houses, was made the unit of organization; it was a small and cohesive unit, and there would be no problem of mistrust involved. Also, the traditional Orangi leadership would not feel threatened if the programme was limited to one lane at a time. Developing one lane at a time without a master plan was considered by planners an invitation to disaster. However, because of innovation and modifications to engineering practice, no disaster took place.

The methodology for developing lane organizations had four stages. First, OPP social organizers (paid employees) would hold meetings in the lane and, using slides, models and pamphlets, explain the programme to the people, along with its economic and health benefits. They would explain that the Karachi Development Authority (KDA), or the Karachi Municipal Corporation (KMC), does not lay sewerage lines free of cost, and their charges could not be afforded by lane residents. The motivators said that, if the people formed an organization in which the whole lane participated, then OPP would give them assistance.

In the second stage, the organization was born and chose its lane managers, who, on behalf of the lane, formally asked for assistance. In the third stage, OPP technical staff surveyed the lane, established benchmarks, prepared plans and estimates (for labour and materials) and handed over these data to the lane managers. Lastly, lane managers collected the money from the people and called meetings to sort out any sociological problems involved in the work. OPP staff supervised the process but at no time handled the people's money.

With no central supervision or controlling agency, and people in many cases doing the work themselves, the only way of guaranteeing quality of work was by educating the people. However, the people's confidence in OPP could develop only over a prolonged association. As a result, some substandard work was done in the lanes, and in mid-1982 there was a lull. Evaluation of the project became necessary.

Research was carried out to identify the causes of substandard work and to simplify engineering designs. The results of this research were taken to the people through a massive extension effort, and hundreds of meetings were held. The people learned about mixing concrete and curing it and about the proper manner of making inverts. This led to a great improvement in the standard of work, and more and more lanes applied for assistance.

Initially only those lanes asked for assistance which were near a natural creek or *nullah*, or which could drain into such *nullahs* easily. It was feared that the programme would end here, unless lanes away from the *nullahs* came together to construct secondary drains. To promote the concept of secondary drains OPP carried out a physical survey of Orangi, done by architects and engineering students. After 30 to 40 students had moved through Orangi, talking to the people and involving them in their work, Orangi became a changed place. The idea of secondary drains registered. The concept of development through community participation also went back to the universities and colleges, whose involvement with Orangi is consequently growing.

The results of the survey were compiled, along with literature regarding the programme, and given to the councillor of each area. The people were informed of this and started to pressurize their councillors to take an interest. This led to a large number of neighbourhood lane organizations coming together and asking OPP for technical assistance for construction of secondary drains.

OPP no longer needs to motivate the people. Lanes now organize themselves and contact OPP for technical assistance. Major changes have also taken place in the relationship between Orangi councillors and KMC. Councillors get grants in aid from KMC for certain development projects in their areas which they have to identify. In November 1984 the people of Orangi Sector 5 got their councillor to use this finance to construct an underground sewer. Although they initially insisted that they should be allowed to use this money themselves, this was not agreed to, and an outside contractor was employed according to KMC regulations. Now well versed in sanitation technology, the people did not permit any substandard work to be done. They also insisted on getting OPP to design and supervise the construction work.

Since then OPP finds itself identifying the location of secondary drains and designing and supervising works financed by KMC, in addition to helping lanes construct primary drains. OPP, it seems, has become a research and extension agency for KMC councillors.

Costs and benefits

Out of a total of 3,181 lanes in OPP's part of Orangi over 1,571 had already built their sewerage system by December 1985. Over 137 secondary drains had been constructed, 107 financed by lane residents and 30 by KMC. The people have invested Rs26,991,950 (US$1,686,996) in this effort, while OPP's investment in research and extension has been about Rs1,500,000 ($93,750) inclusive of capital expenditure. The local authorities would have spent $8,343,980 on this work.

OPP social organizers, lane managers and those who participated in the development work are emerging as an alternative leadership to the traditional one of mainly land-grabbers and exploiters.

Two other squatter colonies in Karachi have applied to OPP for assistance in acquiring a sewerage system through community participation and finance. The Aga Khan Medical University and the Department of Architecture, Karachi, have associated their courses with the programme.

A major environmental and social change has taken place in Orangi. The lanes which have a sewerage system are now clean and healthier. The people have undertaken an improvement of their houses, and the value of property has gone up. Quarrels related to sanitation, common in pre-OPP programme days, have disappeared, and there is more social harmony.

The question of health

OPP realized from its inception that personal and domestic hygiene were keys to good health. It also realized that these aims could be achieved only by organizing the women of Orangi. Therefore in 1981 much time and money were invested in trying to organize women through a programme of home schools and first-aid centres. In 1982 similar attempts were made to form women's and youth clubs to promote hygiene and sports. The director's annual report for 1984–5 deals with the reasons for the failure of these programmes: "the conditions were too anarchic, and our resources too meagre, to establish or sustain stable groups or clubs". However, "OPP's low-cost sanitation programme had spread to hundreds of lanes ... housewives had played a very active role ... they were keenly aware of the health problem of their home and their lane. Their participation provided us with a clue about the future direction of the women's programme." Women were conscious enough of the problems of health and hygiene to pay the sanitation cost from household expenses: "We assume that for changing the attitudes and opinions of segregated women, access is the main problem. Custom requires them to stay at home. Such women generally go out only for emergencies or in exceptional circumstances."

Because of this problem of access, the welfare-centre approach of government agencies and certain NGOs has proved ineffective. There are approaching 80,000 families living in Orangi. Even if four or five centres were established, women would have to cover long distances to get to them. To expect them to do this when their men are away at work is unrealistic. The report noted that "to serve segregated women, a centre should cover only a small area, not exceeding 20 to 30 lanes"; Orangi would require over 100 such centres!

With these factors in mind, Akhtar Hameed Khan introduced the following systems for organizing a women's welfare programme:

(1) *Creation of mobile training teams* which hold meetings in the lane activist's house. Each team consists of a lady health visitor, a social organizer and an expert gardener. The package of advice offered by the team is: further training about sanitation and hygiene; leaflets and training about prevention of 12

common diseases such as diarrhoea, malaria and scabies; immunization of children against six diseases; instructions for growing vegetables in the home and free supply of seeds. Akhtar Hameed Khan calls this, "the street-vendor's approach".

(2) *Selection of women activists or contact people in the lanes.* The woman activist promotes the programme; the women of the lane assemble at her home to meet with the mobile team, and a rudimentary kind of organization is established.

Improved sanitation and health education have reduced the incidence of 12 serious diseases in Orangi.

Conclusion

If municipal corporations and state urban development agencies of Pakistan accept the Orangi model and make it a part of their development strategy, most of the difficulties they face today with regard to sanitation can be overcome. The development cost to the user would be one-sixth of what it is now, and KMC expenditure on research and extension would be 5 per cent of this sum. The problem of collecting high development charges, or recovering loans in instalments, would also be overcome. Maintenance – increasingly a major problem for local bodies – would be taken care of by the residents. No more foreign loans at high rates of interest would be required. Orangi could act as the demonstration area and could house a research and training institute for the development of *katchi abadis*. This proposal has been put forward to the Federal Planning Commission of Pakistan by Akhtar Hameed Khan and has been accepted in principle.

CASE STUDY 31 *Mutual Aid Co-operative Movement, Uruguay*

CENTRO COOPERATIVISTA URUGUAYO

The construction of housing units through the system of mutual aid co-operatives began in Uruguay after the Centro Cooperativista Uruguayo carried out a pilot experiment with three groups from the provinces. Initial difficulties inherent to a system that was practically unknown in the country had to be overcome, but widespread acceptance had been achieved by 1975. The system proved well suited to the Uruguayan tradition of do-it-yourself housebuilding.

The mutual aid co-operative system appears to result in the best solutions at the lowest cost, giving the best results as regards the upkeep and maintenance of the housing developments and the provision of urban amenities. It has also met the needs of beneficiaries and used community spaces effectively. The organization the groups establish during the building period (which is later extended, as most of them have chosen collective ownership) has also led them to approach collectively other common social problems. Thus clinics, day-care centres, libraries and consumers' co-operatives have been created.

Most members of the groups already possessed a high level of organization, discipline and awareness, which turned the co-operatives into an essential bulwark of the struggle to win back democracy in Uruguay. This brought about the withdrawal of official support from the system in 1975, and attacks were made on the co-operative movement. However, experience in Uruguay and other countries of the region suggests that housing co-operatives can constitute an effective solution to the housing problem in Latin America.

Uruguay's housing problem

Rather than to the "housing problem" we should refer to the problem of *habitat* or *living conditions*, in order not to see the problem from an artificially narrow perspective. This problem is closely related to levels of family income; insufficiency of income restricts access to minimum living conditions (housing, health, food and education). More than 7 per cent of Uruguayan families may be classified as indigent and about 50 per cent as poor. It is these people, by and large, who suffer from inadequate housing.

The overall housing deficit has been estimated as more than 105,000 units, out of a total stock of less than a million units. This estimate includes the total number of dwellings that cannot be restored or require upgrading or almost total repairs due to their dilapidated condition. More than half of all Uruguayan housing has at least one serious deficiency (sewage, toilets, drinking water, lighting, kitchen, insufficient number of bedrooms). Lack of community services and inconvenient location in relation to workplace are other disadvantages. A high percentage of family income is usually allotted to paying for housing, for tenants often more than 50 per cent.

Mutual aid co-operatives

History. Most Uruguayan cities, particularly Montevideo, have developed as a consequence of do-it-yourself building, the usual method in Latin America. What is peculiar about the Uruguayan process is that it has not been explosive, as in other countries of the area. On the contrary, growth has taken place in a gradual manner, favoured by the relative economic prosperity prevailing until the 1960s, low demographic growth and legal provisions. Uruguayans are willing to build their house with their own hands, just counting on the aid of a relative or a friend and on the help of a bricklayer or builder in the most difficult stages: the roof, electricity and plumbing.

The economic situation of the country changed radically after the Second World War. Inflation was high, and salaries declined in real terms. This economic deterioration, which affected mainly the working classes, brought about major cut-backs and a serious crisis in housebuilding. The crisis particularly hit the multitude of do-it-yourself builders.

First experiences. People started to be aware that isolated efforts had to be joined together in order to reduce costs, increase effectiveness and be able to pay back loans. A new form of organization emerged to satisfy these needs: mutual aid housing co-operatives. It would pick up, on the one hand, the experience of do-it-yourself builders and, on the other, that of popular organizations such as workers' unions. Mutual aid housing co-operatives are associations of families who, facing a common need for dwellings, contribute their members' effort and initiative to reach a common solution; one of their fundamental resources is the contribution of labour by the families involved. Set-backs and difficulties beset these groups, who were building their own houses and, simultaneously, a new manner of organization where everything had to be invented. However, the results were very positive.

The National Housing Law. When a housing law was approved by Parliament in December 1968, a section was included to provide for the construction of new housing through mutual aid co-operatives. The co-operative system appeared as a marginal chapter, included in the law to ease its approval by Parliament rather than to back up a serious attempt at solving housing problems. Initially, there was scepticism and mistrust towards an alternative that appeared utopian, and many difficulties had to be overcome. Nevertheless, housing co-operatives cropped up and were top of the population's preferences among all the systems the law had provided for as a means of supplying dwellings. In 1975 one out of every two credit applications to the Uruguay Mortgage Bank came from the co-operative sector.

Consolidation and development (1970–3). The 1970–3 period was one of active mobilization when the mutual aid co-operative movement obtained significant achievements in the housing policy of the country; plots were allotted, proceedings were hastened, credit conditions were improved. The movement led the fight for the most profound claims of the popular classes – employment, pay increases and improvements in quality of life – and also strengthened itself internally. A supply board was created, which obtained a significant reduction of costs and an improvement in credit conditions, through bulk purchase of building materials. A prefabrication plant was built to produce building elements by more technical and serial methods, improving quality and lowering costs.

Period of dictatorship. This process was abruptly halted, however, by the change in housing policy occurring after the *coup d'état*, particularly after 1975. Co-operatives were left aside, and priority was given to private capitalistic agents. Thus while the "private promotion" system now got 50 per cent of investment, co-operatives fell below 5 per cent. That was not all; no new legal entities have been constituted since 1976, and loans to existing groups were severely delayed. The conditions for loans also started to be much harder from 1979; interest rates increased three times, and previous savings were made a mandatory require-ment – totally inappropriate for a system meant for poor people.

The movement was also attacked as regards its inner organization. Meetings were hindered, as were members' means of expression. Leaders and members were dismissed from their jobs, and many were imprisoned. People known to act in unions or political parties were forbidden to act as leaders of the co-operatives or even to become members. Despite these events, the essential foundations of the co-operative organizations survived, and they were still able to support the unions when they reappeared after long years of repression and banishment.

Present situation. Democratic institutions have been restored, but the new board of directors of the Uruguay Mortgage Bank is unwilling to take steps that would support the co-operative movement. The "law" passed during dictatorship that provided for individual ownership of dwellings owned in common by co-operatives has not yet been annulled. The governing party does not want to do so if measures are not approved simultaneously to restrict co-operatives' activities. A harsh argument has arisen between the Uruguay Mortgage Bank president and the United Federation of Mutual Aid Co-operatives (FUCVAM); the former has accused co-operatives of all sorts of abuses, ranging from refusing to pay their debts to the bank to persecuting people who express different opinions.

Underlying these confrontations is the wish of the political establishment to undermine those groups and organizations able to question and challenge it. FUCVAM is one of the most firm and active of these. Official policy, on the other hand, seeks support for the establishment from the least privileged through measures of a paternalistic character – measures strongly questioned by self-managed movements such as the co-operatives.

How mutual aid housing co-operatives work

Solidarity, organization, self-management. The resources the co-operative enterprise needs to achieve its economic objectives come from two main sources: the credits the co-operative is granted according to the National Housing Law; and the contribution of labour from group members. Those resources are managed by the members, who receive the technical advice of non-profit interdisciplinary professional teams, their performance being legally provided for and controlled. There is no intermediary trying to obtain any profit – an essential first condition.

A second condition is the contribution of beneficiaries, with their effort, to the solution of the problem. Since that contribution can be made only with work, because they are poor people, it is achieved through mutual aid. Labour is hired only when organization or specialization in the task require it.

Another important factor in achieving the co-operative's economic objectives is the operation of self-management and its relationship with the technical advising team. To achieve self-management, the group needs to receive all kinds of technical advice. Ultimately, however, the decisions belong to the co-operative itself, acting democratically. Thus an organizing capacity is developed, enabling the group to expand its action to other fields.

Mutual aid co-operatives as a social and political movement: FUCVAM. The mutual aid co-operatives have long felt the need to organize themselves to fight. In 1970 the three pioneer co-operatives and eight others established the United Federation of Mutual Aid Co-operatives: FUCVAM. Today FUCVAM is an important organization, covering more than 120 co-operatives and 10,000 families. Together with the Sole Centre of Uruguayan Workers, the Students' Federation and human rights associations, it represents the "social forces" in alliance with the political democratic parties of Uruguay.

Evaluation: why mutual aid cooperatives?

Should building be done by private investors, through the state or by co-operatives? This question probably does not have a single answer, and it would be wrong to think that co-operatives are the only way to build housing with public financing. However, the mutual aid housing co-operative movement in Uruguay, after more than 15 years' experience, deserves a major role, as its comparative advantages demonstrate.

From the social point of view. Mutual aid housing co-operatives' exeriences are indissolubly linked to self-management and participation. Together with the application of the main co-operative principles, they enhance values of solidarity, democracy and mutual respect. Even when mutual aid is not necessary for cutting building costs, it is an important expression of such values. The capacity for co-operation and self-help can be afterwards transferred to the provision of other community necessities. Co-operatives have obtained numerous essential services: infrastructure (water, sewage, electricity, garbage collecting, transportation); cultural (kindergartens, day-care centres, primary schools, physical education, libraries, artistic activities); health (clinics, preventive assistance, dental assistance); food (meals for the people, consumer cooperatives). They have provided solidarity for families with economic or social difficulties.

From the point of view of resource use. Control of programmes' development by those who are most interested in their success (the beneficiaries) encourages a high level of efficiency. Also, the building and administration of the dwellings by the co-operative, eliminating intermediaries and replacing to a large extent the public administration, relieves the latter of a difficult task. Investments needed are lower with mutual aid co-operatives than with other housebuilding systems because (1) between 10 and 15 per cent of the total cost is saved and (2) intermediaries and their profits are eliminated (i.e. contractors, subcontractors and estate agents). Maintenance costs are also reduced, because co-operative members, having taken part in construction, are in a better position to carry out maintenance.

From the point of view of design. The control experienced by the users enables housing design to be better matched to their needs. Users of the housing projects have gradually integrated community spaces – paths, streets and squares. Such contributions, added to improvements made to individual frontages, are establishing areas of character and an enriched urban environmernt. Care for these spaces is much better than in neighbourhoods where housing developments are imposed complete from outside.

From the technological point of view. Mutual aid enables the best output to be obtained from non-specialized labour. Housing units usually consist of only one or two levels. "Traditional" rationalized construction is generally combined with the use of prefabricated elements, such as small stone slabs for roofs and mezzanines, and with simplified finishes. Prefabrication of some elements permits tasks to be carried out by non-specialized (including female) labour, indepenently of work done by hired personnel; it also permits better quality control by concentrating production in one place instead of carrying it out across a widely dispersed area.

Comparison with other alternatives

Informal do-it-yourself building. Much recent writing on housing stresses informal self-help building as a way to prop up – even substitute for – inefficient state building. However, the idea that people who are barely surviving, lack stable work and do not have any organization can confront on their own the task of building on a wide scale is unrealistic. It is true that the number of housing units built informally is several times larger than the number of those formally planned and financed; but the great majority of those housing units show major deficiencies. Also, this type of enterprise is sometimes prolonged over several decades, and efforts are dispersed and generally lack technical support; it is likely that final costs will be considerably larger than those for planned actions where the efforts of many interested people are joined together.

Private participation. It is difficult to imagine private participation with speculative objectives being related to popular housing projects. Adequate "rentability" and low levels of risk imply larger costs, as well as the transfer of risks to the state. This kind of participation has not generally produced satisfactory results, because a sole profit objective leads to inadequate solutions, use of low-quality materials, subsequent high maintenance costs and insufficiency of services. The limited or non-existent participation of beneficiaries in this type of programme means that results do not correspond to needs.

State participation. The above considerations confirm that there is a role for state intervention; i.e. it should be linked to financing, supervision, control and possibly direct production, but management at programme levels should be delegated to the organized beneficiaries. This approach is in between the two extremes of public and private intervention. The co-ordination of state support and organized community management could considerably multiply current levels of action to meet the needed volume of housebuilding.

Is the state able to assume all those roles considered necessary for it to play? Two doubts arise: the economic weakness of the public sector in the peripheral countries, and the inefficiency of state bureaucracy. With regard to the first, Uruguay has invested about 4 per cent of its GDP in housing construction during the last decade. This is enough to solve the problem in the way we propose; the issue is how those resources are used. US$900 million invested during 1980–2 in financing 80,000 housing units could have financed 130,000 popular housing units – 50,000 more than were financed and half Uruguay's housing deficit.

The other doubt, about bureaucracy and inefficiency, would be justified if a centralized state was proposed that would take part in every step and finance every action. However, we do not propose that; the state should carry out only those actions it is able to do well, leaving the rest to organized communities.

Reproduction of the model: a Latin American alternative?

The approach of Uruguayan mutual aid co-operatives is shaped by the characteristics of the society that produced it. The pattern does not suit other social and historical contexts, not even those of other Latin American countries. The basic idea, however, of searching for solutions by means of popular self-management, is valid for every attempt to solve the housing and habitat problems of poor people. Activities are starting in Brazil, Colombia, Mexico and Argentina that take up many aspects of the Uruguayan self-help co-operative model.

CASE STUDY 32 *Unión de Palo Alto Co-operative, Mexico*

ROCIO LOMBERA

Co-ordinator of the Evaluation and Systematization Programme, COPEVI

The Unión de Palo Alto co-operative is the product of the experience of a group of settlers who organized to claim rights to the land they had been living on for more than 30 years. Once the consolidation of the social organization and settlement was achieved, they looked forward to encouraging new generations to stay in the co-operative and to develop housing programmes. They aim to support other groups in the process of organizing co-operatives by transmitting their knowledge and experience and making broader links with other popular organizations.

The Palo Alto co-operative is made up of 317 familes and approximately 2,250 members. Twenty per cent of the co-operative's population works in the industrial sector and 80 per cent in informal service activities, such as street vendors, domestic employees, chauffeurs, mechanics and shoemakers. Palo Alto is located on the Toluca highway, about 15 km to the west-south-west of Mexico City. It is situated in a rugged area, higher than the central part of the city and only slightly urbanized.

Historical process

Background (1940–69). For almost half a century Mexican economic development has been accompanied by constant migration from country to town, producing the staggering growth of Mexico City (to nearly 20 million inhabitants in 1987). From 1940 onwards, peasant families arrived and settled in Palo Alto. Heads of families worked in local industries, particularly sand quarries, where they received a minimum wage for 11 hours' work daily. The employer rented them the land they occupied. They sheltered in shanties, built with locally available stoned, mud and roofing felt. Some lived in abandoned sand quarry caves. The site lacked water supply, electricity and sewage disposal. Isolated, with no external links and no ambition or incentive to produce change, these settlers had a very low level of education and endured a high degree of exploitation and a subhuman level of life.

Struggling for land (1969–75). In 1969 the owner decided to sell the land to combine it with the neighbouring estate, where luxury residential housing predominated. The inhabitants of Palo Alto, who had been living there for 20 to 25 years, rejected the proposal of transferral to another area. Threatened with expulsion, they united and formed the Palo Alto Neighbourhood Union, with the support of Father Escamilla, a Catholic priest.

In 1972 the inhabitants organized themselves into a co-operative and received the assistance of COPEVI (Operation Centre for Housing and Settling), initiating official procedures to legalize the organization. The same year the Palo Alto Union co-operative was officially registered, and an area of 46,242 sq m was granted for a project to house 237 families (1,330 inhabitants). In 1973, after more than two years of negotiations with landowners and authorities and almost one year after the offical assignment of land tenure, the inhabitants seized the land, an act fundamental to their success in keeping the land. The landowners' heirs attempted to prevent the establishment of the co-operative. A financial compromise was reached with the heirs. The co-operative members decided to build homes through mutual aid self-help, with COPEVI responsible for housing design and for monitoring implementation.

Housing and infrastructure (1976–9). Despite the progress made, co-operative members felt they were living in a hostile environment. The owners of the neighbouring estate built a stone wall to avoid all contact with Palo Alto. Elsewhere the site is bordered by the Toluca highway, a high-tension cable, a ravine and a firing range. They felt they would be more secure from the danger of expulsion if they built housing with more substantial materials. For the same reasons, the co-operative wanted buildings to be completed quickly, even before the infrastructure. A two-storey house prototype was built first. Self-help brigades were organized, and professional masons were hired during the week to speed up the works.

Between 1976 and the end of 1985, 189 homes were completed, satisfying 80 per cent of the initial demand. In the remaining 48 plots 144 apartments will be built for the next generation. Basic infrastructure, under way since 1979, is completed (water supply, sewage disposal, electricity). The streets are paved, a few private telephones installed and several trees planted on pedestrian ways and boundaries. Nursery, co-operative store, community hall, chapel, dairy, store-room, small cement block factory, *tortilleria*, playgrounds and sports facilities are already built.

Costs and benefits

Costs. Community participation in this programme has ranged from self-employed economic resources to the production of building materials to the use of labour to build houses and provide services. Housing development costs were $534,250 for 166 houses, or $3,218 per house. Around 60 per cent of the total cost of the project so far has been financed by external agencies, and the other 40 per cent corresponds to the community's contribution in economic resources and labour.

Benefits. Palo Alto's process has benefited not only its specific social group but also other low-income groups of settlers. Some of these benefits are:

- Acquisition of housing with necessary services.
- Reduction of building costs by mutual aid, self-construction and self-management.
- Adjustment of the characteristics of the housing according to priorities and economic capacity.
- Housing accessibility for families with different incomes, including the lowest bracket.
- Security of tenure; family and social identification with neighbourhood and city.
- Employment opportunities for co-operative members.
- Equal distribution of goods and services produced or negotiated by the co-operative; equity in rights and obligations.
- Better capacity for self-action, control and operation of the organizing and settling processes.
- Technical training gained in fields like co-operative administration, financial negotiation, learning techniques, social education, construction procedures, accounting.

Palo Alto has reached and even surpassed most of its initial aims. Compared to the previous 30 years of exploitation, the process does not seem so long. The settlers are still poor, but the improvement in their living standards is unquestionable – from overcrowded, unhealthy shanties and caves to comfortable serviced dwellings; from being an irregular settlement lost between sand quarries, dust and dirt, now Palo Alto is an urbanized neighbourhood on the city's periphery where there are no polluting factories, there are large green areas and contamination is less.

Environmental issues

At the beginning of Palo Alto's process, public concern about environmental issues was low, and the project did not contemplate any environmental goals. However, COPEVI adopted a broader view, taking environmental considerations into account. A common problem for low-income populations in urban settlements is the lack of infrastructure, mainly water supply and sewage disposal. Usually either these settlements are far from the general network, or there is no capacity for supply. Water supply should be optimized and recycled to have more uses, as well as looking for better ways to get it. If there are centralized sewage disposal networks in the settlement, they have to be connected to the general network or through a ravine, polluting air and soil. The use of latrines and septic tanks has some limitations. Garbage is disposed on the street or in idle lots and is partially burned or moved to rubbish dumps.

In Palo Alto all these problems arise. COPEVI looked for new ways of solving them and in 1978 became familiar with the work and research of a group named Alternative Technology (GTA). This team developed a system called Integral

System for Reusing Organic Waste (SIRDO). The system provides an alternative to disposing of urine, excrement and organic waste by processing them together into a highly efficient fertilizer. This product can be marketed to produce significant extra income for the community.

Since 1978 COPEVI has supported SIRDO in several projects. This has provoked discussion over environmental issues and, although limited mostly to the waste-disposal problem, it makes the community aware of the issues. The work of GTA and others has resulted in official support for 60,000 SIRDO programmes in suburban and rural areas of Mexico.

Key factors

Communal organization. The success of the Palo Alto co-operative is strongly based on its organization. The inhabitants, faced with the threat of becoming jobless and homeless, could find no other way to struggle but to unite. Father Escamilla and a group of social workers were motivating agents in the creation of the co-operative.

Seizure of the land. Seizure was the last option used by the settlers to get the land where they had worked and lived for more than 30 years, to make a legal right from a real fact. It succeeded in accelerating the bureaucratic official negotiations and the decision to sell the land in favour of the settlers.

External agents. The Palo Alto case took place in a era when social and political conditions were against this type of process. It is thus difficult to conceive of the process occurring without the participation of two main external social agents. The first is the social workers' team, without whose support and work the Palo Alto co-operative could hardly have come into being. The second is COPEVI, a precursor of professional groups offering communities legal, organizational and technical assistance.

Collective tenure. The organizational level reached by the co-operative, and the security of land tenure, fortified the group. The legal organization they adopted – the housing co-operative – made it possible to hold collective tenure of the land and housing. The decision to have collective tenure was itself a response to, first, the necessity to ensure permanency in the face of constant external pressure to move the co-operative out; and secondly, to avoid the vices of private landownership, (speculation, selling, reselling, etc.) that would make permanence of the organization more difficult and expulsion easier. Fifteen years after this decision, the co-operative is still in control of the property – one of the few organized groups that have got hold of the land despite being in a residential suburban area of Mexico City.

External financing. Until 1975 there were no financial institutions in Mexico that would give credits to shelter groups to build housing – least of all to a group as poor as Palo Alto's community. The group needed to build permanent dwellings because of the constant pressure to uproot them, but they did not have enough resources to begin that task. As a solution, the promoters negotiated a grant with a foreign foundation (Misereor) to create a non-profit organization

(Fomvicoop) to give credits to the housing co-operative. This established a precedent, afterwards accepted by two official housing and community development agencies.

Housing and "progressive dwellings". The need to hold on to the land by building permanent housing, and the lack of economic resources to build finished houses, resulted in the co-operative's fundamental decision: dwellings that can be built in stages (termed "progressive dwellings"), initially with the same core for everyone ("core dwellings"). The decision to build substantial and permanent housing before providing services questions the institutionalization of site and services programmes as a solution for low-income settlers. These official programmes solve land acquisition, sanitary and health problems but end up as middle-class neighbourhoods because of the resultant high costs.

Self-help and mutual aid. The group's democratization involves the participation of the whole community – men, women and children – in decision-making and development. The co-operative took essential decisions such as the basic architectural scheme, the technology and mutual aid.

Project sustainability and replication

Community organization and permanent effort have so far benefited around 200 families. This social organization, although initially promoted by external agents, is now managed and controlled by the settlers. The co-operative maintains strong control over its activities and leaders, and it is not common to find in other shelter groups the high participation and democratic level developed in Palo Alto. Some external initiatives, activities and agents seem to be necessary, however, due to the lengthy and weary process in which the co-operative has been involved and to the satisfaction of basic needs, which have reduced the level of motivation for further action.

Nevertheless, Palo Alto is an important precedent for future integrated co-operative projects, although it would not be desirable to repeat it wholesale due to the high social cost and slow pace. In Mexico City, where the daily need to build equals the number of dwellings produced by this co-operative in more than 15 years, it is important to reconsider work methodology, approach and scale of the social response, to guarantee more vigorous and autonomous social process and more efficiency and speed in achieving results. Palo Alto has served and will serve as a stimulus and learning experience to other shelter organizations and to the popular urban movement. It has shown that the organized struggle is the most viable way to satisfy people's needs. It has introduced alternatives to the professional, technical and official institutions' procedures and methods of carrying out settling and housing programmes, proving that there are possibilities for greater popular control of the development process.

CASE STUDY 33 *Chawama Upgrading, Lusaka, Zambia*

HARRINGTON E. JERE
Human Settlements of Zambia

In 1973 the Zambian government asked American Friends Service Committee (AFSC) to assist in programmes of squatter upgrading in Lusaka, the capital. In 1983, AFSC, Lusaka City Council, UNICEF and others together chose Chawama, Lusaka, to be a demonstration upgrading project. Lessons learned in the Chawama demonstration project contributed to the smooth implementation of upgrading in other areas.

In 1982 AFSC Zambia was transformed into a national NGO called Human Settlements of Zambia (HUZA), whose objective was to continue with the work started in 1973. HUZA's broader objectives are to promote self-help and self-reliance for social and economic development in Zambian society; its work greatly influences the country's development policies. HUZA has focused attention on the promotion of informal economic activities, improvement of nutrition and health, reducing the cost of housebuilding and living, and promoting the conservation of natural resources and their sustainable utilization.

Background to the project

Zambia started experiencing urbanization during the 1930s, when its mining industry was established. Other factors contributing to early urbanization were the expansion of commercial farming and government removal of restrictive laws following independence in 1964. In 1963–9 Zambia's population increased at 2.7 per cent per annum, while its urban population grew from 747,000 to 1,188,000, an increase of 8 per cent a year. Lusaka is said to be the fastest-growing city in independent Africa south of the Sahara and one of the fastest growing in the world. In 1985 its estimated population was 737,500, and the annual growth rate 6.5 per cent.

The post-independence government inherited a lopsided housing policy which was not able to cater for the rapidly increasing urban population. In 1968 the Ministry of Housing and Social Development was created with responsibility to map out a housing policy and set guidelines for urban development. These good intentions to solve the housing problem were largely frustrated by increased demands for housing and related services, lack of finance and shortage of administrative and technical staff. Meanwhile, the temporary grass huts settlements which started before independence grew into large urban squatter settlements.

The origins of the policy of squatter upgrading in Zambia go back to a proposal made by AFSC to the Zambian government in 1970. Influenced by this proposal, a courageous policy was announced in the Second National Development Plan (1972-6), recognizing that squatter areas represent assets in social and financial terms and require planning and services. Squatter area upgrading projects were envisaged to introduce piped water, sewage systems, street lighting, etc.

The first major project to upgrade squatter settlements was undertaken by Lusaka City Council in 1973-8. The exercise was implemented in three major settlements (Chawama and two others); 180,000 beneficiaries were involved. The project was funded by a loan from the World Bank and the Zambian government totalling K26.5 million, with additional inputs from AFSC and UNICEF.

The project aimed at improving the squatter compounds in physical terms. However, the level of community participation was also significant. The infrastructure provided included water supply at two taps for every group of 25 houses, roads, security lights, sanitation of pit latrines, refuse removal, schools, health centres and community centres. Building material loans were provided with technical advice, and those who were displaced as the upgrading progressed were issued plots nearby. Residents were issued full security of tenure.

The Chawama demonstration project

In 1973-4, during preparatory work, Chawama was chosen to serve as a demonstration project. The necessary strategies for community development and self-help would be worked out, experienced staff would be reoriented, and data for project evaluation were to be collected. In 1973 Chawama's population was 36,550, with 6,929 households; today's population is estimated at 50,000, with 11,620 households. In 1973 Chawama had one primary school, one small temporary clinic, four markets and grocery shops. Water wells were the chief source of drinking water, although some piped water was available. There was one dusty/muddy road to which many footpaths were linked. Most houses were of pole-and-*dagga* walls with grass thatching.

Physical basis. Typically the houses of Lusaka's urban compounds are grouped in clusters. This pattern permits the economic and rational provision of water, sewage disposal, streets, mass transportation, electricity and other services. The project plan utilized this existing pattern, showing how the main arteries for services could be installed around the perimeter, with the reticulation designed to service each cluster of houses. The perimeter arteries would be built by contractors, and the reticulation would be installed by residents under supervision of a social and technical assistance agency. The people would together dig the ditches, install the pipes and build the streets to provide their cluster of houses with services.

People power. AFSC's 1970 proposal was predicated on the conviction that urban housing is basically a "people problem", and solutions can best be found when dealt with by professionals trained in community dynamics working with professional urban planners, architects and engineeers. However, it was recognized that it is a major undertaking to stimulate an urban population to initiate mutual help projects and then to sustain that enthusiasm to completion. The proposal recommended, therefore, that the local people be brought into the planning of the scheme. This would be done through existing political, business, religious and traditional community leaders. Project staff would continue with the stimulation phase until everyone involved was conversant with the plan, knew of the government assistance available and was aware of the people's contribution required.

Community dynamics staff would then begin to concentrate efforts on the people living in specific clusters. After careful examination of all the factors involved, the cluster would establish a project priority list, on which basis the arterial systems would be co-ordinated. Cluster groups would carefully consider their financial means in relation to the costs they would be expected to bear; fund-raising activities might become necessary. The group would also consider problems of sharing their labour. Many projects fail because of conflicts over the equitable sharing of work.

The neighbourhood discussions that evolve around the execution of one project often lead to other creative group undertakings, e.g. improved houses, thrift groups, building co-operatives, literacy classes, irrigated gardening clubs and better nutrition. Trained staff would be alert to these opportunities and would encourage the people to follow their interest. In terms of costs relating to project administration, in the first year the community organizers' expenses exceeded well over 25 per cent of the annual cost of K1 million. A total of 86 community workers were employed, making an important contribution to project success.

Goals and achievements

The Chawama demonstration project was seen more as a physical and social exercise than an economic one, although a number of measures were meant to promote informal and formal economic growth in the area.

Community participation

The project and the work of HUZA functioned and continue to develop within the political atmosphere of Zambia's one-party participatory democracy. Project success was largely due to party policies which encourage community participation and grass-roots involvement. The project was able to achieve its goals and objectives as far as community participation was concerned. The residents participated on a self-help basis in trench digging, house construction and other activities.

Participatory project management. Success was made easier by the flexibility and clear vision of the Housing Project Unit (HPU) management team. Although there was no direct representation of the residents on the HPU management committee, their views were fully articulated in the committee by the field team members. Through feedback of the residents' needs and views by the field team, HPU management was able to restructure decisions to accommodate the concerns of residents.

Residents' committee. The creation of a residents' committee in the early stages marked the turning-point of the project in achieving local participation. The residents' committee was called the Road Planning Group, since its functions were at first concerned with road network planning. Later it became responsible for all other decision-making related to squatter upgrading.

Physical achievements

Water. Every group of 25 houses has been connected to clean piped water, and two standpipes are given. The water supply system was designed to allow families to make direct connections to their houses.

Street lighting. All major roads have street lighting. Today many families have connected electricity to their houses.

Roads and storm water drainage were installed in the first year of the project. There has been a tremendous decline in the breeding of water-borne insects such as mosquitoes. Access to Chawama is as good as in better parts of Lusaka.

Health centre. The Chawama urban health centre is now in operation, complete with a maternity wing.

Community centres. Two community centres were built and are used for primary health education, pre-school education and community meetings.

Schools. Since 1973 three new modern primary schools have been built.

Churches. At least ten new churches have been built and many others improved. Some of these churches are used for community meeting and training purposes.

House improvements. 10,000 households have either built themselves new houses in the overspill or made improvements to their existing houses, largely through self-help.

Market improvements. Chawama's existing markets have been improved and new markets built through self-help and by HPU.

Shops. A large state shop was built to provide cheap foodstuffs.

Problems

(1) The Chawama project faces problems of poor maintenance. Roads often are not well repaired, the drainage system needs regular repairs, and refuse collection is far from efficient.
(2) Loan and service charge payment is on the decline. Residents appear to resist paying, particularly service charges, in view of lack of proper repair and maintenance of infrastructure.

(3) The system of collecting loan repayments and service charges using local block leaders failed to work early on due to inefficiency.

(4) Home improvements have been hindered by the rising cost of building materials.

Long-term goals and activities

Care was exercised in ensuring that residents understood that squatter upgrading was not a "one-day wonder" solution but a continuing process. The objectives of the project were to make improvements in existing houses, informal employment activities, health, nutrition and kitchen gardening, continuing repairs and maintenance of the infrastructure and services. HUZA has worked continuously and untiringly to achieve these goals and objectives, concentrating on community-based activities and encouraging the use of locally available human and material resources. Thus HUZA demonstrates that NGOs are well placed to promote grass-roots activities that govenment cannot.

Building materials production as a source of income. HUZA first assisted families in Chawama to produce building materials for their own houses. Today many residents are involved in the production of building materials for sale, earning significant incomes. Thousands of soil/cement bricks are made for sale each month, as well as sisal cement roofing sheets, wooden doors and door frames and simple furniture. Home builders were encouraged to use locally available building stones, and hundreds of women and men have taken to large-scale stone crushing for sale.

Natural resource conservation projects. HUZA has actively promoted programmes of tree planting, food growing, nutrition and health education at Chawama. For this reason the government invited HUZA in 1985 to take part in preparations for the National Conservation Strategy. Since the adoption of the strategy, HUZA has been encouraged to expand its urban conservation activities. At the end of 1986 Chawama residents undertook, as part of the strategy, community education, tree planting and training for artisans in the making of more energy-efficient charcoal stoves.

Community health programmes. HUZA provides training resources in nutrition and health and supports self-help projects.

Women and youth in development. In HUZA's programmes women are acknowledged as a major force in promoting local development. Besides child-bearing, women are skilful managers of household economies and influence and introduce changes in health practices and nutrition. In Chawama women played a critical role in home building when they provided much of the labour and encouragement. They influence and control local market trading and are chief gardeners. After attending courses at the Chawama Skills Training Centre, established by HUZA, many women have gained skills in soap making, design and tailoring and handcrafts production. This has resulted in a number of income-generating activities. In Chawama the majority of the youth are under the age of 15 and out of school. The Chawama Skills Training Centre provides training for them in woodwork and carpentry, designing and tailoring. Former trainees have established a production unit at the centre, producing doors, frames, building equipment and simple furniture which is sold locally.

Wider impact

Valuable lessons and experiences were gained in Chawama, and advantage was taken of these in subsequent squatter upgrading projects. Two further projects were undertaken in Lusaka, and in 1980 the Zambian National Housing Authority undertook six provincial sites-and-services projects elsewhere using the Lusaka experience. In the Third National Development Plan (1979–83) the government encouraged the expansion of the policy of sites and services and programmes of squatter upgrading. Given the constraint of resources, and also with a view to developing self-reliance, communities will be encouraged to provide their own facilities as far as possible.

Key factors in project performance

(1) The formation of the residents' committee and its full involvement.
(2) Community briefing (education) by project community development staff and participating NGOs.
(3) Management flexibility in accommodating beneficiaries' views.
(4) Availability of funds and building materials.
(5) Good response by residents to broaden their participation in self-help projects.
(6) The paramount trust created between residents and project staff.
(7) Zambia's political system, with its emphasis on humanism and self-reliance, allowed the Chawama project to function – for community participation in decision-making is basically a political act.

CASE STUDY 34 *Integrated Community Development Project, Addis Ababa, Ethiopia*

PETTER MYHREN
Resident Representative, Redd Barna, Ethiopia

A large proportion of the 1.5 million or so inhabitants of Addis Ababa live in poverty. The population has more than quadrupled in 30 years, and the slums have multiplied. Many families have to share their tiny shacks; others live in structures so rickety the wind blows through and the rains leak in. It is difficult to keep such houses clean and infections and diseases at bay. There is an acute shortage of clinics, day-care centres, schools, recreation facilities, roads and potable water supplies.

In 1976 the Ethiopian government established urban dwellers' associations, known as *kebelles*. Each of the 284 *kebelles* in Addis Ababa consists of between 2,000 and 7,000 people. The *kebelles* – which elect administrative, youth association, women's association, and development and health committees – at least provide a starting-point for improvement. *Kebelle* administrations are responsible for organizing projects, using money from the municipality and rent collected from the community. They deal with grievances, act as a court for minor offences and are the channel for external aid.

In Ethiopia the urban poor have been given less attention and assistance than their rural brothers and sisters. Sixty-four per cent of households in Addis Ababa live below the urban poverty level. Most homes are of wood and mud structure and lack proper flooring, ceiling, kitchen and toilet facilities. Average life expectancy is 41 years. In view of the plight of these people, the voluntary development agency Redd Barna (Save the Children, Norway) embarked upon the task of seeking appropriate ways to improve the conditions under which they live. Kebelle 41, with 4,200 inhabitants, was the target for the first project.

Project preparation

Project philosophy

The Redd Barna development philosophy recognizes that external interventions should be catalytic in bringing about self-reliant and self-sustained processes of change. Four factors are believed to be of particular importance: (1) linkages with government institutions; (2) choice of technology; (3) establishment of community institutions and development of their capabilities to attain social cohesion around common interests, to conduct assessments on needs and to solve problems; (4) administrative and organizational complexity of activities initiated by the external agent. These points provided the framework for a flexible approach, aiming to produce a process model for development. It was assumed that, despite the deprivation of the target community, Kebelle 41, the people possessed valuable knowledge, information, resources and skills.

The planning process

As soon as the feasibility study, site selection and final negotiations with the Municipality of Addis Ababa were completed, activities were addressed towards improving the environmental conditions, together with a baseline study. The purpose of the study was to establish a participatory and collaborative relationship between Redd Barna project staff and the people and to establish a data base for planning, monitoring and evaluation.

A group from the University of Addis Ababa was commissioned to conduct the baseline study in November 1981. The group was extensively supported by Redd Barna project staff already working in Kebelle 41. Extensive meetings were held with individuals, families, groups of youths, men and women and neighbourhood clusters. In addition to needs and problems that were assessed by the study team, project staff discussed their philosophy and initial plans and stressed the role of the *kebelle* itself in the development process.

People were aware of the complexity of their problems and the magnitude of their needs. They welcomed Redd Barna and were enthusiastic about making their own contributions but took little initiative in strengthening the partnership. The initial activities initiated by Redd Barna seem to have had a catalytic effect, however. The survey data indicated that 94 per cent of families were below the poverty line; 67 per cent stated they had no regular income. Literacy and educational achievement were very low. Environmental and sanitary conditions were extremely poor.

Redd Barna's view was that the social needs were greater than the physical. The physical needs appeared in many ways to be a symbol of social needs, maybe more than basic material needs. No upgrading project would endure without enhancing self-confidence, self-respect and a sense of identity.

Objectives and strategy

The following development objectives were defined for the Kebelle 41 project:

- To create and institutionalize a community development process which will facilitate better access to government services; to help increase income and employment opportunities and improve environmental conditions; to strengthen community institutions.
- To help strengthen the capabilities of residents to assess local needs and to plan, implement and evaluate self-help activities for social, economic and infrastructure development.

- To encourage and strengthen human resource development at community level through effective community leadership and to increase participation of children, youths and women.
- To offer through project activities a functional model of a self-help approach to community-based integrated urban development for possible replication and institutionalization elsewhere in Addis Ababa.

The project strategy involved four major programming sectors:

(1) *Income-generating activities/economic development.* Low income and unemployment were identified by *kebelle* residents as two major problems. Hence, the following strategy was defined: link existing skills with the job market; support skills training in accordance with market needs; support initiatives for individual enterprises and small-scale industries; assist in management training; support establishment of producers' associations/co-operatives; make credits and grants available for small-scale enterprises/industries.

(2) *Physical infrastructure.* Improvement of the physical environment, such as housing, water and sewerage, was expressed as the first priority need in the baseline survey. Important issues for an innovative approach to address the need for limited physical improvements were: strategy for home improvements and renovations, with total reconstruction only when absolutely necessary; aided self-help and community labour combined with skills training and employment opportunities in construction work; the use of low-cost appropriate technology for housing, avoiding the massive use of wood of traditional housing construction; helping *kebelle* dwellers get access to credit in the formal sector and aim to establish a housing improvement revolving loan scheme.

(3) *Preventive health/mother and child care.* The residents seemed aware of the problems related to health, nutrition, education and family planning but emphasized housing, income generation and employment. It was decided that this programming sector would not receive concentrated attention during the first year, but specific sectoral activities would be planned on the basis of detailed studies of family health practices, nutrition, family planning, education and institutional support to children.

(4) *Human development and social awareness building.* Project staff encountered a communiuty which comprised a collection of individuals owing allegiance to nobody but themselves and their nearest relatives. Although the absence of a cohesive community was registered as a hindrance to development, it was felt that the *kebelle* structure and organization showed potential for a change in attitude. The participatory concept could not be projected as a short-term goal but would have to be encouraged and nurtured gradually in a well-planned manner.

Project implementation

The project was launched in July 1981. It was discovered that the first survey, conducted prior to signing the project agreement or any project activity, had several profound biases. People did not know the motives of the interviewers and for what purpose they were collecting information. After confidence started developing between the population and project staff, a second survey was carried out.

People do not live in slums by choice even if the majority of the inhabitants are born there. They live there because they have nowhere else to go. Resources are generally so few among so many that survival is the only primary need. A suddenly introduced planning process has no relevance in this context. Kebelle 41 and Redd Barna had to embark on an exercise of learning by doing, in which expectations of immediate benefits from aid were the greatest obstacle. Process thinking and the need for matching inputs emerged slowly, and the community started taking an interest in the project as new activity components were added.

The project team, which consisted of Ethiopian nationals only, gradually acquired a sense of project ownership through this approach, which was transferred to the reesidents and office-bearers of Kebelle 41. A planning and monitoring system emerged, giving a basis for developing a community-based process where all concerned parties could voice their opinions and through improved relationships influence and contribute to the final result. What slowly emerged over the years was a partnership in community development.

Project costs and achievements, 1981–6

Costs

The financial cost for the project, 1981 to end-1986, is Birr 3,852,256 (US$1,860,993). This includes all overhead costs and staff salaries and implies an overall average investment of Birr 889 ($429) per household per year. The project succeeded in reducing the costs of various construction activities, such as the health post, to substantially less than original estimates.

Achievements

Construction. When the project started there were 788 dwelling units; 368 of these have been repaired, and 153 new houses have been built. Twenty-four kitchens have been repaired, 56 new ones constructed. Twenty-three new communal latrines have been constructed, 31 latrines repaired; a complex of 8 showers, 2 latrines and 5 washstands has been constructed; 5 soak-away pits have been completed; and a sanitary system with 80 bins and 5 collection containers has been put into service. A weavers' and spinners' association house, a mill house, a food processing plant with its own day-care centre, a grain store, a co-operative shop, a health clinic, two bridges, three long retaining walls, a community hall, a nutrition rehabilitation centre, literacy campaign facilities, three multi-faucet tap-water fountains, a workshop, and a 560 sq m kindergarten have been built.

Nutrition and health. Supplementary food sales are made at subsidized prices. Nutrition rehabilitation and educating activities are targeted at marasmic and underweight children. Vaccination has been accomplished for all pregnant mothers, all Kebelle 41 children and most children in the neighbouring *kebelles*.

Communicable disease control and other services have been established in the *kebelle* health clinic.

Community activities. Two grain mills have been installed, providing employment opportunities and mill facilities at well below commercial prices. The community shop generates employment and availability of cheap food. The renovated community hall accommodates large meetings and cultural activities. The small community library makes books available. Eighty children are introduced to woodwork, needlework, carpet-making, etc., in the youth activity centre.

Education. Pre-school education has been provided to over 300 children per year since the kindergarten was constructed. One hundred children attend literacy classes in shifts; the classes are linked with the nearby government school. On-the-job training and special courses have been run in accounting, disabled care and teaching, teaching in kindergarten and teachers' aids production, electrical maintenance and housekeeping.

The greatest achievement is to see the throbbing life, the initiatives and the good cheer among Kebelle 41's inhabitants.

Transferring responsibility to the people

Phase-out and transfer of responsibility received a great deal of attention when Redd Barna first introduced itself to the *kebelle* and to Addis Ababa City Council. The community found the concept both frightening and challenging. The first move towards transferring financial responsibilities away from the organization was to make the *kebelle* administration take full responsibility for employing and paying staff the community needed for running its institutions. Avoiding dependency on strained government budgets must be an aim, and success of the efforts of an NGO depends on local institutionalization. This fact was underestimated by Redd Barna at the start of the project. Social justification was too often accepted, while sustainability and financial criteria were neglected.

To secure the transfer of responsibility to the community, a number of *kebelle* committees have been established and/or revitalized. The project management had also to facilitate the establishment and maintenance of effective links between the community structures and government ministries and authorities – the crucial element for successful institutionalization of what was created in the *kebelle*.

With projects implemented in poor and dilapidated communities, planners, external institutions and project operators often claim all decision-making powers, on the assumption that very little potential exists for an effort aiming to create a productive and self-sustaining community. The Kebelle 41 experience demonstrates that this assumption is false and that, given the chance, poor communities hold the key to the solution of their own problems.

Conclusions

CZECH CONROY

This book has covered a wide range of development activities, from soil conservation to cement production, from land capability assessment to upgrading squatter settlements. The lessons are numerous and diverse, but there are some key themes that recur. There are also general implications in the preceding chapters for aid agencies.

Sustainable development is a multifaceted process, with economic, social and biophysical/technical dimensions. These factors are inextricably related, so it is meaningless to talk of the sustainability of any one on its own. For example, the planting and harvesting of trees, although "technically" feasible, will not happen unless people see its benefits as significantly greater than its financial or labour costs; and people will be confident of that only if the social conditions are right – if they have security of tenure for the land on which the trees are grown or rights to the trees themselves.

Sustainable development is a process rather than a product. A participatory approach, involving local people in decision-making and implementation, is a key factor in sustainability. It prevents inappropriate new technologies, organizations or practices from being foisted upon people by well-meaning but misguided outsiders. Project activities that have been effective in one region will not necessarily be so in another. Thus, it is not project activities that agencies should seek to "replicate" elsewhere, but rather the application of the principles that make projects successful. In particular, projects should be flexible, allowing the local people to select the appropriate path as the project progresses.

"Mega" projects, such as dams, have sometimes had disastrous consequences for local people and their environments. Northern NGOs often complain to the aid agencies concerned that the people affected by the project were not consulted. If they had been given a say in the decision some of these projects probably would not have proceeded. This underlines the importance of democratic processes. As the World Commission on Environment and Development (WCED) concluded, sustainable development requires "a political system that secures effective citizen participation in decision-making" (WCED, 1987).

Sustainable development is not necessarily a harmonious process. David Butcher (Chapter 5) stresses that we need to identify the winners and losers.

Robert Chambers pointed out at the conference that all five of the case studies he had reviewed were probably unrepresentative in that, by and large, they were non-zero-sum situations – everybody was a winner, and hence there were no major confrontations between winners and losers. This is not always the case, and consideration needs to be given to political sustainability. If the poor gain at the expense of the rich, will they be able to hold on to their gains and fend off attempts (by force or other means) by the rich to appropriate them? The commitment and means to stand up against these forces could be a very important factor in sustainability.

The planning technique used by the Organization of American States for regional development (Case Study 19) assumes that development projects will lead to conflict, and that all examples of negative "environmental impact" can be described as conflicts between two or more interest groups. Once potential conflicts have been identified, the technique requires that all involved parties are notified, since only the parties involved in the conflict can provide a satisfactory solution to it. Again, the importance of effective citizen participation is recognized.

Poor people are *not* the problem when it comes to conserving natural resources. Under the right conditions, they can be part of the solution. As Chambers puts it in Chapter 1:

> Contrary to popular professional prejudice, there is mounting evidence that when poor people have secure rights and adequate stocks of assets to deal with contingencies, they tend to take a long view, holding on tenaciously to land, protecting and saving trees and seeking to provide for their children. In this respect, their time perspective is longer than that of commercial interests concerned with early profits from capital, or of conventional development projects concerned with internal rates of return.

Governments should create the conditions (social, legal or financial) that enable the poor to take a long-term view. Official development agencies also have a supporting role to play here, as well as governments.

Implications for aid agencies

The lessons and the recommendations from the preceding chapters can be considered under three headings: project aid; strengthening institutional capacity; and the national context.

One issue should be taken into account when considering all these matters, namely conditionality. Some Third World countries are concerned that extra demands could be placed on their already limited resources if environment-related conditions are attached to aid. Aid agencies should recognize this potential problem, and provide increased support to enable Third World governments to ensure that projects and programmes are environmentally sound. Strengthening the human and institutional capacity is particularly important.

Project aid

Official donor agencies must have the capacity to ensure that all the projects they fund contribute to sustainable development. This requires suitable procedures and adequate numbers of staff with the necessary skills. Project appraisal and evaluation must be changed. As Butcher argues: "There is a clear need for more thinking on how to appraise projects for institutional development, sustainability and environmental impact."

Narrow economic considerations still dominate project appraisal, with the emphasis being on the short term. Environmental costs and benefits, and the goods and services provided by natural resources, are usually accorded less weight because they are difficult to quantify in economic terms. Many of the NGO-funded projects described in this book would not have received funding from official agencies because their benefits, although substantial, are not easily quantifiable. A few agencies, such as the World Bank, the Asian Development Bank, the Swedish International Development Authority and the UK's Overseas Development Administration, have recently begun to examine how these weaknesses of project appraisal methods can be overcome.

Project design and appraisal also need to pay greater attention to institutional aspects of sustainability. When donors withdraw after the first few years of a project, the local institutional capacity is sometimes too weak to maintain project activities and benefits effectively. Institutional capacity is more likely to be strong if local institutions play an active role from the early stages of the project.

Aid agencies should also increase the proportion of aid going to "investments needed to enhance the environment and the productivity of the resource sectors", as the World Commission on Environment and Development recommended. Such projects are usually people-centred, and include soil conservation, agroforestry, watershed protection, small-scale agriculture and low-cost sanitation measures.

Unfortunately, various aspects of the way official agencies operate discourage increased funding for these projects, and make it difficult for them to achieve their intended benefits. Perhaps the most important obstacle is that the main concern of official donors is "to disburse funding, spending a minimum amount of time designing projects and paying little attention to the long-term financial soundness of the projects" (Rees, Chapter 4). Pressures to reduce administrative costs result in "ever-increasing amounts of funds per project officer. Staff are rewarded for the amount of funds programmed rather than the impact of those funds" (Kramer, Chapter 2). This situation could be aggravated if aid volumes increased, something that advocates of increased aid flows would do well to consider.

The above factors lead to pressures for "off-the-shelf" projects with a minimum of deviation and innovation, especially large capital-intensive ones such as dams, roads or power-stations. On the other hand, innovative, people-centred projects tend to require more staff time, and cannot absorb large volumes of capital, so agencies are less keen to fund them.

Large volumes of money can undermine these projects in various ways. They may encourage projects to expand more quickly than they are capable of doing, or to incur recurrent costs that are not sustainable after donor funding is terminated. Or subsidies to local people (either cash or food for work) may lead them to perpetuate activities that they do not regard as being in their best interests; and their perpetuation may give the impression to outsiders responsible for the project that the activities are in the people's interests.

The conference had some suggestions for dealing with the pressures to disburse large amounts of money quickly. A kind of partitioning was suggested by Robert Chambers's group. A few big-spending projects could use up the bulk of the agency's funds, so that there can be a staff-intensive and more creative, more micro-level set of activities with the remaining funds. Correspondingly, it was suggested that perhaps there should be two accounting systems, or two parts of the organization, with different budgetary targeting procedures. One would behave conventionally according to normal economic and planning criteria, and the other would be able to be much more creative and flexible.

A similar suggestion is made in Chapter 2 by John Michael Kramer. He suggests that bilaterals should have a separate funding system for small-scale, experimental projects that reduces "requirements for preparation, funding approval and administration of these projects". He cites USAID's Guesselbodi forest management project as evidence that bilateral agencies can "act small". This project "had a relatively small budget and just one long-term expatriate adviser who fought for and won a remarkable degree of flexibility".

Inadequate numbers of staff are the other major constraint on the funding of people-centred projects by official agencies. The obvious solution is to increase staffing levels; but this is politically unpopular in most Western countries, and the pressures are very much in the opposite direction at present. This situation needs to be changed. Perhaps counter-pressures will build up as more people become aware that the quality of aid is suffering as a result. One of the conference groups suggested that, as the number of people in the development business committed to changing aid agencies increases, a "critical mass" might be reached within certain agencies that leads to their transformation. That time may seem a long way away, but it is something to work towards.

Even if agencies are committed to funding people-centred projects, they may be unsure how to design and implement them effectively. The authors of this book have tried to address this issue. Chambers identifies five complementary requirements for projects aimed at enhancing sustainable livelihoods: a learning process approach; putting people's priorities first; secure rights and gains for the poor; sustainability through self-help; and high calibre, commitment and continuity of staff. Kramer and Butcher identify similar sets of factors that are important to project sustainability. Other recent publications also contain useful material for aid agencies (Harrison, 1987; Dankelman and Davidson, 1988). This growing amount of case-study material, combined with enough staff with appropriate experience and qualifications, should greatly improve the success rate of projects.

Staff are not usually sensitive and knowledgable about social and environmental aspects of projects, and training is required. Some agencies have started to do this, but training programmes need to be further developed and applied more systematically. There is also a need for more specialist staff to advise on various aspects of sustainability. Most official agencies have only one environment adviser, who often has other responsibilities as well, and there is far too much work for her/him to process thoroughly. More social advisers and resource and environmental economists are also badly needed.

It is often suggested that official agencies should channel more funds through international NGOs, such as Oxfam and Save the Children, since they are generally thought to be better at identifying and managing small projects in a socially sensitive way. In some cases bilateral agencies could usefully increase the amount of funds disbursed via NGOs, but this should not be seen as a substitute for the agencies improving their own performance in this area. NGO aid flows are insignificant compared with the volume of official aid, and international NGOs could absorb only a limited additional amount. Some people are also concerned about NGOs losing their independence if a large proportion of their funds comes from official agencies.

Increasing the amount of aid flowing from official agencies to Third World NGOs would also be useful. But Third World governments often dislike agencies bypassing them and giving money directly to NGOs, so funding of NGO projects usually has to meet with the approval of the government concerned. Kramer suggests that their concern can be reduced if the recipient NGOs work through government counterpart agencies.

Kramer also notes that it will remain difficult for official agencies to deal directly with local Third World NGOs, and suggests that instead they should fund them through international development NGOs. Potential conflicts between international and local NGOs arising from competition for funds can be minimized if both receive funding. The Haiti Agroforestry Outreach Project provides a good example of how this approach can work.

Strengthening institutional capacity

Indigenous institutions, from NGOs and community groups to local and national government, will ultimately determine whether or not Third World development is sustainable. This is why the World Commission on Environment and Development recommended that aid agencies should fund "special programmes for strengthening the institutional and professional capacities needed for sustainable development" (WCED, 1987).

Aid agencies do not usually give institutional strengthening the emphasis it deserves. The appropriate technology and industry group at the IIED conference concluded that there was a need for donors to move from short-term project support to longer-term programme and institutional support.

In addition, project aid should be compatible with institution-building. The human and institutional development group concluded that projects should ideally be integrated within existing institutions rather than create new ones. This point has been made many times before, particularly in relation to integrated rural development programmes, but it is so important that it bears repeating. Donors must take this point on board if they are to strengthen institutional capacity rather than weaken it.

Good examples do exist. Kenya's Soil Conservation Programme illustrates how a sectoral ministry can be strengthened to tackle a major threat to natural resource productivity; the Zambian Integrated Rural Development Programme shows how local government can be strengthened; and the Lampang Applied Nutrition Programme demonstrates how an NGO can work with government to increase the effectiveness of health services at the provincial level.

The national context

Livelihoods can be sustainable only if the policy and institutional context is conducive to this. Donor agencies have a potential role to play in helping or encouraging Third World governments to achieve this, but it is one that they have hardly begun to explore.

Donor agencies have a responsibility to ensure that any policy changes they encourage Third World governments to make will not damage the environment. The World Bank is the most important lending agency in this respect since it exerts the most influence on recipient governments. The WCED report stressed that sustainability considerations must "be taken into account by the Bank in the appraisal of structural adjustment lending and other policy-oriented lending directed to resource-based sectors – agriculture, fishing, forestry, and energy" (WCED, 1987).

In 1987 the World Bank launched a pioneering initiative in this area, a series of thirty country-based environmental management and strategy studies. These studies cover resource assessment, identification of priority environmental issues and policies and projects designed to address them.

The sustainable development conference identified the following issues as important for consideration in policy dialogue:

- questions of rights and access to land, and land reform;
- community control of resources, particularly for pastoralists;
- rights to trees and their products.

Regarding community control of resources, Kramer points out (Chapter 2) that "when communities manage their own resources and when the people directly receive the benefits of those resources, the likelihood of achieving sustainability is increased". He argues that donor agencies can assist community management of resources by supporting land reform, both of common lands and large private landholdings.

Chambers also considers this issue (Chapter 1) and observes that "Approaches to the management of commons are vulnerable to simple dogma, with privatization currently in vogue." The simplistic political dogma of some donor agencies is liable to lead to inappropriate policy recommendations. Kramer suggests that since international development NGOs carry "less political baggage", and because they have "the field experience that is often poorly represented in policy setting", they too should engage in policy dialogue with recipient-country governments.

The appropriate policy prescriptions are still not fully understood. This is true of the development process in general. Many would agree with Colin Rees when he said at the conference that "the development process has been forced to shed its somewhat falsely deterministic character and is now becoming something of a learning process. I would suggest that this presents us with an exciting intellectual challenge made all the more compelling by the horrendous problems in developing countries today."

IIED hopes that this book will make a valuable contribution to that intellectual challenge, and that it will guide development agencies and governments towards helping more of the world's poorest people to achieve sustainable and prosperous livelihoods.

References

Harrison, Paul (1987), *The Greening of Africa: Breaking Through in the Battle for Land and Food*. Paladin, London.

Dankelman, Irene, and Davidson, Joan (1988), *Women and Environment in the Third World: Alliance for the Future*. Earthscan, London.

World Commission an Environment and Development (1987), *Our Common Future* (the Brundtland Report). Oxford University Press, Oxford and New York.

Abbreviations

AA	Agroecosystem analysis
ACORDE	Association for the Co-ordination of Development Resources (Honduras)
ADBN	Agricultural Development Bank of Nepal
AFSC	American Friends Service Committee
AKRSP	Aga Khan Rural Support Programme (Pakistan)
ANP	Applied Nutrition Program (Thailand)
AOP	Agroforestry Outreach Project (Haiti)
ARC	Aid recipient country
ATDA	Appropriate Technology Development Association (India)
BAMB	Botswana Agricultural Marketing Board
BAS	Business Advisory Services (Kenya and Ghana)
BASIG	Business Advisory Services in Ghana
BASIK	Business Advisory Services in Kenya
BBP	Baudha-Bahunipati Project (Nepal)
BCCI	Bank of Credit and Commerce International
BMOA	Botswana Mill Owners' Association
BTI	Butwal Training Institute (Nepal)
BYS	Balaju Yantra Shala (Nepal)
CABEI	Central American Bank for Economic Integration
CAOTACO	Organic Agriculture and Appropriate Technology Centre for the Community (Dominican Republic)
CAT	Centre for Appropriate Technology (India)
CBO	Community-based organization
CCU	Centro Cooperativista Uruguayo
CDC	Commonwealth Development Corporation
CIDA	Canadian International Development Agency
COPEVI	Operation Centre for Housing and Settling (Mexico)
COTESU	Swiss Technical Co-operation Mission (Bolivia)
CRI	Cement Research Institute of India
CPRs	Common property resources
CSWCRTI	Central Soil and Water Conservation Research and Training Institute (India)

CUMAT	Centro de Investigación y Estudio de la Capacidad de Uso Mayor de la Tierra (Bolivia)
DC	District council (Zambia)
DCS	Development and Consulting Services (Nepal)
DDCC	District development co-ordinating committee (Zambia)
DR	District representative (Zambia)
EIA	Environmental impact analysis/assessment
EMDI	Environmental Manpower Development in Indonesia
EPCOM	Environmental Pollution Advisory Committee (Hong Kong)
ERL	Environmental Resources Ltd (UK)
FAAD	Farmer Associations and Agribusiness Development (Ghana)
FAO	Food and Agriculture Organization of the United Nations
FD	Forest Department
FDJC	Federación de Desarrollo Juvenil Comunitario (Dominican Republic)
FGR	Fédération de Groupements Ruraux (Mali)
FIA	Inter-American Foundation
FLUP	Forest and Land-Use Planning Project (Niger)
FUCVAM	United Federation of Mutual Aid Co-operatives (Uruguay)
FUDECO	Fundación para el Desarrollo Comunitario (Dominican Republic)
FWS	Fishermen's Welfare Society (India)
GOK	Government of Kenya
GP	Gifford & Partners (UK)
GP	Gifford & Partners (UK)
GTA	Alternative Technology Group (Mexico)
HIC	Habitat International Council
HPU	Housing Project Unit (Zambia)
HUZA	Human Settlements of Zambia
IARC	International Agricultural Research Centre
IDRC	International Development Research Centre
IFAD	International Fund for Agricultural Development
IIED	International Institute for Environment and Development
ILO	International Labour Organization
IRDP	Integrated Rural Development Programme
IRDP SMC	Integrated Rural Development Programme in Serenje, Mpika and Chinsali (Zambia)
ITDG	Intermediate Technology Development Group
ITTU	Intermediate Technology Transfer Unit (Ghana)
IUCN	International Union for Conservation of Nature and Natural Resources
KCJ	Kenya Ceramic Jiko
KDA	Karachi Development Authority

KENGO	Kenya Energy Non-Governmental Organizations' Association
KMC	Karachi Municipal Corporation
LWR	Lutheran World Relief
MBBC	Muttom Boat Building Centre (India)
MCP	Mini-cement plant
MDB	Multilateral development bank
MFM	Meals for Millions
MKLH	Ministry of Population and the Environment (Indonesia)
MPPU	Multi-Purpose Processing Unit (Nepal)
NCS	National conservation strategy
NGO	Non-governmental organization
NORAD	Norwegian government aid agency
OAA	Official assistance agency
OAS	Organization of American States
ODA	Overseas Development Administration (UK)
ODC	Oficina de Desarrollo de la Comunidad (Dominican Republic)
ODH	Operation Double Harvest
OECD	Organization for Economic Co-operation and Development
OPP	Orangi Pilot Project (Pakistan)
PADF	Pan-American Development Foundation
PAF	Projet Agro-Forestier (Burkina Faso)
PMU	Project management unit
PPA	Indonesian Nature Conservation Department
RIIC	Rural Industries Innovation Centre (Botswana)
RRA	Rapid rural appraisal
SFDP	Small Farmer Development Project (Nepal)
SIDA	Swedish International Development Authority
SIFFS	South Indian Federation of Fishermen Societies
SIRDO	Integral System for Re-using Organic Waste (Mexico)
STMP	Small Turbine Mill Project (Nepal)
SWC	Soil and water conservation
TA	Technical assistance
TA	Technical assistant (Kenya)
TCC	Technology Consultancy Centre (Ghana)
TCO	Technical co-operation officer (Zambia)
tpd	Tonnes per day
TPS	Technical Planning Secretariat (Paraguay)
T&V	Training and visit system
UMN	United Missions to Nepal
UNCHS	United Nations Centre for Human Settlements
UNDP	United Nations Development Programme
UNEP	United Nations Environment Programme

UNICEF	United Nations (International) Children's (Emergency) Fund
USAID	US Agency for International Development
USDA	US Department of Agriculture
UST	University of Science and Technology (Ghana)
VSK	Vertical shaft kiln (India)
WCED	World Commission on Environment and Development
WCS	World Conservation Strategy
WHO	World Health Organization
WWF	World Wildlife Fund

Index